RAILWAYS OF THE WORLD

2   Railways of Australia

In Windmill Cutting: Western Australian Government Railways 'V' Class on
Midland-York goods in 1966

RAILWAYS OF THE WORLD

2   *Railways of Australia*

O. S. NOCK

B.SC., C.ENG., F.I.C.E., F.I.MECH.E.
PAST-PRESIDENT, I.R.S.E.

WITH 109 PHOTOGRAPHS
AND 8 COLOUR PLATES

ADAM & CHARLES BLACK · LONDON

FIRST PUBLISHED 1971
A. AND C. BLACK LIMITED
4, 5 AND 6 SOHO SQUARE LONDON WIV 6AD

© 1971 O. S. NOCK

ISBN 0 7136 1190 1

MADE AND PRINTED
IN GREAT BRITAIN
BY BUTLER AND TANNER LTD
FROME AND LONDON

Contents

Illustrations

IN COLOUR

The Author and Publishers wish to express their indebtedness to the following for permission to use photographs as follows:

To Commonwealth Railways for plates 37c, 41b.

To the New South Wales Government Railways for 1a, 1b, 2a, 3a, 3b, 8a, 9a, 9b, 10a, 10b, 17a, 20a, 20b, 21a, 21b, 21c, 33c, 41a.

To the Queensland Railways for 12a, 12b, 13a, 13b, 14a, 14b, 23b.

To the Victorian Railways for 23a, 23d, 23e, 27, 29a, 32a, 33a, 33b, 37a.

To the Western Australian Government Railways for 23c, 23f, 39b, 39c, 40b, 42, 43, 44a, 44b, 46a, 46b, 47b.

To Beyer Peacock & Co. Ltd. for plate 4.

To D. Budd Esq., for plate 18.

To C. A. Cardew Esq., for 2b, 2c, 6, 7a, 7b, 7c, 8b, 11a, 11b, 15a, 19a, 19b, 22, 24a, 24b, 25a, 25b, 26a, 31a, 31b.

To R. M. Carlisle Esq., for 28b

To Mortimer H. Clark Esq., for 30a, to h inclusive.

To Donald A. Colquhoun Esq., for 26b, 35a, 35b, 36, 38a, 38b, 38c.

To C. L. Craig Esq., for 28a.

Plates 5a, 5b, 5c, 15b, 17b, 29b, 31c, 31d, 32b, 34a, 34b, 37b, 40a, 45a, 45b, 45c, 47a, 48a, 48b, 48c, are from photographs by the Author.

Plate 39b is reproduced from a painting by Percy F. S. Spence in *Australia* (published by A. & C. Black Ltd. in 1910).

The colour plates, painted by Jack Hill, are from photographs supplied by the Commonwealth Railways, the Queensland Railways, the Western Australian Government Railways, the A.R.H.S. South Australian Section, C. A. Cardew, Mortimer H. Clark, and the Author.

The plate of N.S.W.G.R. locomotive No. 1210 at Canberra is from a colour transparency by the Author.

Indebtedness is also expressed to Mrs. C. Boyer, who prepared the various special maps.

16

This book is in many ways the result of a journey of exploration. Many facets of the railways of Australia were familiar to me beforehand. Even before I reached the status of a teenager I had a copy of the first edition of the *Wonder Book of Railways*; I had read of the Lithgow Zig-Zag, and had enjoyed a colour plate of the 'Interstate Express' which at that time was the only through train connecting any two of the Australian State capitals. But to visit Australia in 1969 was to gain the most inspiriting experience any railway enthusiast could ever wish for. It was to travel in a country where new railways were being constructed over vast distances, as integral parts of great new industrial projects; it was to travel in a country where the express passenger train is so popular a means of travel that one has to reserve seats and sleeping berths months in advance.

My wife and I had manifold tasks ahead of us when we arrived in Sydney on a wet and blustering morning in mid-August; but from the moment we set foot on Australian soil our path was made smooth and delightful, even if the pace was a bit hectic at times. When I first met John T. Taylor, the United Kingdom Representative of the Railways of Australia, in London, some months before the intended time of our departure, and sketched out my idea of a tour, at the same time telling him a little of the form I hoped this book would take, I little thought of the 'magic carpet' that would be put at our disposal, thanks initially to Jack Taylor. Through the courtesy of the Commissioners of Railways in all the States we were able to make a very extensive tour. No limit was put on distance or route, and had we been able to stay longer in Australia we could have travelled even further.

There was another cogent reason for visiting Australia in 1969, for in April of that year I had been elected President of the Institution of Railway Signal Engineers. There is a strong section of that Institution in Australia, and it was an ideal time to visit them, and to meet many men who had been no more than pen-friends hitherto. Collecting data for this book and carrying out Presidential duties became a pleasantly integrated task, which brought me into touch with railwaymen of diverse callings, from Rockhampton far up on the Queensland coast to Melbourne; from Adelaide to Port Pirie and Perth. I should like to thank the very senior railway officers who gave of their time to talk to me, and of others who spent long days taking me to see many railway sights. Their enthusiasm was infectious; the railways they were running, and the new ones they were building, were magnificent.

I cannot obviously mention everyone by name, but I must especially thank Mr. N. McCusker, Commissioner of Railways New South Wales, and Mr. R. J. Fitch, Commissioner of Railways, South Australia, for granting me very pleasant interviews, while the help given to me by Mr. L. Reynolds, Assistant Commissioner, Victorian Railways is mentioned particularly in Chapters 10 and 12. In Brisbane I was made especially welcome by the Secretary for Railways, Queensland, Mr. Girard, and in Perth, my last call, Mr. Reeves, the Secretary for Railways, Western Australia, certainly saw to it that my limited time there was fully occupied! With the Signal Engineers in all five States I naturally had special bonds. They and their wives extended hospitality far beyond railways, and the talking of 'shop'. To all of them, and to many of their senior assistants we were most grateful. Harold Bourne, New South Wales; Keith Cousin, Victoria; Frank Jones, Queensland; Bob Carmichael, South Australia; and Donald Curtis, Western Australia.

In addition to railway officers I was made very welcome by members of the two railway enthusiasts societies, the Australian Historical Railway Society, and the Association of Railway Enthusiasts. At meetings in Sydney and Melbourne I faced a barrage of questions on how railways were doing in the United Kingdom. It was absorbing to find how closely British railway literature is read in Australia, and how thoroughly locomotive history has been studied. Although several members, in New South Wales, Victoria, Queensland and South Australia have helped me a great deal, I am especially indebted to Mr. C. A. Cardew, formerly Assistant Chief Mechanical Engineer of the New South Wales Government Railways. Cardew was not only a mine of information on steam locomotive history and practice in New South Wales, but he had made available to me a magnificent selection of his action pictures, many of which are reproduced in this book. I am also much indebted to

Mr. Mortimer H. Clark for help in connection with early Victorian Railways locomotives. We are also indebted to the joint authors and publishers of the book *Railways of Australia* for permission to reproduce the diagrams on pages 74 and 75.

In the original prospectus, when this series of books on world railways was first announced, this second volume was specified as dealing with 'Australasia'. As it is, many important fields of activity on the mainland of Australia remain unvisited, let alone Tasmania, and the fine railways of New Zealand. We hope to return again, and travel far more extensively in Queensland; to penetrate up the Commonwealth line to Alice Springs, and perhaps to visit the great privately-owned industrial lines in the northwest. Tasmania will then also be a 'must', and also New Zealand.

In the present book, Olivia my wife has been my partner to a greater extent than ever before. Her presence beside me through all our tour of the Australian railways is mentioned at many stages, and when the book came to be written I think she typed it with more than usual relish. It was an experience of which we shall always carry the most vivid memories.

Silver Cedars   O. S. Nock
High Bannerdown,
Batheaston,
BATH   July 1970.

CHAPTER ONE

Introduction

The big turbo-jet in which we were crossing the Pacific took off for the last time; next stop Sydney. As we climbed away from Nadi, Fiji, and the 'Fasten seat belts' notices were extinguished fellow passengers settled down to make the best of what remained of the night. Some were wearing garlands from a holiday in Hawaii; others were seasoned business travellers, while my wife and I were going to Australia in all the eager anticipation of exploring a new country, to be reunited for a few weeks with members of our own family, and to meet face to face many kindly people who had been pen-friends for years. Railways were of course to be the focal point of nearly all our activities. We were to travel vast distances, to see even vaster prospects, and almost entirely by train. We were to meet senior railway officers, and sometimes their families too, in every State on the mainland of Australia; I was to ride locomotives of all kinds. What would it all be like? In one respect our first contact with Australia was something of a surprise. Travelling at mid-August we left behind in England one of the finest summers in memory, and a brief stay-over in San Francisco had been blessed with cloudless weather. But after leaving Fiji increasing evidence of turbulence was amply confirmed when daylight came and we saw below great banks of cumulus cloud. At one time our Captain thought it might not be possible to land at Sydney, so rough was the weather, and so strong the cross-wind over the runway at the Kingsford Smith Airport. We might have to divert to Brisbane. But in the event all was well, and dead on time at 7 a.m. on a cold, wind-swept airfield, in torrents of rain, we first set foot in Australia. Any chilliness that the bleak weather might have instilled in us was however dispersed in a flash once we were done with the formalities of travel and into the reception lounge. Three senior officers of the New South Wales Railways, and a former colleague of mine now settled in Australia, were there to meet us, and the warmth and friendliness of their greeting set a pattern that was to be followed wherever we went in five thrilling weeks.

In the previous book in this series, dealing with Southern Africa, I explained how modern air travel tended to land one at the goals of railway enterprise rather than at its points of origin. No such strictures apply in this case of Australia, because in Sydney we were close to the very birthplace of the Australian nation, and even if Melbourne claims priority where railways are concerned it is priority by a very narrow margin. Our hosts in Sydney saw to it that we had a very proper introduction to Australia, and before lunch on that very first morning, despite the squalls of rain sweeping in from the Pacific, we were standing on the shores of Botany Bay at the spot where Captain Cook first landed in 1770. Our hosts that morning were both signal engineers, and I told them of the English signal box on the East Coast main line north of Retford which bears the name 'Botany Bay'. They told us also how great preparations were being made for the Royal visit in 1970, in celebration of the two hundredth anniversary of the landing of Captain Cook, and one could not help reflecting upon how much had happened in that brief two hundred years. In England it marked almost the entire span of the steam age in transport, for within a few months of that momentous landing on the shores of Australia, in the shadow of Carn Brea in Cornwall there was born Richard Trevithick.

The development of railways in Australia was as uncoordinated and individualistic as any of the early enterprises at home. The pioneer settlements took place at points on the coast where a sheltered anchorage and good water was available, and the early railways were driven for short distances inland. Independent enterprises began over a span of some twenty years from Melbourne, Sydney, Newcastle, Brisbane, Adelaide, Albany and Fremantle, to be followed in the same general pattern from Rockhampton and Townsville. Except in the State of Victoria there seems to have been no coordinated plan. In the Mother Colony of New South Wales, for example, the lines gradually extending inland from Sydney and Newcastle were not linked up until the year 1889. It was no more than natural that in this piecemeal development many disjointed and inconsistent practices grew up, among which the most outstanding was the diversity of rail gauges. Clever fellows, being wise many, many years after the event, have written quartos about the muddle-headedness of

22

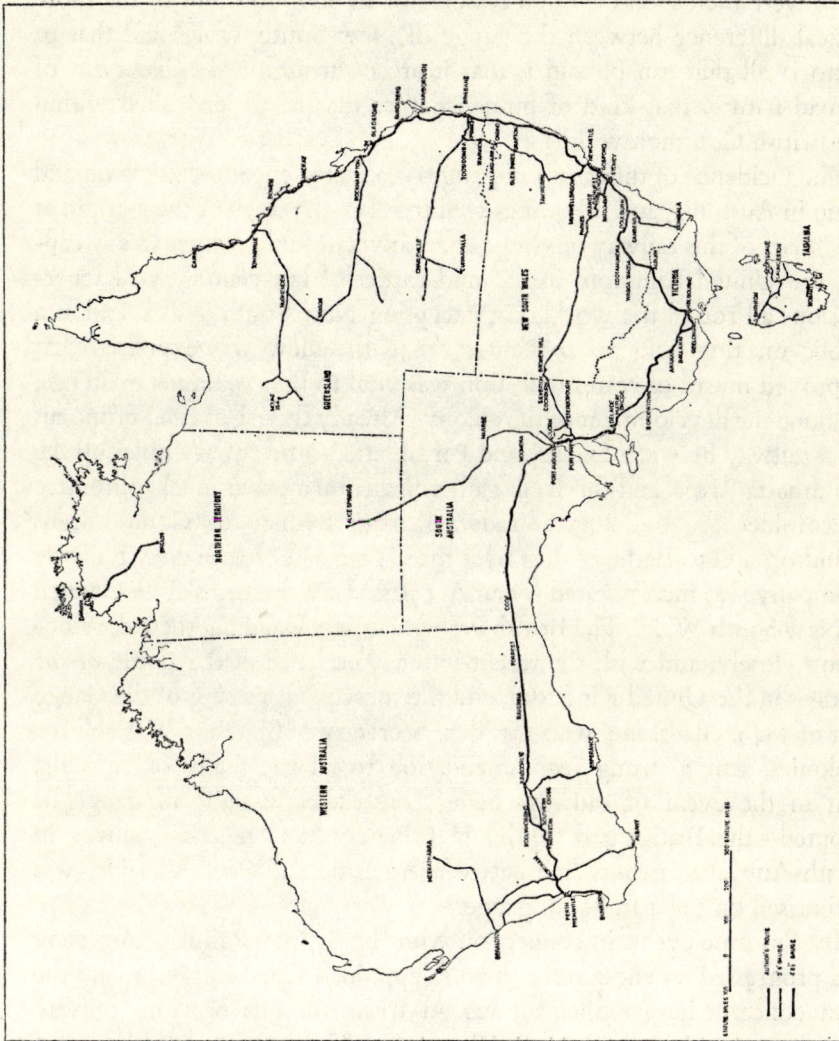

Railways of Australia: map showing principal lines and author's route

pioneer Australian railway managements in allowing such a situation to develop. With the 3 ft. 6 in. gauge in Queensland and Western Australia there were then sound enough reasons for its adoption; but of the more critical difference between the gauge of New South Wales and that of Victoria all that can be said is that it arose through a peculiar twist of human nature, that kind of human nature that is still cherished within the British Commonwealth!

The incidence of different rail gauges is a factor encountered again and again in Australia, and it is just as well to relate the story of their origin at the outset of this railway odyssey. The Railway Mania, which was sweeping the United Kingdom in the mid-forties of last century, had repercussions all round the world, not excepting New South Wales, and at a public meeting held on 29 January 1846 the view was expressed that improved means of communication was vital to the continued existence, let alone the development of the colony. Already there had been proposals for a railway between Sydney and Parramatta, some twenty miles up the Parramatta River, and this fresh gathering set up a provisional committee to consider the building of railways from Sydney to Goulburn, to Windsor, and to Bathurst. Just over three years later the Sydney Railway Company was incorporated by an Act passed by the Legislative Council of New South Wales. The British Parliament was watching these developments closely, and with the recent bitter experience of the Battle of the Gauges in the United Kingdom, and the subsequent passing of the Gauge Act of 1846, Gladstone, who was then Secretary of State for War and the Colonies, sent a strong recommendation to all the States of Australia that in the event of railways being constructed a uniform gauge be adopted—the British 4 ft. 8½ in. In February 1850 the first railway in South Australia, a short line between Adelaide and Port Adelaide, was authorised on the 4 ft. 8½ in. gauge.

By this time events in connection with the Sydney Railway Company had progressed far enough for them to appoint a Chief Engineer, and the man concerned, one Sheilds, was an Irishman. His previous railway experience had been with C. B. Vignoles, and he seems to have been just such another stormy petrel! He vehemently declaimed that the Irish gauge of 5 ft. 3 in. was superior to the British; and his views carried such conviction that the directors of the Company wrote to the Colonial Secretary in London stating that they wished to adopt the 5 ft. 3 in.

gauge. No railways had actually been constructed at the time, and the British Government of the day, having no reason to argue about actual dimensions, agreed to the change. So long as there was uniformity the Palace of Westminster, in modern slang, 'couldn't care less'. So, on 27 July 1852 an Act was passed stating that the gauge of the railways in New South Wales should be 5 ft. 3 in. Victoria and South Australia, both uncommitted so far as purchase of equipment was concerned, followed suit, and adopted the 5 ft. 3 in. gauge. Before this time however it would seem that the Sydney Railway Company was finding its vehement Irish chief engineer a trifle hot to hold, while the financial prospects were gloomy. The early records are not clear on the precise chain of events, but the fact remains that his salary was reduced, and as a natural consequence he resigned. There would have been nothing significant about this except that he had been the special advocate of the 5 ft. 3 in. gauge, and this was to have the most profound significance.

In his place there was appointed a Scotsman named Wallace, who came to Sydney fresh from experience on railway building in the United Kingdom and on the continent of Europe. Over the question of rail gauge he was as dour and uncompromising in favour of 4 ft. 8½ in. as Sheilds had been eloquent on behalf of 5 ft. 3 in., and so far as New South Wales was concerned he secured the repeal of the 1852 Act, and a reversion to 4 ft. 8½ in. It was evidently not in Wallace's nature to advise the neighbour States of Victoria and South Australia of what he was doing; they learned of it only when the measure for repeal came before the Legislature. Both States were furious, and the two small railway companies being by that time committed in respect of orders for rolling stock, they stood their ground, and the Melbourne and Hobson's Bay Railway and the Adelaide and Port Adelaide Railway both went into service on the 5 ft. 3 in. gauge. At the time the Australian colonies were quite independent of each other. The British Parliament saw no grounds for interference, although at that time the commitment so far as the 5 ft. 3 in. gauge was very small indeed. One would have thought that a very small amount of compensation to the two small companies in Victoria and South Australia would have been enough to tip the balance, and secure the uniformity of gauge. It must be remembered however that by that time, 1854–5, the home Government was embroiled in all the complexities, muddles and disasters of the Crimean War, and a disagreement

25

over rail gauges between two small colonies on the other side of the world could well have appeared as an insignificant trifle. Yet from this trifle arose the great stumbling block of gauge diversity, which even today has been no more than partially resolved. Such was the origin of the century-old confrontation on rail gauge between Victoria and South Australia on the one hand, and New South Wales on the other. But what of Queensland and Western Australia?

Today, with the immense facility of long-distance air travel it is perhaps difficult for those living in Europe to appreciate the extremely primitive state of communications that existed in Australia well into the latter part of the nineteenth century. So far as Queensland was concerned it was not until September 1824 that the site of its capital city was even discovered; then John Oxley, landing from the sea in search of good water, came upon the splendid natural site astride the winding course of the river, which was subsequently named Brisbane. At first it was established as a penal settlement, and it was not until 1842 that an adjoining area was thrown open to free settlers. Seventeen years later matters had developed sufficiently for Queensland to be granted separation from the Mother Colony of New South Wales. Six years later, in July 1865, the citizens of Queensland flocked to witness the opening of their first railway, 21 miles long, from Ipswich to Grandchester. Though a mere handful of settlers in the vast territory delineated by the new colony, they quickly began to show a spirit of stout independence, and in nothing stronger than over the question of railway gauges! To the consternation of the older established colonies farther south, Queensland, on the strong advice of Mr. Fitzgibbon, engineer to the 'Southern and Western Railway', adopted the 3 ft. 6 in. gauge.

At the time there was little thought of the inconvenience that would eventuate when it came to linking up with the railways of New South Wales, because the Brisbane district, more than 700 miles from Sydney, was as relatively remote as the Outer Hebrides were from London. Furthermore, Brisbane was only just beyond the State boundary. To the north there extended more than 2000 miles of coastline that was virtually unexplored, let alone settled. Fitzgibbon, having regard to the special circumstances of Queensland, considered that the British standard of 4 ft. 8½ in. gauge would make railways too costly for the economy of the colony to bear. He had very clearly in mind the task of crossing the

26

mountain ranges running parallel to the coast in order to reach the interior, and like those who planned railways many years later in the Cape of Good Hope he felt that a narrower gauge than standard was desirable in the mountain regions. And so, for good or ill, the Legislature of the young colony decided that the 3 ft. 6 in. gauge was adequate. Thus was originated a *third* main line railway gauge on the mainland of Australia.

Then there was the already amazing colony of Western Australia, with an area equal to roughly one-third of the entire continent. Yet at the time its Legislature was set up, in 1868, the total population of this vast area had only just topped the 15,000 mark. Its earliest railways, of which the first was opened in 1871, were short, privately-owned affairs built to assist in the logging trade. Such enterprises naturally paid no heed to any ideals of gauge standardisation, and when the first Government-sponsored railway was built in the mid-seventies the gauge was originally 3 ft. This was soon altered to 3 ft. 6 in., and this latter became the standard gauge of the colony. It could well have remained a quiet little local system, serving the agricultural needs of the fine farming and forest country around Perth, but for the sensational discoveries of gold at Southern Cross in 1887, at Coolgardie in 1892, and finally the world-famous 'Golden Mile' between Kalgoorlie and Boulder. This led to a rapid expansion of the railway system to such an extent that by the turn of the century there was a far greater mileage on the 3 ft. 6 in. gauge—taking Queensland and Western Australia together—than on either of the two wider gauges. At that time the striking figures were:

3 ft. 6 in. gauge	5280 miles
4 ft. 8½ in. gauge	2531 miles
5 ft. 3 in. gauge	3615 miles

The individual total mileages for the five states were:

New South Wales	2531
Victoria	3122
South Australia (5 ft. 3 in.)	493
,, ,, (3 ft. 6 in.)	502
Queensland	2503
Western Australia	2275

After the initial manœuvring and passing of the necessary legislation each colony had gone ahead with its railway development regardless of what was happening elsewhere in Australia; but as the end of the nineteenth century approached and the proposals for an Australian Commonwealth began to take shape the question of the unification of railway gauges assumed great importance. In 1899 *The Railway Magazine* printed the following paragraph:

The question of a uniform gauge for the railways of the proposed Commonwealth received and occupied much of the time and attention of the collective wisdom of our Australian Conventional 'Decades' and their specially appointed committee during the sittings of each session; and despite the evidence tended to them by our accredited railway experts of the highest grade, including the late Mr. E. M. G. Eddy, it was ultimately dropped as being beyond the grasp of Conventional solution.

Subsequently the probable cost of bringing Victoria and South Australia into line with New South Wales was estimated at £2,400,000; but to convert all Australian railways to the 4 ft. 8½ in. gauge was estimated at around £8 million. It seems that this central conference was very near to agreement in respect of the conversion of the 5 ft. 3 in. gauge lines in Victoria and South Australia to the 4 ft. 8½ in. gauge, but in 1898 the Queensland Chief Commissioner for Railways was brought into the discussions. He stood out resolutely against the making of any change to the gauge in Queensland, and proposals for general unification of gauges were allowed to lapse. The case for the retention of the 3 ft. 6 in. gauge in Queensland attracted a good deal of attention abroad. In England, in 1899, *The Railway Magazine* carried two long articles setting out the case for Queensland's 3 ft. 6 in. gauge, comparing the cost of railway construction per mile in that colony, and pointing out that if she had adopted the 4 ft. 8½ in. gauge, on the basis of costs in New South Wales, it would have been possible to build only half the mileage then in existence for the money that had been expended. There was, in addition, very little difference in speed, and the same article quoted, as the average speed of all principal trains:

New South Wales	24½ m.p.h.
Victoria	22 m.p.h.
Queensland	21½ m.p.h.

The article wound up thus:

It is too late in the day to think of altering the Queensland gauge—at all events, we would require some greater advantage than can at present be seen on the surface, especially if it means raising the passenger fares and live-stock rates to the level of those charged in New South Wales. The gauge in New South Wales will not be altered either, nor do I believe will any of the main lines in the other colonies. . . .

The publication of these articles caused a considerable amount of interest, even of excitement, in Australia, and the author, writing under the pen-name of 'Rebus', contributed a further two articles in 1900, giving a vivid account of the inauguration of the pioneer line in Queensland. Railway openings in mid-Victorian times were much the same in the colonies as they had been earlier in the United Kingdom itself, but the opening of the Ipswich and Grantchester line was marked by some speeches of exceeding length. However boring they must have been to the great majority of those gathered around, they included one or two highly significant sentences. Fitzgibbon, the engineer, went to some length to defend his recommendation of the 3 ft. 6 in. gauge, which in 1865 was not adopted in Queensland without some considerable opposition; but he was followed by W. T. Doyne, a Member of the Institution of Civil Engineers, who had commanded a British Army works corps in the Crimea, and who had been a personal friend of the great Thomas Brassey. On the question of gauge he said: 'There can be no question as to the great inferiority of a railway laid with a gauge of 3 ft. 6 in. in respect of power when compared to the broader gauges, and I should not adopt it in any case in which the character of the country would permit of the construction of full gauge railways at a moderate cost. . . .'

He then went on to enlarge upon the merits of the 5 ft. 3 in. gauge in Victoria, where he was then engaged on constructional work. By that time some of his hearers must have been getting uneasy. But then he continued:

I now come to the question of the Queensland Railways, and I have much pleasure in being able to say that I believe the course that has been adopted here is a wise one, and I do not venture that opinion on light grounds. It has been arrived at after a careful study of the question, with all the facts before me. The position of Queensland appears to me to be simply this. It possesses a great territory inland which is cut off from the ports on the seaboard by mountain ranges, which have to be crossed by any system of communication which may be adopted. The present means of the Colony are inadequate to provide a system of broad-gauge railways, while the wants of the community demand some power superior to the bush tracks of transit. A medium course has, therefore, been introduced—I think, wisely. A railway is being constructed at a moderate cost, which will amply meet the needs of this community for many years to come, which is perfect so far as its powers extend, and will, I have no doubt, act as a pioneer to develop the resources of the Colony, and enable it to carry out superior works when necessity demands them, without having in the first instance loaded it with the incubus of a debt which would retard its progress in other matters.

In its early years *The Railway Magazine* had a remarkably wide coverage of events in many parts of the world, and it is very interesting to find that in the first four years of its existence references to Australian railways were confined entirely to those of Queensland and Western Australia. Furthermore, another three years were to pass before detailed reference was made to the working in any other of the States, and then no more than briefly, to South Australia. Queensland had, of course, been a focal point of interest in the mild 'Battle of the Gauges' that had preceded the establishment of the Commonwealth of Australia, in 1901; but Western Australia was then an isolated outpost, in which railway working was on somewhat primitive lines. The wheel has certainly come full circle, and before I come to the end of this book of mine Queensland and Western Australia will once again have been very fully written up; but while seventy years ago, although so well documented, they were the lesser lights of the Australian railways firmament, today both States are fairly 'hitting the headlines' in their magnificent railway developments.

So fair-minded a commentator as W. T. Doyne would no doubt be ready enough to alter his views on the subject of *power* had he seen the triple-headed coal trains of today coming down from Moura to Gladstone: sixty hopper wagons, conveying a pay load of 3000 tons, and representing a gross trailing load of 4150 tons, and running at speeds up to 50 m.p.h. on the 3 ft. 6 in. gauge. This is no freak effort. Last August when I was at Rockhampton it was not unusual to run more than twenty of these giant trains in a single week! But I must not anticipate. This is no more than an introductory chapter. It was in New South Wales that we first set foot in Australia, and it is appropriate that in this one-time 'Mother Colony' our explorations should begin. One of the disadvantages of long-distance railway travel in Australia for those who would see both the country and the railway system is that so much of most journeys is made at night.

With journeys of some 600 miles between Brisbane and Sydney, 600 miles between Sydney and Melbourne, and 500 miles between Melbourne and Adelaide, the inter-state expresses leave in the early evening and reach their destination around breakfast time next morning. So far as seeing the country is concerned New South Wales is in many respects a notable exception, for in addition to highly scenic shorter expeditions, to Newcastle and to the far-famed Blue Mountains, there is the splendid 'Intercapital Daylight Express', running between Sydney and Melbourne, which as its name suggests does most of the long journey between the two cities in daylight.

The ease of communication nowadays between the State capitals of Australia makes an extraordinary contrast to the situation that existed a hundred years ago, even after the construction of railways had commenced. A railway map of Australia, even if carried forward to the year 1875, would show no more than a few ribbons of track extending inward from coastal districts. No appreciable progress had then been made in connecting up one colony with another. It so happened that the inception of railways in Australia roughly coincided with the inauguration of the first Anglo-Australian steamship mail. Hitherto, the post, conveyed by sailing cutters, had taken anything between 120 and 130 days on the journey from London to Sydney. The Peninsular and Oriental Steamship Company secured the first Government contract for conveyance of the Australian mail, and then it was considered of such relatively minor importance that the contract called for no more than a branch run, operated once a month from Singapore in connection with the main P. & O. run to China and Japan. These early mail steamers called at Albany, Melbourne and Sydney. To the disgust of South Australians Adelaide was by-passed, while in Western Australia Albany was preferred to Fremantle, because the latter then had little more than an open roadstead. The fact that an English mail was received no more than once a month serves to underline the isolation in which Australia as a whole then existed, and fills in yet another detail of the background against which railway development began.

CHAPTER TWO

Sydney—The West line

It was certainly appropriate that my exploration of the railways of New South Wales should have begun by travelling over the Sydney–Parramatta line. This pioneer stretch, now an intensely busy section of the Sydney suburban complex, has recently attained a far greater significance even than that of springboard for the Main West line. Not only does it make an arduous way through the great barrier of the Blue Mountains, but now, having for long extended across the great inland plains, and served the distant mining area of Broken Hill, 699 miles to the west of Sydney, it forms the great standard-gauge transcontinental link right across Australia. I had no opportunity to explore beyond Lithgow, a mere 97 miles on the way to the west; but this section includes the utterly fascinating ascent of the Blue Mountain range. Armed with a footplate pass, and with some delightful railwaymen as companions, the cab of one of the fine '46' class electric locomotives provided a grandstand view of all the passing scene. We travelled by the 'Central West Express' leaving Sydney Terminal station at 8 a.m., and at this stage in my explorations there was time for little more than a glance at the huge station, and its intensely varied traffic, before we were on our way.

Electric multiple-unit commuter trains were coming in thick and fast; the 'Intercapital Daylight Express' left for Melbourne; and amidst the plethora of diesel and electric locomotives several tough old 4–6–4 steam tank engines were engaged in shunting. One of the massive '38' class steam 'Pacifics' was taking out an empty stock train. These notes are no more than incidental to the present chapter, however. The Sydney suburban area is discussed in some detail in a later chapter. My own train consisted of five air-conditioned coaches, no more than 223 tons tare. This was an easy enough load for the opening stages of our journey, but a

PLATE I.

(a) Sydney Central Station, showing the through suburban lines leading to the harbour bridge in the foreground and the buildings of the main line section in rear

(b) Testing Sydney Harbour Bridge before its opening in March 1932, with four lines of locomotives totalling 7000 tons

PLATE 2. Vintage New South Wales trains
(*a*) A McConnell 0–4–2 of 1855 (now preserved)

(*b*) Two 4–4–0s of Class '79', dating from 1877, on A.R.H.S. Special to Canberra in 1962. The leading engine is now preserved at Canberra

(*c*) Two 0–6–0s of Class '93' also of 1877 on A.R.H.S. special on Gilmore–Batlow line

different proposition when we began our ascent of the Blue Mountains. Out of Sydney Terminal, over the sextuple track through the suburban area the course is very winding, but at speeds of 50 to 55 m.p.h. the locomotive rode splendidly, and we quickly reached the outer-suburban station of Strathfield. The station names are a constant source of interest to an English visitor, and in this first short run of $7\frac{1}{2}$ miles we had passed Stanmore, Lewisham, Petersham, Ashfield, Croydon and Burwood. Strathfield is the junction for the north main line leading to the Queensland border. It is the entraining point for passengers in the western suburbs joining main line express trains, as Ealing Broadway and Willesden Junction used to be in outer London, and as Watford Junction is today. The main line to the south traversed by inter-state expresses diverges at Lidcombe, a further three miles to the west.

At this hour in the morning all six tracks were being heavily utilised. The sextuple line ended at Homebush and the quadrupling continued to Granville, $13\frac{1}{2}$ miles out of Sydney, where the original main southern line, which is now an alternative line, diverges to the south, and a branch line diverges northwards to Carlingford. A mile beyond Granville lies Parramatta, and here we made our second stop. The atmosphere was still definitely suburban, with many multiple-unit electric trains. Their colour is a plain red, almost identical to the iron-ore red of the former Furness Railway locomotives at home. From Parramatta we really began to head out into open country, or more correctly through a succession of countrified suburbs. The track is excellent, and we were running steadily at around 60 m.p.h. The station names are equally intriguing, and it does not need much guesswork to imagine from what part of the United Kingdom the original settlers came when passing stations such as Pendle Hill, Doonside, Werrington, and Kingswood. Soon after Rooty Hill the lofty ridges of the Blue Mountains can be seen far ahead, lying athwart our general direction, while over a fine and practically level track we were heading straight for them. After the cold squally weather that had greeted our arrival in Australia this second day was more promising, with patches of sunlight beginning to light up the ridges that lay ahead of us. The good speed we had made from Parramatta was reflected in the smart time for the 20-mile run to Penrith, $21\frac{3}{4}$ minutes start to stop, with a maximum of 67 m.p.h.

Penrith is the terminal point of the multiple-unit electric suburban

c

services from Sydney, and although it was not yet nine o'clock in the morning many train sets were already stabled, having coped with the early morning peak period. The problems of commuter traffic are as great in Australia as everywhere else in the world, as details of the working around Sydney given in Chapter Five of this book will show. Although Penrith, New South Wales, looks so different a town from Penrith, Cumberland, it is similar in lying at the foot of a severe incline on the railway, though to be sure the southbound ascent to Shap is a mere hillock compared to the ascent that now faced us. Immediately ahead of us now, extending in endless array to both left and right, was a solid wall of mountains rising to nearly 4000 ft. The escarpment is tremendous, and to climb Lapstone Hill it was first proposed to use a gradient of 1 in 20. This route was abandoned as likely to impose too great a task upon locomotives. So also was the second proposal, using a minimum inclination of 1 in 30. No contractor was prepared to tender for a tunnel nearly two miles long through the solid rock of the mountainside, and even if the bore had been driven, no one could suggest any means of transporting the ten million bricks that would have been necessary to line it. So John Whitton, the engineer, designed a zig-zag location to climb the mountain face, climbing part way on a moderately severe gradient, then reversing direction and continuing upward on the second arm of the zig-zag.

It was an expedient, but the two reversals of direction made for slow and tedious operation and in later years a direct line was constructed. So, on a continuous ascent at 1 in 60 we climbed a double-track railway cut on a ledge from the solid rock. Below and to the left we saw the plains gradually receding; to the right of the line the solid rock rose vertically for many hundreds of feet. We passed a heavy coal train coasting gently down towards Penrith; seventeen great bogie wagons conveying between them some 1200 tons of coal in a single load. With regenerative braking on the locomotives the descent was easy and safe. This was my first introduction to the mighty Australian freight trains of today, though I was soon to learn that 1200 tons is now considered quite a light load! We were making a comfortable 40 m.p.h. up the hill, and soon we began to leave the region of the precipitous escarpment, and come out into a glorious tumbled upland country. On the station name-boards the heights above sea level are quoted, and these alone showed the rapidity with which we were climbing. From 89 ft. at Penrith we were up to 535 ft. at Glenbrook, 768 ft. at Blaxland, and 1056 ft. at Valley Heights, where we were only 14 miles on our way from Penrith. Here we were climbing a ridge among the mountains. With a major highway running close alongside, the land fell abruptly on both sides of the track, and we looked out over range upon range of densely-wooded hills.

It was difficult to assimilate fully the geography of this strange and beautiful region. The stations lay beside clusters of splendid villas served by excellent shopping centres, and yet all the time we were climbing higher and higher into the mountains. It was the Australian spring. Flowers were everywhere, and the blossoms of the almond and wattle trees gave an almost exotic look to the countryside. As our powerful electric locomotive took us with effortless ease up the steep gradients I listened to stories of steam days on these great banks. The line was electrified as recently as 1957, and although my companions in the cab appreciated the speed and efficiency of the new power I sensed they were all steam men at heart! Higher and higher we climbed: Faulconbridge, 1465 ft.; Woodford, 1992 ft.; Hazelbrook, 2210 ft. Still the railway was carried on this curious ridge formation, and the higher we mounted the wider and grander became the prospects to both left and right of the line. The gradients were by this time much steeper, with a high proportion of 1 in 33. There was hardly a length of straight track, and still the villages remained like so many opulent residential suburbs. Even on these slopes speed was rarely less than 35 m.p.h., and when we approached Wentworth Falls, at an altitude of 2844 ft., glimpses of some of the most spectacular ranges of the Blue Mountains began to open out, with sheer cliffs, and immense clefts thickly wooded with the all-pervading Australian gum trees. One could appreciate also how these dramatic heights got their name, because a distinctive blue haze rises to the upper crags from the forests below.

In one and three quarter hours running from Sydney, now 68½ miles away, we reached Katoomba, 3336 ft. above sea level, and a very charming mountain resort. It is also the terminus of some of the longer-distance residential trains from Sydney. In addition to its popularity in this respect it has become a major tourist centre because of its proximity to some of the greatest sights in the Blue Mountains. So far as the railway is concerned the worst of the climbing is over by the time Katoomba is attained, and the next 17 miles can be described as a mountain switchback in glorious

35

country, with a ruling gradient of 1 in 75, constant and severe curvature and station altitudes varying between the 3336 ft. of Katoomba and the 3501 ft. of Bell. Actually the highest point on the line is reached about 1½ miles west of Bell, at 3584 ft. Despite the easier gradients this is not a stretch for fast running, and because of the curves the maximum attained is around 45 m.p.h. A continuous descent begins at milepost 86½ from Sydney, though at Clarence, 89 miles, the altitude is still 3468 ft. Then the line comes to the western escarpment, with an abrupt natural fall to the town of Lithgow; and here John Whitton was faced with an even more formidable task than on the Lapstone cliff face. He surmounted this great task with a piece of engineering that in its day was as famous as the spiral tunnels of the Alps, or the Victoria Falls Bridge in Rhodesia; the great Lithgow Zig-Zag.

Gliding down the gradient today over the 'new line', even though riding in the cab, it is difficult to appreciate the nature of John Whitton's task. Just after the highest point on the line a descent on the very moderate gradient of 1 in 90 begins, and through an increasingly rocky defile, with far more straight track than we have experienced so far on this line, we cut through a succession of no fewer than ten tunnels. Most of them are quite short, but all had to be blasted through solid rock and with the limited local experience at the time the original line was built, tunnels were things to be avoided if possible. Leaving the last tunnel and emerging into a densely-wooded glen, above which rise great beetling cliffs on either side, we pass Zig-Zag signal box, and with no more than a glimpse at this stage of graceful viaducts high up among the trees a precipitous descent of 1 in 42 is entered upon. Speed is now held to no more than 22 m.p.h. and so we come to the outskirts of Lithgow. There is a large, and one-time well-equipped yard for steam locomotives, where a few of the celebrated 2-8-0 engines of Class '50' may still be seen today, and then we enter the island platformed station of Lithgow, just 97 miles from Sydney. The journey has taken 2 hr. 36 min. inclusive of six intermediate stops. Lithgow is the limit of electric traction on the west main line; thenceforward the haulage is diesel or steam.

From Lithgow we retraced our steps to Katoomba by road, and this proved an unrivalled way of seeing the Great Zig-Zag. We first of all made our way to the present Zig-Zag signal box on the electrified line. This is now opened only on special occasions because the line is completely equipped with automatic colour light signals, and no train has occasion to stop at 'Zig-Zag' unless closely following another one, and receiving a momentary check. The problems of working have been greatly simplified since electrification. In steam days many heavy east-bound freight trains had four locomotives from Lithgow up the 1 in 42 gradient to Zig-Zag box. Such trains were triple-headed, with the fourth locomotive banking in rear. At Zig-Zag box a stop was made for the leading engine and the banker to be detached. Then the train continued up the 1 in 90 ascent through the ten tunnels with two engines at its head. 'Zig-Zag' is typical of the smaller signal boxes on the line, of an all-timber design strongly reminiscent of the Lancashire and Yorkshire Railway. In 1911 C. B. Byles, the Signal Engineer of the latter railway, was invited to go to New South Wales as signalling adviser to the Chief Commissioner of Railways in that State, and he was subsequently appointed Signal Engineer. A connoisseur of mechanical signalling equipment can detect many features that would at one time have been familiar on the L. & Y. R. at home.

From an inspection of Zig-Zag signal box we took to the road once again, and then proceeded to climb the face of the great escarpment on a road made over the route of the original railway zig-zag. It was an absolutely fascinating experience. We drove slowly over the viaducts, looking down to the double-track main line of today, passing through a short tunnel, and stopping to inspect the present roadway at the site of one of the reversing places. The great Zig-Zag was entirely single-tracked, but the viaducts are wide enough to permit cars to pass abreast. Today the slopes are densely wooded, and even from vantage points of the viaducts it is not easy to discern the alignment of the original railway; but when first constructed the slopes were quite bare, and the complete extent of the zig-zag seen from either side presented a truly magnificent spectacle. Driving slowly over the track today I was very conscious of being in the presence of railway history of the very first importance. Although there was a minimum of tunnelling some tremendous blasting operations were necessary. Two masses of rock in particular, one estimated to weigh 40,000 tons, and another 45,000, had to be dislodged. The events were publicised well in advance and large numbers of spectators came to Lithgow to see the 'blasts'. The second blast was of such importance that the Countess of Belmore, wife of the Governor-General, was invited to fire the charge, by pressing an electric button. By a coincidence the section of line including the great Zig-Zag—20 miles from Mount Victoria to Bowenfels—was opened for traffic in October 1869, almost exactly 100 years before my own first visit.

Although this is anticipating to some extent the contents of the next chapter the reader will be naturally a little curious to know how such an exceptional stretch of line was operated in the earlier days of steam. In approaching Lithgow attention was drawn to some of the veteran Class '50' 2-8-0 locomotives still in use on shunting and secondary duties. They were the freight counterparts of the very celebrated Class 'P6' 4-6-0s, later known as Class 'C32'. These were the 'maid-of-all-work' passenger engines and worked over all sections of the New South Wales railway system; but, in particular, the way in which they hauled passenger trains over the fearsome gradients of the Blue Mountains was at times quite astonishing. In those primitive days on the New South Wales railways, just before the turn of the century, there was considerable rivalry between British and American interests as to which would exert the greatest influence on locomotive practice. The British influence might have been much greater than it eventually turned out to be if Dugald Drummond's temperament had been otherwise. Despite the great publicity given to Crewe and the Webb compounds, to the speed achievements of the Great Northern, and to the striking developments on the North Eastern under Wilson Worsdell and Walter M. Smith, in the eyes of the railway world at large the personality and achievements of Dugald Drummond, in his Caledonian days, were quite outstanding. So that when Eddy, as Chief Commissioner of Railways in New South Wales, was dissatisfied with the motive power situation, and sent Mr. Thow, the Chief Mechanical Engineer, to the United Kingdom to discuss the supply of new locomotives, it was with Dugald Drummond that many of the discussions took place.

It was known in Australia that Drummond in collaboration with certain other gentlemen was actively considering the formation of a locomotive building establishment near Sydney; but while the business negotiations were protracted and difficult, Thow and Drummond together schemed out the basic design for a new main line passenger locomotive. The discussions took place in Glasgow in October 1890, and the eventual outcome was the celebrated 'P' class 4-6-0. But long before the final design took shape, and the time came for contracts to be placed, Drummond and the Government authorities in Sydney had completely failed to come to terms, and the Australians broke off all negotiations. Nevertheless Thow had the design of the 4-6-0 'in his pocket' as it were, and when examination of existing Caledonian passenger and goods engines showed that such designs would be unsuitable for the conditions in New South Wales the outline of the proposed new 4-6-0 was discussed with various British manufacturers and tenders obtained.

Studying the line through the Blue Mountains and having had some first-hand experience of the train working—albeit with modern electric haulage—it is fascinating to work through the old records, and discover the extent to which Scottish practice was examined in the search for a satisfactory solution. Excellent though the Drummond 4-4-0s were on the Beattock bank the climb from Penrith to Katoomba was infinitely more severe, and many times longer, and however well they might have done elsewhere in New South Wales they would not have been much good in this terrain. As things turned out the 4-6-0 design roughed out between Thow and Dugald Drummond was copied, with quite remarkable fidelity, in the celebrated 'Jones Goods' 4-6-0 for the Highland, and it gained special fame as being the first British 4-6-0! So far as the New South Wales 'P' class was concerned the circular side window was an original feature, but the chimney was pure Drummond. The first engines of the 'P' class took the road in New South Wales early in 1892, nearly three years before 'Jones Goods' on the Highland Railway, and by British standards they were considered a very large engine indeed. In fact the Manchester firm of Beyer, Peacock and Company, who secured the contract to build the first fifty engines of the class, expressed grave doubts about the whole design. They thought that the engines would be very heavy, difficult to make, and not very satisfactory in service. I have referred in my previous book *Steam Railways in Retrospect* to the remarkable freedom from teething troubles enjoyed by the 'Jones Goods' 4-6-0s on the Highland Railway; I wonder how many features that could have been troublesome were sorted out on the 'P' class 4-6-0s in New South Wales!

I must not dilate upon steam locomotive power at this stage; but the heavy gradients and magnificent scenery of the Blue Mountains are a constant reminder of the nineteenth-century affinity between the Caledonian, the Highland and the New South Wales railways. The sight and sound of a 'P' class 4–6–0 pounding its way up the cliff-edge near Lapstone, or fighting the 1 in 33 gradients above Springwood, had worthy counterparts in Scotland, on the Forres–Dava bank, on the Dingwall and Skye line, or in climbing the last bleak miles up to the Slochd. These reflections were vividly brought to mind on travelling through some of the grandest scenery of the Blue Mountains. In the central *massif*, between the great escarpments that run east and west of the range, the scenery is extraordinarily Scottish in character, though with blue gums replacing the larches, rowans and silver birches. We got back to Katoomba in time to catch the 2.56 p.m. fast electric train for Sydney, and from the driver's cab once again, with an unrivalled view of the line ahead, I was able to take a different look at the details of this most compelling line of railway.

The weather had by this time cleared beautifully, and on an afternoon of bright spring sunshine we made our way down the bank. This train stopped at all stations between Katoomba and Penrith, and as well as noting in more detail the unfamiliar geological formations in the mountain country, the equipment of the railway itself was of much interest. Until Lapstone all the stations were formed of a single island platform, with pleasant architecture that reminded me very much of the West Highland line in Scotland. At Lawson, nine miles down the bank from Katoomba, is the electrical control room from which electric traction current supplies over the whole line from Parramatta to Lithgow are regulated. The traction system is 1500 volts direct current, as used on the Manchester–Sheffield–Wath lines at home, and on the earlier main line electrification schemes in France. We had a wonderful effect of light and shade in the late afternoon sunshine as we rounded the dramatic curve on the rock face of the Lapstone escarpment, and then I saw more clearly the ground formation of the old single-track line leading to the one-time zig-zag between Lapstone and the foot of the incline, at Emu Plains. Unlike the more spectacular zig-zag near Lithgow the one-time route near Lapstone is now almost completely overgrown.

The 34½ miles down the bank from Katoomba to Penrith took just over 70 minutes, with fifteen intermediate stops—a smart piece of railway working even though the continuous descent made no particular demands for tractive power. The section does provide a remarkable instance of the way in which electric traction, skilfully designed, can completely 'flatten

New South Wales Government Railways Class 'C79' 4-4-0 No. 1210 as now preserved at Canberra. This engine was the first to work the Queanbeyan–Canberra branch on its opening in 1913

out' difficult gradients; for these local passenger trains are worked to precisely the same timings in the reverse direction! On the 'Central West Express' by which I had travelled in the morning the time allowance from Penrith up to Katoomba is 59 minutes, inclusive of two stops; but the local trains which have to make the full fifteen intermediate stops, still climb that 34½ miles in 71 minutes, with a vertical rise of 3247 ft. in the process.

At the time of my visit there were five other named trains running over this route on Mondays to Fridays. Two residential expresses leave Sydney at 5.15 and 5.17 p.m. and follow each other at close headway out to Penrith. The first goes by the name of 'The Fish', and the origin of this unusual name extends back almost to the earliest days of the line. The story generally accepted today is that the regular driver, John Heron by name, got the nickname of the 'Big Fish'. Railwaymen in all countries are ever ready to apply tags to train workings, buildings, and so on, and somewhere in the 1880s with John Heron continuing as a daily institution the train itself gradually came to be known as 'The Fish', Today the 5.15 p.m. from Sydney to Mount Victoria is officially printed so in the public timetables. It is one of those residential expresses on which the clientele is so regular as to make it more like a travelling club. Calling only at Strathfield in the Sydney suburbs it then runs non-stop to Penrith, and from there takes the first part of the climb over the Blue Mountains also non-stop: 15½ miles up to Springwood in 24 minutes. After that it calls at all stations onwards to Mount Victoria. The immediately following 5.17 p.m. from Sydney is appropriately and officially known as 'The Chips'. This follows hard on the tail of 'The Fish' out to Penrith, and then calls at all stations up to Springwood, where it terminates. The two trains between them provide a splendid evening service to the residential areas in the Blue Mountains, while the corresponding inward services in the morning leave Mount Victoria at 5.54 a.m., due at Sydney at 8.5 a.m., and 6.57 a.m. ('The Chips') from Springwood, due at Sydney 8.20 a.m. These trains do not run on Saturdays, but a train performing the combined work of the two, calling at all stations from Mount Victoria to Penrith, is run instead.

In my own brief visit to this most fascinating line I was able to see no more than the first hundred miles, to Lithgow. This is merely the start, for beyond the mountain barrier a whole series of lengthy branch lines

41

spread out, in addition of course to the main transcontinental line to Broken Hill and beyond. The lines west of Lithgow are served nightly, except on Saturdays by three separate mail trains. At 9 p.m. the 'Through Mail' leaves Sydney, taking the west main line as far as Orange, and then taking the line through Wellington to terminate at Dubbo, 287 miles distant, at 6.53 a.m. next morning. This is followed at 10.10 p.m. from Sydney by the 'Forbes and Cowra' mail, covering distances of 296 and 227 miles to its two separate destinations. Finally, there is the 'Mudgee Mail' at 10.15 p.m. diverging from the main line at Wallerawang, barely 10 miles beyond Lithgow. Mudgee, 191½ miles from Sydney, is the daily destination of this train, but on four days a week it continues to Coonabarabran, 316 miles distant, and on three days still further to Gwabegar, 375 miles away, and reached at 1.42 p.m. I am afraid these distant stations in the Australian 'outback' are still no more than names on the map to me, and I would dearly have liked to have the time to explore these remoter branches. There is something intensely symbolical about them, because they all feed their traffic into the parent stem of all railways in New South Wales, the Sydney and Parramatta line.

CHAPTER THREE

Sydney—North Coast line

The present trunk line between Sydney and Brisbane differs considerably in its origins as compared with the West line described in the previous chapter. In that case the railway was the natural sequel to colonial development. In the endeavour to seek further grasslands for the settlers to occupy, expeditions sponsored by the Government had sought ways of crossing the barrier of the Blue Mountains. Having discovered the great, almost limitless plains to the west, and established new settlements in many hitherto isolated places, it was no more than natural, once railways were introduced, for tracks to be pushed westward in the wake of colonial agricultural settlement. Along the coast north of Sydney the situation was quite otherwise. The township of Newcastle grew up as an independent entity, with its own developing industries, its coal, and its own seaborne trade. Still farther north was Brisbane, and its stout independence, so far as railway development was concerned, has been emphasised in an earlier chapter.

The first and natural railway development from Newcastle was along the line of the Hunter valley, which was rich in coal, and in its upper reaches contained large and highly productive vineyards; and by the year 1878 the railway had been extended up the valley as far as Tamworth, 183 miles from Newcastle. A further extension was made towards the Queensland border, and this was reached by the inland route via Glen Innes in 1888, the border station being Wallan-garra. This however was not the future Interstate main line, although connection was made there with the Queensland railway 3 ft. 6 in. gauge system. It was not until 1930 that the standard-gauge line now known as the 'North Coast' line was completed, and continued for nearly 70 miles in Queensland territory to its terminus in South Brisbane. Prior to that the journey was

43

made via Wallan-garra, a distance of 715 miles. The fastest journey times over the two sections were Sydney to Wallan-garra, 492 miles, in 17 hr. 8 min., and Wallan-garra to Brisbane, 223 miles, in 9 hr. 50 min. Although the time occupied in changing from 4 ft. 8½ in. to 3 ft. 6 in. gauge occupied less than half an hour it was a marathon journey from Sydney to Brisbane, even as recently as 1925 occupying nearly 28 hours. At that time, also, there was no alternative of going by air. It must have been almost as quick to go by sea!

In referring to through communication between Sydney and Brisbane however I am somewhat anticipating, because at the time contact was established between the New South Wales and Queensland railways at Wallan-garra it was not then possible to travel between Sydney and Newcastle by train. The independent development of the railway networks from the twin ports had progressed rapidly, except to the extent of linking the two together. This linking up might have taken place much earlier had it not been for the exceptional geographical barrier that lay roughly midway between them—namely the great estuary of the Hawkesbury River. It is a place of truly astonishing beauty; an inlet even more extensive and including a far greater diversity of creeks than the Parramatta River at Sydney itself. But whereas the great anchorage at Sydney is surrounded by relatively gentle slopes the Hawkesbury River is bounded by steep hills on every side, densely wooded right to the water's edge. It reminded me of our beautiful West Country estuaries of the Dart and the Fal, but with surrounding hills much higher, and all the waterways—both main river and creeks alike—infinitely wider and deeper. The first time I saw it was in the early morning, with a grey-green mist hanging over the hills and the water so still as to mirror the forests of gum trees to an almost uncanny perfection.

Scenery apart however, here was a nice little problem for the railway engineer when the time eventually came for the link-up between Sydney and Newcastle. In 1881 a sum of £2 million was voted by the legislature for a line from Homebush, on the Sydney–Parramatta line, to Waratah, on the line from Newcastle up the Hunter valley. The distance was 95 miles, and separate contracts were let for the sections from south and north to the banks of the Hawkesbury River. The section from Sydney to the river was completed in 1887, and over this I rode in the cab of an electrically-hauled Newcastle day express, leaving Sydney at 9.22 a.m.

We took the West main line as far as Strathfield, and then turned on to the North main line. Passing through highly-industrialised suburbs we crossed the Parramatta River on a long bridge at Rhodes, and then commenced a steep ascent into the Pennant Hills. Except for a brief descent for about 1½ miles after Epping most of the gradients were around 1 in 40 and 1 in 50. Although our electric locomotive was making short work of it, even though we had a substantial seven-coach train of some 330 tons, I can well imagine what a gruelling start this would have provided for even the most efficient steam locomotives starting 'cold' on the journey north. We were climbing mostly between 40 and 45 m.p.h.

More level ground, albeit at a high altitude, is reached after Pennant Hills station is passed. We called at Hornsby, where the suburban line taking the short cut across Sydney Harbour Bridge joins in. The ramifications of the Sydney suburban district are described in a later chapter. We continued, at 55 to 60 m.p.h., on the fringe of the Sydney outer suburbs, through stations with such appealing names as Mount Colah and Mount Kuring-gai, till we came into a region of rocky hills. We passed a summit point near Berowra station of 670 ft., and then on the left got some first glimpses far below of Berowra Creek, in all its sylvan beauty; then we began the descent to the Hawkesbury River, on the formidable Cowan bank. There are many speed restrictions due to the curves, and nearing Cowan station we eased down to 35 m.p.h. Down the 1 in 40 gradient through the four successive Boronie Tunnels the regenerative brake was in action, and we glided smoothly down, with ever more broadening and beautiful vistas across the Hawkesbury River. Finally, round an 11-chain curve in a short tunnel, we came to Hawkesbury River station, and after crossing the causeway to Long Island, so to the bridge itself.

This was the temporary terminal point of the railway from Sydney, and within a few months of its opening the northern part of the line had reached Gosford, 12 miles to the north and lying on one of the picturesque creeks. Having got thus far, so anxious was the Government to establish through communication that a ferry service was put on between Long Island and Gosford. This service was maintained by a glorious old stern-wheeler vessel, like one of the celebrated Mississippi ferry boats. It was named the *General Gordon*. After about six months however the northern part of the railway had been extended, by the waterside to Mullet Creek, only four miles from Long Island. The site chosen by the engineer, John Whitton, for the crossing of the river was at a point seven miles from the sea, where the estuary had a total width of 6600 ft. Although the constructional problems were difficult enough in themselves the engineer and the contractors were not troubled with matters of providing for navigation on the river. The Hawkesbury, despite its majestic situation and proportions, carries no waterborne traffic.

When the time came for considering the placing of contracts for the original bridge there is no doubt that the Government of New South Wales developed the proverbial 'cold feet'. The disaster to the first Tay Bridge in Scotland was fresh in the minds of all railway administrations, and although the Hawkesbury River was relatively sheltered, and the coast of New South Wales was not generally subject to very severe storms, the Government was not willing to accept a design prepared by their own chief engineer; instead they threw the problem open to world competition. To judge the various proposals, and the prices submitted for them, a Board was appointed to adjudicate. This Board consisted of Captain Douglas Galton, a former Inspector General of Railways to the British Board of Trade, and a former Royal Engineer officer with a distinguished record of railway work. In conjunction with the celebrated American engineer George Westinghouse he had conducted some of the most significant early tests on continuous automatic brakes. His colleagues on the Hawkesbury River Bridge Board were W. H. Barlow, a Past President of the Institution of Civil Engineers, and G. Berkley, Consulting Engineer to the Great Indian Peninsula, and to the Natal Government Railways. As if this were not enough the Government's own consulting engineer, Sir John Fowler, joint designer of the Forth Bridge, was required to make an independent assessment, while when it was all over John Whitton, the Railway's own chief engineer, was to make the final recommendation. He would in any case have had the responsibility for invigilating during the course of the constructional work.

The design eventually accepted consisted of seven lattice girder spans of most handsome appearance. They were originally intended to be of equal length, 416 ft.; but during construction of the large masonry piers one of these latter had shifted slightly from its designed position, and in consequence one span was 2 ft. shorter than the rest. A great task facing the engineers was the extreme depth the piers had to be sunk below water

46

level to reach solid rock. The estuary had a great depth of sand and the foundations had to be carried to a depth of between 101 and 162 ft. below high-water level where the bed was actually solid rock; where the bed was in sand the piers had to be carried to nearly double that depth. The original bridge was opened in 1889, and was undoubtedly the greatest railway civil engineering work in Australia at the time. Like all other great bridges it was subject to constant and stringent routine examination, and in the years 1937–8, after nearly 50 years' continuously heavy service, some deterioration was noted in the masonry work of the piers. Examination was intensified and some of the cracks were found to be extending, and new ones appearing. On each of the piers there were expansion bearings, with rollers, to permit free longitudinal movement of the girders in response to changes of temperature, and on one pier the cracks were preventing this action. In cold weather the contraction of the girders was tending to split the piers.

The trouble could scarcely have developed at a worse time. In 1938 the threat of world war was growing more serious, and yet there seemed no solution but to construct an entirely new bridge, taking advantage of the 50 years' experience at the Hawkesbury River, and providing also main girders of greater strength in anticipation of still heavier train loads. In the meantime the old bridge was subjected to a speed limit of 15 m.p.h., which later had to be reduced to 5 m.p.h. before the new bridge was completed. The design and construction of the new bridge was a triumph of railway civil engineering practice. In general appearance the new bridge is not greatly dissimilar from the old one, except that having regard to the rock strata in the river bed it was considered to use spans of varying lengths so that the piers would be sited to the best advantage. The design adopted was thus:

2 spans	445 ft. 1 in. long
4 spans	347 ft. 6 in. long
2 spans	147 ft. long
2 reinforced concrete arched approach spans each	75 ft. long

The most advantageous site was found to be about 200 ft. upstream from the existing bridge, but due to the hilly nature of the river banks two new tunnels had to be bored on the approach lines.

There was a very striking difference from that of 1889 in the way in which the construction was approached. Fifty years later there was no question of setting up Boards of experts; the Chief Civil Engineer's department of the New South Wales Railways tackled the job entirely on their own. They carried out all the preliminary surveys, designed the new bridge, fabricated all the steelwork, and then did all the difficult erection work on this tidal estuary. When I add that construction was started in July 1939 and continued unbrokenly through all the difficulties and anxieties of World War II the tremendous nature of the achievement will be fully appreciated. It was entirely a case of 'do it yourself' so far as the railway was concerned, and wholly indigenous, for the steel for the new spans was all rolled in Australian mills. The need was critically urgent, for war conditions placed a burden of greatly enhanced traffic on this important main line, and the necessary imposition of such severe speed limits over the old bridge was a serious handicap.

The erection of a great bridge is always a fascinating business, and the new Hawkesbury River project was no exception. On the rocky shore of Long Island, just upstream from the old bridge, a special erecting site was prepared. This involved the cutting of a broad ledge out of the solid rock, wide enough and long enough to accommodate the largest of the new girders. The sinking of the new piers involved no problems other than those connected with their colossal size. The caissons on which the piers are founded weigh between 3312 and 12,100 tons, and they were sunk in sand to a depth of between 100 and 183 feet below high-water level. Five of the caissons are founded exceedingly deep in sand, and the remaining three on rock. The erection of the girders on the river bank, and floating them out into position, recalls the classic works of Robert Stephenson at the Britannia Tubular Bridge over the Menai Strait, and of I. K. Brunel at the Royal Albert Bridge over the Tamar, at Saltash. But the Australian engineers had one advantage over the two great pioneers; the Hawkesbury River is not navigable by large vessels, and the railway is carried at no more than 40 ft. above high-water mark. The girders were therefore erected on the special riverside platform at the height they would eventually occupy on the piers, and then they were transferred to floating trestles of the requisite height. At the Hawkesbury River there was no question of raising the girders to their correct height when they were actually in position, as had to be done at the Menai Strait and at Saltash.

PLATE 3. On the West Main Line
(a) Penrith station in the 1880s, showing an early form of semaphore signal
(b) The great Zig-Zag looking eastwards

PLATE 4. Climbing westwards into the Blue Mountains: one of the huge 'AD 60' Beyer–Garratt locomotives on a freight train near Lapstone

When the new bridge was completed and before it was opened for traffic, deflection tests were carried out with six 'C38' class Pacific locomotives, three in tandem on each track and steaming across precisely abreast of each other, first at 5 m.p.h. and then at 38 m.p.h. Deflection tests were made with this massed weight, 201 tons for each locomotive and tender, representing a total moving load of 1200 tons; these proving eminently satisfactory, the new bridge was opened for traffic on 1 July 1946. On the electrically-hauled Newcastle express by which I travelled we crossed the bridge at 50 m.p.h. I was more fortunate than many long-distance travellers in not only crossing the river in broad daylight, but to be able to see it from such a splendid vantage point as the cab of an electric locomotive. The Brisbane sleeping car express crosses at night, and on the southbound journey although it is daylight one imagines that few passengers would be in the mood to enjoy a great spectacle of nature, soon after daybreak after a night in the train.

For some distance after reaching the north shore the line runs at water level, providing a series of charming glimpses of the wooded creeks, of oyster beds along the shore, and of vistas that remind an Englishman more than ever of some secluded Cornish estuary. From Wondabyne there is a sharp ascent for a mile at 1 in 40. No one seemed afraid of stiff gradients when this line was laid out, and right at this particular summit we came to Woy Woy tunnel, the longest in Australia. It is just over a mile long, and quite straight, and on a descending gradient we were soon running at 50 m.p.h. The scenery, by the creek side, remains delightful, and on generally level track we bowled along at 50 to 60 m.p.h., until nearing Gosford, where the electrified line ends. Running into this station we completed the 29·3-mile run from Hornsby in 40½ minutes, an excellent performance having regard to the difficult country traversed. Engines were now changed, and I was most interested to find that the crew of the electric locomotive were going to transfer to the steam Class 'C38' Pacific that was taking over haulage of the train. These are very large and powerful engines, and I was glad of the opportunity to ride one of them on a fast express duty. Their design is discussed in a later chapter, and at this stage I will say no more than they reminded me of the British Railways 'Britannias' in their rugged simplicity on the footplate.

Making the abrupt change from diesel or electric locomotives to steam is always somewhat of a chastening experience, especially as this engine had to be worked hard to keep the sharp timing over a generally undulating road with severe gradients. Fortunately there are no appreciable speed restrictions, and the engine was taken fast downhill to charge the subsequent inclines. It was an exhilarating spin, amid all the hurly-burly of steam working, dashing through typical Australian bush country, topping 70 m.p.h. on the favourable stretches, and then enjoying the fierce rhythmic tattoo of the exhaust beat hammering up the 1 in 44 gradients after Dora Creek. The $38\frac{1}{4}$ miles from Gosford to Fassifern were covered in $43\frac{3}{4}$ minutes start to stop, but of that distance $31\frac{1}{4}$ miles were run in no more than $33\frac{3}{4}$ minutes. I was leaving the train at Fassifern, because my Australian friends had other railway sights for me to see in the neighbourhood of Newcastle; but as I had a quick wash in the station house I could not help contrasting in my mind's eye this wayside main line station in the Australian bush with that other Fassifern far away in the West Highlands of Scotland by the side of Loch Eil. There must surely have been Camerons among the early settlers in this part of New South Wales! To heighten the contrast with the Scottish Fassifern, and the modest traffic that passes to and fro on the Mallaig extension line, a seemingly endless freight passed briskly through headed by one of the huge 'AD 60' Beyer–Garratt locomotives.

On the following day, a Sunday, I was able to visit Broadmeadow locomotive shed, on the outskirts of Newcastle, and I found this a positive parade ground for these giant Garratts. A number of them were 'off duty' on this Sunday, and were parked like the spokes of a wheel pointed towards the 'hub' of the roundhouse turntable. The New South Wales Railways had already introduced some very large and heavy freight engines of the 4–8–2 type; but these could not be used on all lines due to the high concentration of weight on the driving axles, and the Beyer–Garratt system of articulation permitted of the production of a very powerful engine with a maximum axle-load of only 16 tons, in contrast to the 22 tons of the orthodox 4–8–2s. With the gradual extension of diesel and electric traction the sphere of activity of the giant Garratts has lessened, and the majority of those remaining in service are based on Broadmeadow, for the coal traffic in the Newcastle district.

Newcastle itself is a terminus, and the main lines to the north provide connections to it from Broadmeadow. The main north line continues for some 18 miles, to Maitland, and it is at this junction that the North Coast line diverges. The 'Brisbane Limited Express' leaving Sydney at 6.30 p.m. traverses this part of the line in darkness. On the occasion of my journey by this latter train we had a heavy load of fourteen coaches out of Sydney: five of the splendid air-conditioned 'sleepers'; six air-conditioned sitting cars, a buffet dining car, and two vans. To haul this lengthy train we had three diesel-electric locomotives of the '44' class, each of 1800 engine horsepower. On our long journey through the night I slept well, and was roused as we were nearing South Grafton, 432 miles from Sydney, having been nearly eleven hours on the run. I was due to ride in the cab from Casino onwards, and there was time for a wash and a shave, and an early breakfast before we were due to arrive at the latter station at about 7 a.m. From South Grafton we were running through thick bush country, and I saw for the first time the incredible sight, for an Englishman, of a kangaroo in full career. We were running a little behind time, and when we reached Casino I found we then had two '44' class diesels, Nos. 4448 and 4465, working a load of 570 tons. It was now after 7 a.m. and a fine clear morning, and I was able to enjoy to the full the non-stop run of nearly three hours from Casino to Brisbane from the driver's cab.

For the first 30 miles the line is on a very gradual rising gradient. The altitude increases from 84 ft. above sea level at Casino to 287 ft. at The Risk. We were travelling over open grass lands, sometimes on a very winding course requiring reductions in speed to 40 m.p.h. or even less; but as soon as we got on to any appreciable straight away we would go to 65 or 70 m.p.h. It was single-line throughout, with electric tablet working and mechanical exchange at the passing loops. The names as usual were interesting: Nammoona, Fairy Hill, Cedar Point, Kyogle. I could see that our locomotives were driven up to the limit of the road; it was the curves, not the tractive power that governed our speed on this section of line. It was evident too that from the green, spring-like countryside of New South Wales we were passing into a much drier land, and at The Risk we were entering mountain country. We were now getting to the northern border of New South Wales, and having passed The Risk, $29\frac{3}{4}$ miles from Casino in $38\frac{1}{2}$ minutes, the scenery began to grow distinctly wild.

We passed Mount Lion, and soon after we were entering upon an ascent of 1 in 66. The trees with their white stems looked like silver birches in the Highlands of Scotland but they were, of course, the

51

all pervading Australian blue gums. We were crossing and recrossing the narrow rivulet of Crady's Creek, across which there are no fewer than five small bridges. These are very narrow structures with the supporting girders immediately beneath the rails. There is no walkway at the side of the track, and no parapet; the sleepers themselves mark the outermost extent of the bridge. In this rough country we were climbing on a continuous ascent of 1 in 66. The actual inclination is rather less steep than this, but some compensation is included for the continuous and severe curvature, and the effect so far as traction is concerned is that of a continuous 1 in 66 gradient on straight track. The speed was now a steady 33 m.p.h.—excellent work with a 570-ton train—and just over a mile beyond Cougal station we began to negotiate the spiral by which the gradient leading to the summit marking the New South Wales–Queensland border is maintained, at a compensated 1 in 66. There are two tunnels on the spiral, and so we came to the Border Loop, 890 ft. above sea level and 543·8 miles from Sydney. The 43·5 miles from Casino to this summit point had taken just 55 seconds over the even hour.

Immediately beyond the summit the line enters a long straight tunnel, about three-quarters of a mile long, and we emerged in the State of Queensland. The line descends on a very curving alignment, again at a compensated 1 in 66; speed was held back to about 35 m.p.h. and at Glenapp we slackened further to 25 m.p.h. to exchange tablets. By this time the country ahead was beginning to open out, though there were some rocky peaks on the skyline. These were of most curious formation, and were similar to some I saw at close quarters on the coast north of Brisbane, where the existing peak was the 'core' of an extinct volcano; all the surrounding rock having been eroded away in the course of time. After Glenapp we began to 'run' again, enjoying considerable spells at 60 to 65 m.p.h. through thick bush country. Although we were running fairly close to the coast we did not get any glimpses of the sea, though stretches of rich farming land on the right-hand side of the line made an interesting change from the 'bush' landscape. It was evident also that we were getting into more tropical regions. In places there were palm trees at the lineside, and by this time the sun was well up on a glorious cloudless day. When we were checked to 10 m.p.h. for permanent way repairs I noticed the surfacemen were all wearing shorts, and battered old trilby hats to shade their heads from the hot sun.

PLATE 5. The transformed Zig-Zag as a scenic roadway

(*a*) One of the viaducts

(*b*) 'Tunnel No. 1'

(*c*) A former reversing station

PLATE 6. An eastbound stock train, double-headed with two 2–8–0s, climbing the 1 in 42 gradient from Lithgow to Zig-Zag signal box. One of the viaducts of the old 'Zig-Zag' can be discerned through the trees above the train

Prior to this check, and another to cross a southbound freight, we had been making excellent speed, keeping up a general average of 55 to 65 m.p.h. on long straight stretches of track through beautiful woodland country. The road was in splendid condition, finely ballasted, and permitting of most comfortable riding of the locomotive. I learned later from my wife, who was travelling in the train, that the coaching stock was riding equally well. It was on this train, while I was on the footplate, that she had her first experience of what an 'Australian breakfast' is. Making her way to the buffet–dining car to have the modest Continental breakfast that is customary for both of us she was pardonably astonished to see some of her fellow travellers—ladies too!—tucking into enormous repasts of steaks, chops, and goodness knows what else, that put the heartiest English 'bacon and eggs' completely in the shade. In the meantime we on the footplate were baulked of our scheduled non-stop run from Casino to South Brisbane. At Greenbank a southbound freight that we were to cross had not quite cleared into the loop, and we were stopped for a minute at the home signal. The 93·5 miles from Casino to this point had taken 123 minutes, a very good average of 46 m.p.h. from start to stop. When the freight had come to rest and we could draw forward into the loop we had to wait another $1\frac{1}{2}$ minutes before the signalman brought us the tablet and gave us the right-away.

From Greenbank, as the driver put it, it is 'timber country' right into Brisbane. Beautiful woodlands extended on both sides of the line, but having passed the 600th milepost from Sydney the scene began to open out, and the city of Brisbane could be seen ahead. There is little in the way of suburban complex on this line however, and from Greenbank there is not a station for 13 miles; then, when only five miles from journey's end a 3 ft. 6 in. gauge line of the Queensland Railways draws alongside, and we passed Clapham Junction. We had made up a considerable amount of our lateness on leaving Casino, but the check at Greenbank had taken its toll. At that location a distance of two miles had taken us $10\frac{1}{2}$ minutes, and but for this I think we should have been very nearly on time at journey's end. As it was we were only 8 minutes late: 613 miles from Sydney in 15 hr. 38 min., an overall average speed of $39\frac{1}{2}$ m.p.h. The terminus is a modest station compared with some of the great city terminals of Australia; but it deals purely with the standard-gauge through trains from New South Wales, and that means only two regular trains in each direction daily. There is one single long platform, finely equipped nevertheless with all the facilities for long-distance travel. Three Queensland railwaymen, hitherto only pen-friends, were on the platform to meet and greet us, and their welcome was the prelude to four memorable days in that delightful country. Before writing of the splendid railway activities that we saw I must for the moment return to New South Wales; for in making the long run on the 'Brisbane Limited Express', with New South Wales carriages and locomotives, I have somewhat run ahead of many intense activities around Sydney that remain to be described.

CHAPTER FOUR

New South Wales motive power

In Chapter Two of this book I referred to the first engineer of the New South Wales Railways, John Whitton. Like the majority of the early Australian railway officers he came out from the United Kingdom, and in his case from none other than the Oxford, Worcester and Wolverhampton—the 'Old Worse and Worse'! But however the company itself may have been struggling it certainly had some great men in its employ, of whom David Joy, the locomotive engineer and valve gear designer, was certainly one. Whitton was another, and some of his work has already been described, in the crossing of the Blue Mountains and the bridging of the Hawkesbury River. It was considered advisable to get the first engines from England, and the specification given to the English agents of the young company was for locomotives with four wheels coupled, and having six-wheeled tenders. The instruction was issued in 1853.

Now the New South Wales Government had wisely decided to seek out a railway engineer of high eminence to be their consultant engineer in England, and the choice had fallen upon J. E. McConnell, Locomotive Superintendent of the Southern Division of the London and North Western Railway. He was generally considered to be one of the foremost locomotive designers of the day, though his 'big engine' policy was not entirely to the liking of certain members of the North Western Board, who desired to get their equipment as cheaply as possible. Any feelings in this respect did not influence McConnell's recommendations to the New South Wales Government, and in response to the specifications for locomotives he put forward his standard Wolverton 0–6–0. As a four coupled engine was asked for he merely altered the wheel arrangement to 0–4–2. The L.N.W.R. 0–6–0s were first built in 1854 by Kitson's; the N.S.W.G.R. 0–4–2s were delivered in 1855. Connoisseurs of English locomotive design will note the precise similarity of the two classes, except for the wheel arrangement. Details such as the shape of chimney and dome, and the number carried on the front of the chimney, were identical. The four Australian 0–4–2s were built by Robert Stephenson and Company, then in Newcastle-upon-Tyne.

In their early years the New South Wales Government Railways went through all the vicissitudes of changing fashions in engine design that beset so many other railways, and when the McConnell 0–4–2s were found too heavy, and unnecessarily powerful for some routes on the expanding railway system, it was interesting to find that those in charge also turned to London and North Western practice, and purchased from the celebrated Leeds firm of E. B. Wilson and Company some Allan 'singles' complete with the outside cylinders and the fore-end double framing that was so characteristic of the type. As if this were not enough, some further Allan engines of the 2–4–0 type were added to the stock in 1863. Up to this time it could not be said that anything approaching a standard design had been evolved. There were many different classes, some of no more than two or three locomotives. In 1865 the first steps towards a continuous locomotive policy were taken in the purchase of the first examples of the Beyer, Peacock outside-cylinder 2–4–0s of the so-called '23' class. These engines, with their inclined outside cylinders, with pony truck immediately beneath, and the characteristic Beyer chimneys and domes, looked like a large tender-engine version of the narrow-gauge 2–4–0 tanks on the Isle of Man Railway and on the Belfast and Northern Counties. Thirteen of these pretty little engines were put into service in 1865–70 and they worked the bulk of the main line passenger and mail traffic until the introduction of the 'C79' class in 1877.

The 'C79' bore a remarkable resemblance in its wheel spacing to the celebrated Beyer, Peacock 4–4–0 'Metropolitan' tank engines used on the London Underground lines in pre-electrification days. This latter design dated from 1864, and one of its most noticeable features was the very short wheelbase of the bogie. This was faithfully copied in the New South Wales 4–4–0s of 1877, and it was necessitated by use of the Bissell type of bogie. This did not pivot about its centre, or near the centre, as in more modern designs, but had its pivot some distance to the rear, and it swung on a long radial arm. This type of construction, and its consequent action when a locomotive was rounding a curve, made it necessary to have the wheels close together; otherwise the wheels would not adjust themselves readily to a curve. No fewer than sixty engines of this class were supplied from the United Kingdom, thirty-four from Beyer Peacocks and twenty-six from Dübs, while a further eight were built at the Atlas Works, Sydney, in 1882. They were powerful engines for the day, with cylinders 18 in. diameter by 24 in. stroke, although with coupled wheels 5 ft. 6 in. diameter they were not very well suited to the mountain sections. They were able to run very freely on the more favourable stretches of line.

After forming the mainstay of the main line passenger and mail motive power stud for some fifteen years these excellent little engines were moved to the inland branch lines, where their light axle-loading and easy action enabled them to be effectively used on lines where the track was unballasted. Some of them were also retained as main line pilots on the heavily-graded sections, in circumstances of exceptional loading. Three of them have been preserved. One of these, No. 1243, has been kept in full working order and is retained for use on departmental Vintage Train specials; engine No. 1243 not with its original number 176 is destined for permanent exhibition at the Museum of Applied Arts and Sciences, at Sydney, while No. 1219 will be on exhibition at the New South Wales Transport Museum at Enfield Depot. In addition there is No. 1210, of special interest as the first locomotive to work the then newly-opened branch line from Queanbeyan to Canberra, in 1913, after the establishment of the Federal capital city. Engine No. 1210 now stands on a plinth outside Canberra station, and I had the pleasure of examining and photographing it during the course of an interesting visit to the district in August 1969. Although standing in the open the engine is beautifully maintained, and shows off to great advantage the quite distinctive grey-green livery standard on the New South Wales Government Railways. It is a colour unlike anything used on the home railways. In tone it is not unlike that of the Glasgow and South Western; but the latter had a distinct bluish tinge, and was of a richer shade. The Australian colour is a much *colder* hue.

From the year 1882 the New South Wales Government Railways reverted to inside cylinders for their principal express passenger locomotives and a series of 4-4-0 designs, with 6 ft. diameter coupled wheels, was introduced from various British builders, of a kind closely similar to

57

some currently being supplied to the Victorian Railways. The latter were of course adapted to the 5 ft. 3 in. gauge. The N.S.W. engines were of thoroughly characteristic English appearance, with handsomely tapered chimneys, polished brass domes, a straight running plate with deep splashers over the coupled wheels. The earlier varieties of this new general design had the Bissell type of bogie but in 1884, when a further variety was introduced, having the Joy valve gear instead of the hitherto standard Stephenson's link motion, the Adams swivelling and sliding bolster type of bogie was adopted. This not only gave a greatly improved appearance, and an air of striding elegance to the engine as a whole, but it was a superior type of guiding device mechanically, and was used in all subsequent N.S.W.G.R. passenger locomotives. Although having larger cylinders than the 'Peacock High-Flyers', as the inside-cylinder 4-4-0s of 1882 were known, they had a reduced boiler pressure, and the tractive effort was therefore practically the same. Both varieties, 'Bissell' and 'Adams', were used turn and turn about on the fast trains on the southern main line, and from the inception of through railway communication between Sydney and Melbourne, following the extension of the line from Wodonga across the Murray River at Albury in 1883, the 'High-flyers' were used on the Albury–Sydney part of the run.

In readiness for the opening of the Hawkesbury River Bridge, and the establishment of through railway communication between Sydney and Newcastle, a new design of outside-cylinder 4-4-0 was introduced in 1887, having a tractive effort considerably greater than that of any previous passenger engine on the line. The old '79' class as now exhibited at Canberra had a tractive effort of 13,000 lb. and the inside-cylinder 'High-Fyers' a little less, because of their larger coupled wheels. The new engines, built by the Vulcan Foundry, had 16,800 lb., with 5 ft. 6 in. coupled wheels and 19 in. by 26 in. cylinders. They had the Adams-type bogie and the cylinders were horizontal, instead of inclined, with outside overhead steam chests. They were originally distinguished by very large extended smokeboxes, which admitted of hard driving without getting the lower tubes blocked up with an accumulation of ash in the smokebox. Although strong and powerful engines they immediately exhibited all the traits of outside-cylindered 4-4-0s of considerable power, being hard and rough riding, and consequently unpopular both with the footplate men and with the civil engineer. In later years, when the need for exceptional power from a 4–4–0 engine had receded, they had the cylinder diameter reduced to 18 inches, and they were fitted with modified boilers with short smokeboxes and Belpaire fireboxes. One of these engines, No. 1709, has been preserved in full working order, and is used in conjunction with No. 1243 for trips with Vintage Trains. This engine has been painted in a red livery known as 'Victoria Maroon', almost exactly the shade of the Furness locomotives, and matching the standard passenger carriages colour of the N.S.W.G.R.

By the year 1890 we come to the beginning of an entirely new era on the New South Wales Railways. In Chapter Two of this book I have referred briefly to the inception of the celebrated 'P6' class of 4–6–0. These splendid engines represented a tremendous advance in size and power over anything previously used in the colony; they had a tractive effort of no less than 22,180 lb., and with the original six-wheeled tender weighed 88½ tons in working order. The cylinders were 20 in. diameter by 26 in. stroke, and the coupled wheels 5 ft. diameter. A feature of some significance was the use of the Allan straight-link motion, instead of Stephenson's. Some years ago a British locomotive engineer of wide experience once remarked, on a public occasion, that he had never heard of a bad engine with Allan valve gear. Certainly the N.S.W.G.R. 'P6' could rank as the most successful ever with Allan gear, ranking even higher than the Highland 'Jones Goods' and 'Castle' classes. The 'P6' class were handsomely finished in black, with red lining. Later engines of the class were fitted with large bogie tenders, superheating and cylinder diameter increased to 21 in. This brought the tractive effort up to 26,000 lb. and the total weight to 110 tons. In all, no fewer than 191 of these engines were purchased, between 1891 and 1911; of these 106 came from Beyer, Peacock; 20 from the Baldwin Locomotive Company in the U.S.A.; 45 from the Clyde Engineering Company in Sydney, and 20 were built at the railway workshops, Eveleigh, Sydney. A special tribute to the efficiency and generally high reputation of the 'P6' class engines was paid in 1914 when the design was adopted as the first standard passenger engine for the Commonwealth Railway, to inaugurate the Trans-Australian service on the 4 ft. 8½ in. gauge line then within sight of completion between Port Augusta and Kalgoorlie. In view of the extremely severe and isolated conditions anticipated in crossing the Nullarbor Plain the choice of the 'P6' was a great 'feather in its cap'.

Mr. Thow produced an enlarged version, the 'N' class, for running on the fast stretches of line south of Junee. These engines had larger coupled wheels, 5 ft. 9 in. diameter, but the same characteristic spacing and also the Allan valve gear. These were 'special purpose' engines, and only five were built, all at Eveleigh Works, in 1909–10. They were extremely handsome engines, but when drafted to the North Coast line, for running the through Brisbane expresses in 1927, they did not take kindly to the continuous curvature of parts of that line, particularly between Casino and the Border Loop. In due course they returned to Junee. In 1911 Thow retired, having been in office for more than twenty years, and he was succeeded by E. E. Lucy, from the Great Western Railway, and it was not surprising that under his able direction the development of the 4-6-0 type for the heaviest express passenger service continued. He held the office of Chief Mechanical Engineer until the end of 1932. It is of interest to recall that Lucy came from a very old English family, the Lucys of Charlecote, near Warwick. It was before an ancestor of E. E. Lucy that the youthful William Shakespeare was summoned for poaching deer. In later years Shakespeare caricatured Sir Thomas Lucy as 'Justice Shallow' in *The Merry Wives of Windsor*. All this is rather aside from locomotive development on the New South Wales Government Railways, but this twentieth-century Lucy certainly made his mark on the motive-power situation on the Australian railways. As with Thow's 'P6' 4-6-0, one of Lucy's most successful later developments was also adopted as a standard on the Trans-Australian line of the Commonwealth Railways.

Lucy's first main line express locomotive, the 'NN' class of 1914, represented a substantial advance in tractive power over previous 4-6-0s, for with cylinders no less than $22\frac{1}{2}$ in. in diameter the tractive effort was 29,186 lb. Students of locomotive lineaments detected a certain likeness to Great Western practice in these heavy and powerful locomotives; but the only feature that can now be likened to the Swindon style was the partially coned boiler barrel. This had three rings, and the hindmost was coned to the top of the Belpaire firebox. The latter was rectangular in plan, and not of the trapezoidal shape developed to such a high degree of perfection at Swindon. For the rest, the 'NN' class was a simple hard-slogging two-cylinder job, which, after a good deal of early teething troubles, did much first class work. All the thirty-five engines of this class were built at Eveleigh Works. As recently as 1965 all of them were still

PLATE 7. New South Wales steam in action

(a) One of the famous 'P6' 4–6–0s

) A heavy goods, Sydney to Goulburn, near Campbelltown, hauled by a '55' class 2–8–0, fitted with the 'Southern' valve gear

) One of the 'AD 60' class Beyer-Garratt engines on an up coal train near Minto, Southern line

PLATE 8. Eveleigh Running Sheds, Sydney

(a) A daytime view showing one of the 'C38' class Pacifics in the foreground

(b) A night scene, showing main line passenger and suburban tank locomotives

in service on the northern sections of the line beyond Gosford, and particularly between Newcastle and South Brisbane. Despite the intrusion of war conditions twenty-five engines of this class were built at the railway shops in 1914–16, though construction of the second batch of ten extended over the years 1917–23. In the meantime post-war developments foreshadowed heavier demands upon the locomotive department. Non-stop runs of more than 100 miles were projected, and with the completion of the North Coast line through to South Brisbane a massive speed-up of the inter-state services between New South Wales and Queensland was planned. The 'NN' class, powerful engines though they were, had not proved ideal for the class of service then envisaged, and under Lucy's direction, a new design of 4–6–0 was prepared, and in January 1925 the first of the 'C36' class was completed at Eveleigh Works.

The nominal tractive effort was no more than slightly increased over that of the 'NN' class, which in 1924 had been re-designated 'C35'. But the 'C36' incorporated a number of features which experience had shown were desirable to give hard trouble-free service. At last inside valve gear was discarded, and all 'the works' made readily accessible by use of outside Walschaerts gear. The boilers were very much larger, and to permit of long non-stop runs without taking water intermediately the tenders were extremely large. Furthermore, they were made of the so-called turret type, in which the coal bunker was set inwards from the line of the water tank so as to give the crew a clear view backwards along the train when running, or an equally clear view when setting back on to a train. With their large tenders the new engines weighed no less than 159 tons in working order—considerably heavier than the English Gresley Pacifics, which were then coming into general service on the London and North Eastern Railway. The 'C36' class proved a splendid investment, and after the teething troubles had been ironed out with the ten original engines built at Eveleigh Works an order for a further 65 was placed with the Clyde Engineering Company. The entire class of 75 engines was in service by the end of 1928. They were hard-worked and fast-running engines, and although having coupled wheels of no more than 5 ft. 9 in. regularly attained speeds in excess of 70 m.p.h. The 'C36' was chosen by the Commonwealth Railways for service on the Trans-Australian line, and for this duty they were provided with enormous tenders running on two six-wheeled bogies and weighing 120 tons when fully loaded with coal and water. The reasons for such provisions will be apparent when I come to describe a journey over this line, from Port Pirie to Kalgoorlie, in a later chapter.

In a chapter such as the present one, attention is naturally centred upon the long-distance passenger engines, though the railway revenue is derived to a great extent from freight haulage, and no less from the rapidly-growing commuter traffic around Sydney. The most powerful steam suburban engines were a class of 4–6–4 tanks with outside cylinders, of somewhat similar appearance to the 'P6' class of main line 4–6–0. First introduced in 1903, there were eventually 145 of these useful engines, and some are still to be seen around Sydney Terminal station today on shunting duties. Like the main line 4–6–0s they had the Allan straight-link motion. The third member of this trilogy of the early 1900s, with the 'P6' 4–6–0s and the 4–6–4 tanks, was the 2–8–0 goods class, later designated 'D50'. This was another outstandingly successful design, originating in 1896 with a small batch of five from Beyer, Peacocks. The class eventually numbered 280, and many are still in service today. These engines had the Allan valve gear, but a later development of 1912, the 'D53' class, had the coned boiler barrel of Mr. Lucy's introduction, and Allan straight link motion. There were 190 of this latter class, and a still further development was the 'D55' class of 1918. These are also 2–8–0s, and are distinctive in having the 'Southern' valve gear. In all by the end of 1925 there were no fewer than 590 engines of the 2–8–0 type, of these three classes alone, in heavy freight service in New South Wales.

Successful though the various 2–8–0s had been the need was felt for a still more powerful locomotive for heavy freight service, and in 1929 the first of the enormous 'D57' class 4–8–2s took the road. They had three cylinders $23\frac{1}{4}$ in. diameter by 28 in. stroke, with Walschaerts valve gear for the outside cylinders, and the steam distribution to the inside cylinder regulated by the Gresley conjugated gear. Unlike the famous range of three-cylinder engines on the London and North Eastern Railway the two-to-one combination lever was in full view beneath the smokebox and just above the buffer beam. As these engines came pounding slowly up gradients along the Southern main line the distinctive action of the conjugated lever could be watched by a lineside observer. These huge engines which with their tenders weighed 227 tons, had a tractive effort of 56,000 lb. There were twenty-five of them, all built by the Clyde

Engineering Company and put into service between 1929 and 1930. They were the most powerful non-articulated engines ever built for service in Australia. In Chapter Two of this book I referred to the working of the heavy eastbound freight trains from Lithgow up to the Zig-Zag signal box. When four locomotives were used on this arduous stretch they included a 'D57' as train engine, with two 2-8-0s ahead and another 2-8-0 banking in rear. To deal with the heavy traffic arising from World War II a further twenty-five engines of the 4-8-2 type were ordered in 1943; but shortage of funds and materials precluded an immediate execution of the order. Eventually no more than 13 were built, all in railway shops, from 1950 onwards. This class, designated 'D58', was similar to 'D57' but with smaller cylinders and a modified version of the conjugated valve gear. They could readily be distinguished from class 'D57' by having a valance below the running board.

The final wholly indigenous steam locomotive design on the New South Wales Government Railways was the 'C38' class Pacific, introduced in 1943. As mentioned in connection with my own journeys on the North main line they are a massive, extremely simple two-cylinder job, carrying the high boiler pressure of 245 lb. per sq. in. They were designed for long through workings, and prior to the introduction of diesel traction they worked through from Sydney to Dubbo, over the Blue Mountains, a run of 287 miles, being re-coaled *en route*, at Lithgow. On the South Main Line they worked right through from Sydney to Albury, all but 400 miles. On this run they were re-coaled at Demondrille, 243 miles from Sydney. My own brief experience on the footplate of one of them left very favourable impressions. The first five engines of this class of thirty had a moderate degree of air-smoothing applied to the upper part of the boiler, shrouding the chimney, sandbox and dome beneath a continuous longitudinal casing. The smokebox front was also slightly coned. This gave the engines a 'modern' look, especially as the pleasing green livery was set off by yellow lines springing from the headlight. This latter was mounted in the middle of the coned smokebox door. I can't imagine this so-styled streamlining made the slightest difference, except to provide a modicum of publicity value. They did excellent work on the Sydney–Newcastle flyers when these were steam-hauled throughout; but owing to their great weight they were soon restricted to working south of Broadmeadow.

63

The introduction of the gigantic 'AD60' class Beyer–Garratt articulated engines of the 4–8–4 + 4–8–4 type has already been mentioned in Chapter Three, in connection with the coal train workings in the Hunter valley, and so far as main line passenger locomotives were concerned it remains for me to describe the '44' class diesel electrics, now used on the principal inter-state expresses from Sydney, and the '46' class electrics, used on the expresses climbing over the Blue Mountains as far as Lithgow. The '44' class are nose-cab Co + Co's first introduced in 1957. They were built by the Australian firm of A. E. Goodwin Ltd., with ALCO diesel engines, and traction motors variously from A.E.I. or General Electric. They have proved a great success in general service, both express passenger and fast goods. I made some extensive journeys in their cabs, both north and south of Sydney, and enjoyed their fine riding and efficient performance. Only one end has the nose-type cab; but when two locomotives are coupled in multiple-unit the nose cabs are arranged outwards. The individual locomotives can be driven from either end—flat end or nose end. The engine horsepower is 1800, indicating a maximum drawbar horsepower of about 1500, and the maximum speed permitted is 70 m.p.h.

The '46' class straight-electric locomotives, on one of which I rode over the Blue Mountains, are of approximately the same size and weight as the '44' class diesels, but possess the vastly greater tractive power inherent in full electric traction. They were designed for working over the mountains between Sydney and Lithgow, and for the heavily-graded first stretch of the northern interstate main line between Sydney and Gosford. The specification required a speed of 35 m.p.h. on a 1 in 33 gradient with a 400-ton train. The all-up weight is 108 tons, as compared with 106 tons on the '44' class, but while the diesels are capable of a continuous output of about 1500 at the drawbar these remarkable electric locomotives can exert some 3500 horsepower continuously and for short periods their output can be considerably greater. They were designed and built in England by the Metropolitan Vickers company, and were first introduced in 1956. At the present time there are 40 of them in service, and they are doing splendid work. Both electric and diesel-electric locomotives are painted red, to match the colour of the passenger rolling stock, and with smart yellow striping they look most attractive.

PLATE 9. Hawkesbury River

(a) The *General Gordon* stern-wheeler ferry boat, used before completion of the bridge

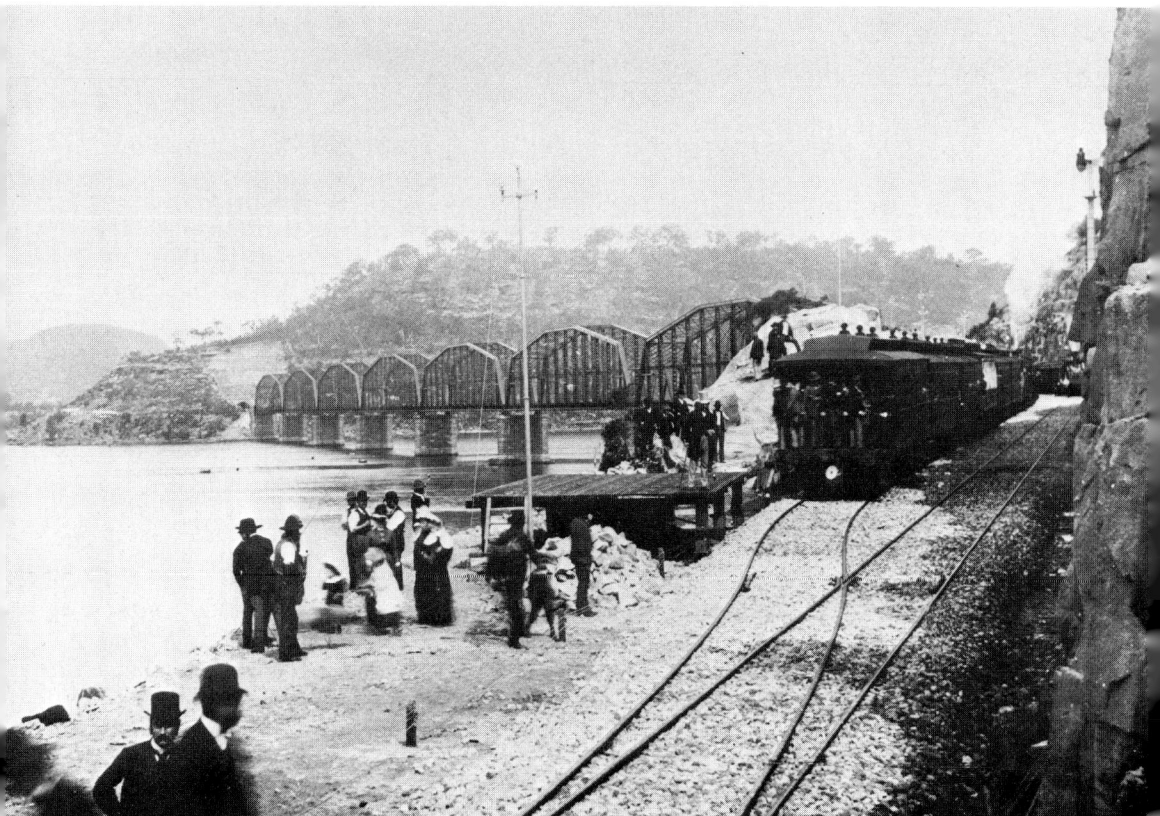

(b) Opening Ceremony at the bridge, 1 May 1889

PLATE 10. Hawkesbury River

(a) Building the new bridge: the largest span being floated into position. The old bridge is seen on the right

(b) Testing the new bridge: the first pair of a *posse* of six 'C38' class Pacifics steaming on to the bridge

CHAPTER FIVE

Sydney suburban

From the revolving restaurant at the top of the Summit Tower in Sydney I looked out over the astonishing panorama of city offices, dwellings and factories; of riverside wharfs, creeks, landing stages, and dockyards to the open sea. We had been in Australia for no more than a few days; but in that time we had gone from one appointment to another, by taxi, private car, and local train, and amid the enthusiasm of our Sydney friends we had found little time to see the city itself, and to get our bearings. But from the 'Summit' the fascinating geography of Sydney was made crystal clear. We were taken up there to lunch, on a blustering spring day, and could see the ramifications of the Parramatta River, and the amazing 'settlement' that has taken place around it. Mere statistics, phenomenal as they are, take a little grasping, for within a thirty-mile radius of the point where we were lunching there lives one-fifth of the entire population of Australia. One-fifth! Two and a half million people out of a total of twelve million. It can readily be appreciated why the Sydney suburban lines occupy so huge a proportion of the operating and engineering activities of the New South Wales Government Railways. There is also a further startling fact to be borne in mind. Although a span of two hundred years has elapsed since Captain Cook first set foot on the shores of Botany Bay, it is only during the last thirty years that the positive 'explosion' of population has taken place. In 1938 the population of Sydney and its surrounding suburbs was 1·25 million; today it is more than *double*. Railways have to take their share in transporting the vastly increased numbers of commuters, and so, while the historic build-up of the suburban railway network is highly interesting, the way in which the urgent problems of the last thirty years have been met are perhaps even more absorbing.

A large-scale map reveals a decidedly complicated geographical situation;

E

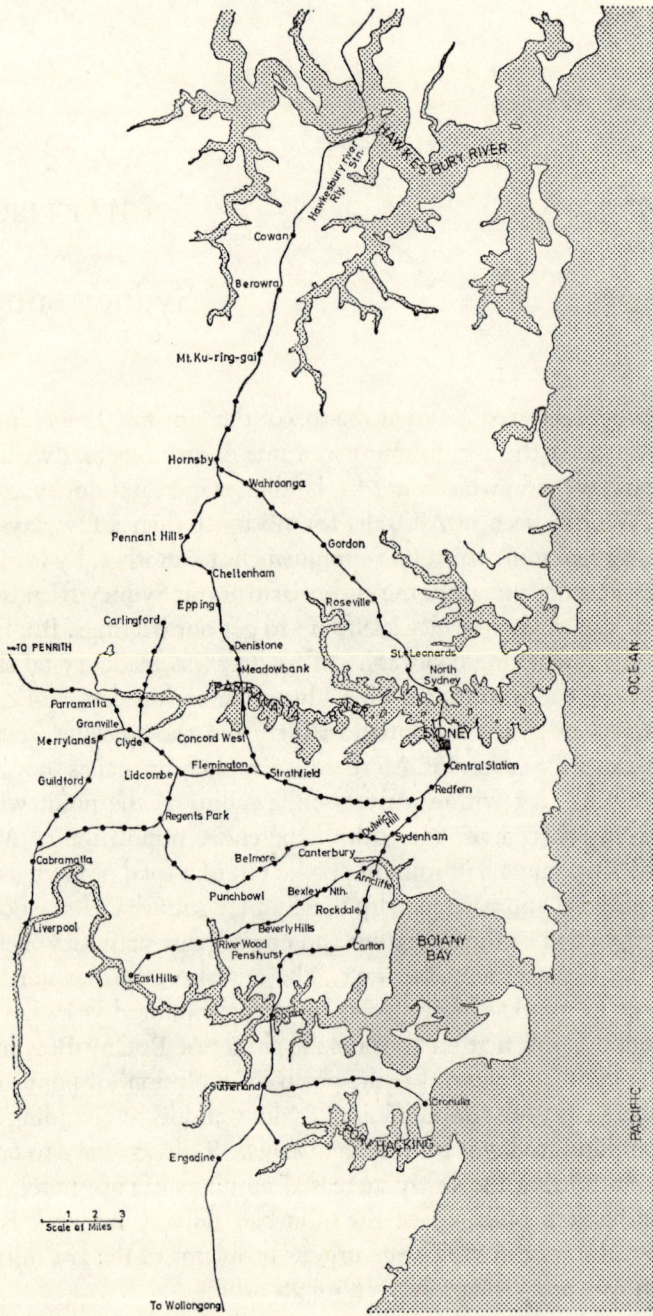

The Sydney suburban area, and line to the crossing of the Hawkesbury River.

but to see the whole Sydney 'complex' at one's feet from the 544-ft altitude of the Summit Restaurant is to appreciate even more vividly how the spreading residential areas have grown up, and how that growth has complicated the railway network. First of all there is the broad, deeply-indented estuary of the Parramatta River, which seawards from the world-famous Sydney Harbour Bridge broadens out into the magnificent anchor-age of Port Jackson—large enough to accommodate comfortably the entire British Navy at its pre-1914 greatest. Everywhere from the water's edge the land rises, not precipitously but enough to provide problems in layout and operating railways. Furthermore, there are no continuous land areas to north and south of the great central waterway. To the south is the windswept waste of Botany Bay and beyond that the considerable inlets of the George's River, and Port Hacking. To the north of Port Jackson is Middle Harbour. On the hilly ground between these numerous water-ways have grown up populous and flourishing suburbs.

I need hardly explain that the present extensive railway network did not grow up overnight. As everywhere else in the world where there is a high density of population it was developed gradually; but three com-paratively recent landmarks in this development may be specially men-tioned as they formed important links in the establishment of the system as it is today. These three events were:

1932: Opening of the Sydney Harbour Bridge and thus providing the direct link-up between the suburbs north and south of the har-bour.
1939: Opening of the branch line from Sutherland to Cronulla.
1956: Opening of the Circular Quay loop on the Sydney underground line.

With the completion of the last mentioned the suburban network as shown in the accompanying map was finally established, and the train services as now operated can be readily appreciated. The entire area thus represented is served by multiple-unit electric trains working on 1500 volts d.c. with overhead-line current collection. The Sydney underground line is an integral part of the New South Wales Government Railways, and as will be explained a large number of outer residential trains traverse part of the underground lines.

The Sydney suburban services are operated in seven well-defined groups,

67

which it will be convenient to refer to under their numerical references in the public timetable. These groups are:

1. Cowan–Chatswood–City–Penrith and Campbelltown (64)
2. City–Strathfield–Hornsby–Cowan (6)
3. Wynyard–Clyde–Carlingford (2)
4. City–Cronulla–Helensburgh (16)
5. City–Riverwood–East Hills (6)
6. City–Bankstown–Lidcombe (8)
7. City–Blacktown–Richmond (2)

Some idea of the relative activities in the seven groups may be gained from the figures quoted in brackets after each route description, which are the number of pages the services occupy in the public timetable. It will be seen that Group 1 is immeasurably the largest, and provides services originating as far north as Cowan, via the northern suburbs line through Gordon and Chatswood, over the harbour bridge, and through the central city area. Thence the Group 1 services proceed, some to Campbelltown on the south main line or to Penrith on the west line. Some of the south line trains travel via Granville, and some via Regents Park. It should be appreciated that by no means all trains on this service originate at Cowan. Many start from Hornsby, and others from Gordon and Chatswood. On the south side Liverpool is a terminal point for many trains, but throughout the day there is an hourly service to Campbelltown. A train running through from Cowan to Campbelltown, roughly 62 miles, and calling at all stations except those between Redfern and Burwood on the intensely used central section between Sydney Central and Strathfield, takes $2\frac{1}{2}$ hours on the journey. In the present timetable there are no trains running from Cowan to Penrith. Blacktown is the furthest point served on the west line, though there are through trains to Penrith from Hornsby and Gordon.

One could not, of course, imagine any one travelling from end to end of this far-flung suburban area, but by very good connecting trains one can travel from Cowan to Penrith in a few minutes over the $2\frac{1}{2}$ hours, which is remarkably good for a journey of 65 miles, stopping at nearly all intermediate stations. On this particular route there are no fewer than 48 of them, this not including another eight which are passed by the longer-distance suburban trains between Redfern and Burwood. In the central area there are a number of trains that in the public timetable appear to originate at Museum and proceed round the underground City Circle anti-clockwise to the Central station, continuing thence to various destinations on the south lines in Group 1. In fact, these trains come from Bankstown and/or East Hills and pass through Central on their way to Museum. It would confuse the public if two Central times were shown for each train on the City Outer or Inner line (City Circle). These trains, coming from the southern or western lines, arrive at Central then pass around the underground loop to Central again and on to the western or southern destinations. As befits a city with a population of more than $2\frac{1}{2}$ million the services provided on these routes are lavish. From the northern suburbs line, together with trains proceeding from Museum round the City Circle, a total of 50 trains arrive in Central station between the hours of 6.30 and 9 a.m., while during the same period, on the Group 1 services, 81 come in from the various routes that converge at Lidcombe. These figures indicate an average headway, over $2\frac{1}{2}$ hours, of 3 minutes from the north, and only $1\frac{7}{8}$ minutes from the south and west. In their approaches to the Central station both routes are double-tracked.

The Group 2 services relate to stations on the main north line from Strathfield to Cowan. The majority of the trains originate at North Sydney, cross the Harbour Bridge, proceeding thence via Wynward and Town Hall to the Central station. They then run fast to Strathfield, forming an 'express' component of the Group 1 network, and then turn on to the north line to serve all stations, either to Hornsby or Cowan. During the morning peak period, between 6.30 a.m. and 9 a.m., 21 trains arrive at Strathfield from the northern main line suburban stations, and then form part of the Group 1 procession into Sydney Central. The Group 3 trains, from Carlingford, feed into the Group 1 complex at Clyde, where passengers have to change trains. The local service between Carlingford and Clyde includes seven trains with connections due to arrive in Sydney Central between 6.32 a.m. and 9.8 a.m. Group 4, 5 and 6 are to a large extent linked operationally in the central area, as all using the busy line between Redfern and Sydenham. Trains in Groups 4 and 5 appear in the public time-tables to originate at Town Hall and proceed clockwise round the circle, and from 4.30 p.m. until 6 p.m. there are 21 service 4 trains, and 9 service 5 leaving, an average headway, for $1\frac{1}{2}$ hours of 3 minutes. The trains shown to start at Town Hall pass Central

69

on their way in from Bankstown, via Lidcombe or via Sydenham, or from East Hills, or Sutherland. A train may run from Bankstown via Sydenham, swing over to the Main Suburban Local line at the flyover junctions outside Central, go round the City Circle and back to Bankstown via Sydenham. The Group 6 trains originate at Museum, and proceed anti-clockwise round the circle, with 13 departures in the $1\frac{1}{2}$ hours from 4.30 p.m. Finally there is Group 7, which is a non-electrified offshoot of group 1, operated as a shuttle service between Blacktown and Richmond, in connection with Group 1 trains on the Penrith line.

These necessarily statistical details will give a broad picture of the general operating strategy of the Sydney suburban lines. Richmond is the furthest point from the Central station, lying $37\frac{1}{2}$ miles away, though Penrith is the furthest point regularly served by the multiple-unit electric trains. The limit of the electrified line so far is Gosford, 50 miles out on the north line, but this is beyond the suburban area. On the West line, of course, electrification extends to Lithgow, nearly 100 miles out. It is an area of tremendous activity; of 'slick' and efficient working, and from this introduction we can pass with enhanced interest to some details of the rolling stock, fixed equipment, and stations. Brief mention was made in the previous chapter of the steam 4-6-4 tank engines that carried virtually the entire burden of the suburban service in pre-electrification days. Their basic dimensions were, cylinders $18\frac{1}{2}$ in. diameter by 24 in. stroke; coupled wheels 4 ft. 7 in. diameter; boiler pressure 160 lb. per sq. in.; total weight of engine in working order 72 tons. They were tremendously strong and trouble-free engines. The original batch consisted of 35 engines, delivered from England in 1903–4; but between 1905 and 1917 a further 110 were added to the stock. As preparations for electrification proceeded after World War I, new and heavy rolling stock intended for inclusion in multiple-unit electric trains was put into service and to cope with the heavier train loads 104 of these engines had their power boosted, by enlargement of the cylinders to 19 in. diameter, and boiler pressure increased to 175 lb. per sq. in. The electrification of the main suburban area made a number of these engines redundant; but they were far too valuable to scrap, and 77 of them were converted into 4-6-0 tender engines and transferred to light branch duties.

The new coaching stock built for the electric services, though similar in general appearance to the latest main line carriages, was of the exceptional width of 10 ft. 6 in. The New South Wales Government Railways were experiencing to the full the problems of peak-hour traffic, and the new electric trains were designed for maximum passenger accommodation. There is seating for 70 passengers in each trailer vehicle, but with ample circulating space to permit considerable standing room. Furthermore, every consideration was given to the task of getting the passengers in and out quickly, and each coach had two entrances on each side with two sliding doors to an entrance. The platforms, at all stations, are made up to full height, with the surface only about six inches below carriage floor level. Even before electrification some 150,000 passengers passed through Sydney Central station in each direction daily. The running performance of the multiple-unit electric trains will be well appreciated from the details I have already given about the scheduling and service frequency on the various lines.

The tremendous increase in the population of Sydney, and the fact that much of this increase took place in the outer districts, led to an exceptional problem so far as rail transport was concerned. To commuters making relatively short journeys morning and evening overcrowding, and the diminishing chance of getting a seat at all, are just tolerable; but when it is a case of travelling in from Hornsby, Gordon, Blacktown, or even farther afield it is another matter, and it is this problem that has greatly exercised the management in recent years. On the suburban railways of Paris double-decked coaches have been in use for many years, and in England that most original of mechanical engineering designers, O. V. S. Bulleid, built some experimental double-decked carriages for the suburban services of the Southern Railway. These latter were unpopular, both with the travelling public and with the operating department. Although they carried more passengers seated they took considerably longer to load and unload. In Sydney advantage has been taken of the higher loading gauge to introduce double-deck coaches, seating 132 passengers as against 70 in previous standard stock. These double-deckers have proved successful, and now the principle has also been applied to motor coaches to provide the world's first complete saloon-type double-deck multiple-unit trains with a total passenger accommodation of 2250.

Preparations for the electrification of the Sydney suburban area in matters other than rolling stock began even before World War I had ended. C. B. Byles was then signal engineer, and within the British Empire he was then one of the most forward exponents of the day. At that time rapid progress was being made in the United States of America with the introduction of three-position signalling, with semaphores working in the upper quadrant. They showed horizontal for 'stop', arm inclined diagonally upwards for 'caution', and arm pointing vertically upwards for 'clear'. On the American railways many busy sections of line were being equipped with automatic signalling, in place of the traditional block working on the British style. Sections were being provided with a succession of three-position upper-quadrant semaphores, showing indications leading sequentially from one to the next. In the United Kingdom this strong American trend was greatly discussed. During the war years there was little opportunity for any experimental installations to be made, but generally speaking the idea of the three-position upper-quadrant signal was not favoured. Except for one installation on the South Eastern and Chatham Railway it was purely a case of discussion, though naturally the engineers of all railways were looking towards post-war developments, and were endeavouring to formulate future practice. In Australia Byles had a freer hand, and he decided to adopt the three-position upper-quadrant semaphore as a standard for automatically signalled sections of the suburban area, with a signal layout arranged to provide the frequency of service planned when the electrification actually took place. It was a splendid piece of forward planning, and the first installations of the new electrically-operated three-position signals were made as early as 1916.

From the same period a start was made in converting major junction interlockings in the central area to power operations, to ensure the speed of actuation essential in the working of such intensive train services as were then contemplated. Two British signalling firms closely associated at the time and both eventually incorporated in the present Westinghouse Brake and Signal Company had strong representation in Australia. These firms were McKenzie and Holland, and the McKenzie, Holland and Westinghouse Power Signal Company, with manufactories at both Melbourne and Brisbane. Largely in consequence of this association the electro-pneumatic system was recommended for point operation and the first major interlockings to be treated, at Sydney Terminal station and Illawarra Junction, were both brought into commission in 1910. Later interlockings in the Sydney area however showed strong evidence of the American influence, being of the General Railway Signal Company's type, with

PLATE C

A Queensland Railways Moura to Gladstone coal train winds its way through the Calliope Range. The tail of the train can be seen in the top left-hand corner of the picture

'pistol-grip' handles instead of conventional levers, and a modification of this type was afterwards standardised and built in the railway administration's shops.

In using the three-position upper-quadrant type of signal a set of indications that would seem very curious to us today was adopted. At that time the amber light, so familiar now from its use in road traffic signals, was non-existent in New South Wales, and while the positions of the upper-quadrant semaphore arm, as previously described, gave the 'stop', 'caution' and 'clear' indications plainly enough in daylight, special measures had to be taken at night, because the only colours available were red and green. A lower light was fitted, which would display red or green, and the night aspects were thus:

STOP	Red above red
CAUTION	Green above red
CLEAR	Green above green

From this it was realised that although the upper-quadrant semaphore had three roundels, corresponding to the three positions of the arm itself, two of those roundels were green and the other red.

The entire pattern of railway working in the suburban area was changed by the construction of the Sydney Harbour Bridge. Proposals for such a bridge had been made since the very inception of railways in New South Wales, and for upwards of sixty years successive schemes had been turned down. Eventually in 1922 the Government of the day asked the Railway Commissioners for a report as to the urgency for a bridge from their point of view. The reply was brief, and very much to the point:

The congestion of both the passenger and vehicular traffic on the northern side of the Harbour has reached saturation point, and it can only be relieved by the immediate construction of the Bridge which will also open up the Northern suburbs and give them direct railway communication with the City and Eastern and Southern suburbs.

This largely settled the matter. The necessary Bill was quickly passed through Parliament and the contract for construction of the bridge was awarded to Dorman Long and Company, of Middlesbrough, England. Plans were immediately drawn up for important railway developments in the central area. The existing Sydney Terminal station, with its nineteen

73

platforms, was a terminus with its 'back' towards the harbour. To provide for the very large influx of additional traffic that would enter the city over the harbour bridge a new through station was built beside the existing terminus, and this new station had no fewer than eight running lines. The present through suburban services operated from north to south of the harbour have already been outlined, but the connection of the tracks concerned with the City Circle line also need detailed references. The tracks are shown diagrammatically in the accompanying sketch map, and it will be seen that in passing towards the harbour two tracks run towards the station originally known as Liverpool Street, and now Museum, while

SYDNEY CENTRAL FLYOVERS

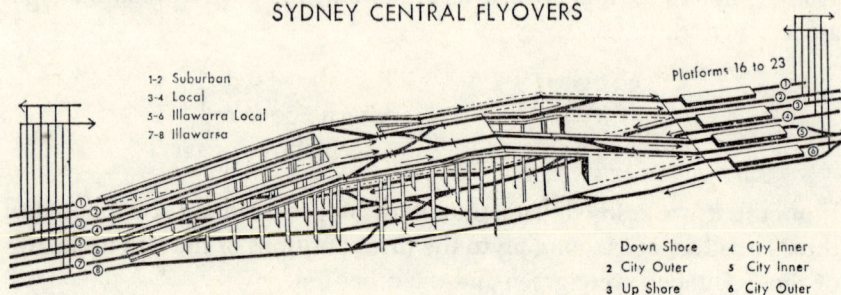

Sydney Control: Fly-over junctions south-east of station

four others diverge to pass through 'Town Hall'. Beyond this there is a grade separation to reach the upper and lower levels of Wynyard. The tracks on the upper level proceed to the crossing of the Sydney Harbour Bridge while the lower level form the first part of the City Circle, which passes through Circular Quay, and then sweeps round through St. James to pass Museum and re-enter Central station. All these lines were electrically operated from the outset and include some steep gradients such as 1 in 40 and even 1 in 30. I should mention however that the 'circle', although projected and shown on a plan dated 1926, was not completed through Circular Quay until 1956.

The terminal section of Sydney station which caters for the main line traffic in all directions as well as many suburban terminating trains, was completed in 1906, and is a splendid affair. It is a remarkable example of the forward-looking policy of the New South Wales Government Railways in so many respects. The layout of platforms, concourses, booking

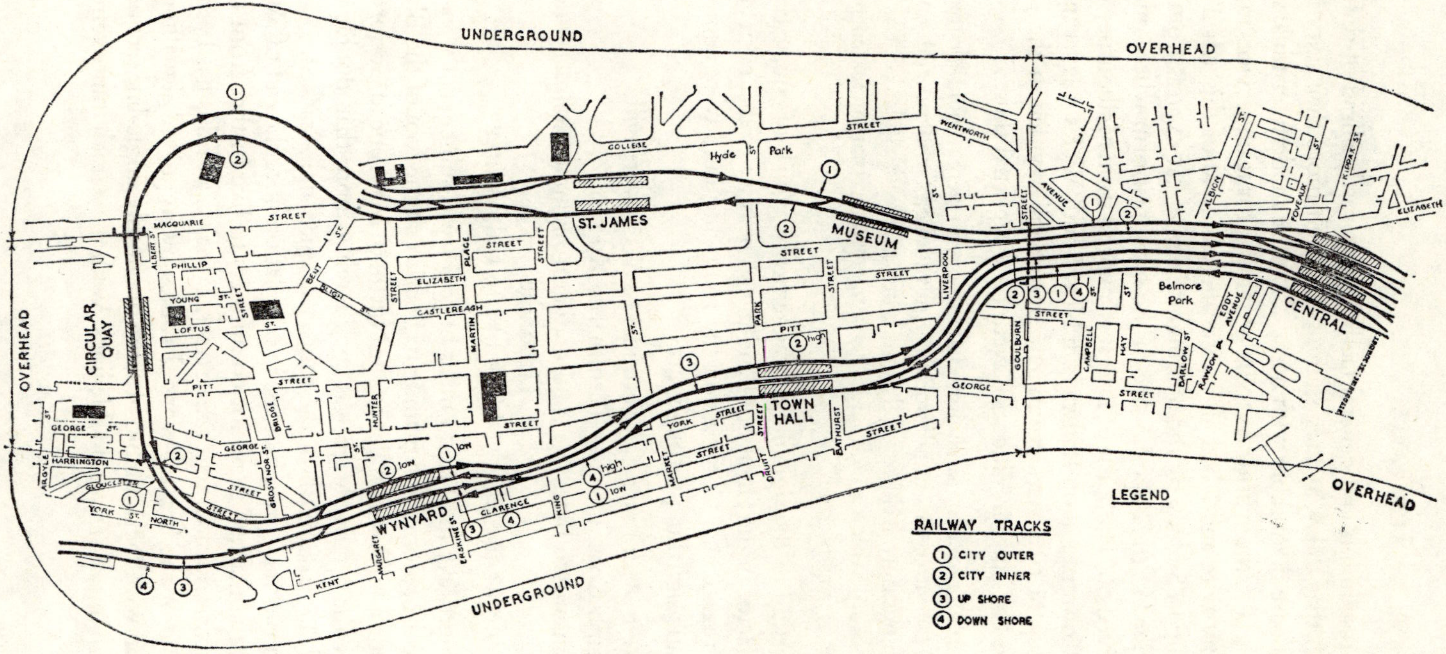

RAILWAY TRACKS

LEGEND

① CITY OUTER
② CITY INNER
③ UP SHORE
④ DOWN SHORE

OVERHEAD

OVERHEAD

OVERHEAD

UNDERGROUND

UNDERGROUND

CENTRAL

TOWN HALL

MUSEUM

ST. JAMES

WYNYARD

CIRCULAR QUAY

offices, restaurants and general facilities was vastly ahead of the times; so much so that today Sydney station, although more than sixty years old, can compare favourably with many far more modern terminal stations in other parts of the world. As to its providing for train services in all directions, my wife and I had an interesting example of this when we were travelling to Sydney by the overnight sleeping car express from Brisbane and arrived at the opposite face of the same platform where our son had just arrived on 'The Spirit of Progress' express from Melbourne. When the Royal Commission on Railways in New South Wales was set up in 1924, consisting of two very prominent British railwaymen in the persons of Sir Sam Fay and Sir Vincent Raven, they reported thus:

It is a matter for congratulations that those who were responsible for the building and layout of this important terminus looked far ahead and gave Sydney a station not only architecturally good, but so effectively laid out as to be able to deal easily with a much larger passenger traffic than appeared probable at the time it was erected.

Reverting to the signalling arrangements, which of course constitute a major factor in the facility of handling so heavy a traffic, even at the time of the 1924 Royal Commission the following lines were equipped with automatic signalling throughout:

West Main Line:	Terminal to Wentworthville
South Coast Line:	Terminal to Kogarah
Bankstown Line:	Automatic throughout Campsie Junction to Lidcombe
South Main Line:	Lidcombe to Cabramatta

This impressive total of 46 miles of route was subsequently increased by 18 miles of automatic signalling to Penrith, at the foot of the Blue Mountains, and a further 43 miles on the Northern Main line to Gosford. Around Sydney the total mileage was considerably more than double the figure quoted, because much of the route was quadruple-tracked.

With the very great increase in population since the end of World War II, and the marked trend for commuters to live further from the central area, it was essential to increase track capacity, and this has been achieved on some of the heavier-worked routes by improved signalling, in conjunction with the doubling of some previously single-line sections and the quadrupling of certain double lines. With these track improvements there has been a general change from upper-quadrant semaphores to colour light signals. Prior to the extension of the electrified area, which began in 1950, a review was made of the signal indications then in use, having particular regard to the general adoption of the 'amber' or 'yellow' light as used in colour light systems in many parts of the world. First of all there was the possibility of economy in capital expenditure if the necessary indications could be provided from a single signal head instead of the two then required with the standard New South Wales code of aspects. Secondly there were the very important extensions of the 4 ft. 8½ in. gauge then projected in other States of the Commonwealth; any alteration that would tend to conform to the indications of other States was desirable. In view of this the familiar red, yellow and green aspects were adopted for 'stop', 'caution' and 'clear' respectively, with the addition of an extra red marker light, illuminated only when the red stop aspect is being displayed.

Over lengthy mileages, when I was travelling in locomotive cabs I saw both the old standard upper-quadrant signals, and the new colour lights, and I could not fail to be very impressed by the very comprehensive nature of the signals displayed to the drivers: clear, excellently positioned, and unmistakable in their meaning. In the suburban area the signals have automatic train stops co-acting with them in exactly the same manner as standard on the London Underground railways. These train stops are electrically operated, and the multiple-unit electric trains are fitted with trip-cocks for making immediate application of the brakes in the event of a train over-running a signal at danger.

Since the year 1939 all new signalling installations have been of the relay-interlocking type, with individual thumb-switches to operate signals and points; but in 1968 an interesting change to a route-setting panel installation was made at Campbelltown. I was able to observe the working at this busy signal box on the south main line. The station marks the terminal point of the suburban services in the extensive Group 1 complex, so that in addition to the through main line passenger and freight traffic there is a great activity, particularly in the peak hours, with the terminating of multiple-unit trains, reversing them for their return journeys. The signal box is mounted on a gallery high above the station platforms with a clear view of the tracks below. The method of operation of the panel is on the 'push–push' principle; at the commencement of the route to be set up the appropriate button is pressed, while the selection of the respective button

77

at the terminating point sets up the intervening route—providing of course that the interlocking of the points and signals involved is free.

Such is no more than a brief sketch of a very busy and efficiently operated railway complex. While I have concentrated in this chapter on the purely suburban aspects of the area, it is important to appreciate that unlike some of the busiest commuter traffic elsewhere the peak hours, particularly around 8 a.m., have to accommodate many important long-distance express trains, both arriving and departing at Sydney station, and the smooth and punctual working of these very heavy trains amid a swarm of multiple-unit electrics is an impressive feature in itself.

CHAPTER SIX

Queensland: around Brisbane

In the opening chapter of this book I referred briefly to the general situation of railways in Queensland at the time of their origin. A glance at the map of the present network is enough to show how lengthy trunk lines stretching far into the interior have sprung from Brisbane, Rockhampton, and Townsville. Linking the coastal railheads is the 1043-mile main line between Brisbane and Cairns. The distances alone provide a vivid impression of the vastness of the 3 ft. 6 in. gauge system in Queensland: 604 miles from Brisbane to Cunnamulla; 537 miles from Rockhampton to Winton; 603 miles from Townsville to Mount Isa—not to mention the 202 miles from Brisbane by the old route to the New South Wales border at Wallangarra. The system is appropriately organised in four divisions each with its own general manager, though control of engineering work and operation is centralised at the Brisbane headquarters. The Chief Mechanical Engineer is responsible for all workshops throughout the system, while the Chief Engineer includes signalling with all the civil engineering of the line. The General Manager of the South Eastern Division is also Chief of Operations.

As described in Chapter Three we arrived in Brisbane by the overnight standard-gauge sleeping car express from Sydney, and embarking almost immediately upon a comprehensive tour of railway establishments I very quickly gained a good outline picture of Queensland railway working. In no State of Australia has the process of modernisation been more rapid; and although a historian could regret the rapid disappearance of steam locomotives, the territory served is exceptionally favourable to the diesel. In later chapters I shall have much to say about the remarkable mineral traffic developments in the north. It is in no spirit of disparagement that I assert that the steam locomotive was perhaps the least developed in

GULF OF
CARPENTARIA

NORTHERN TERRITORY

SOUTH AUSTRALIA

STATE BOUNDARY

NEW SOUTH WALES

SOUTH PACIFIC OCEAN

Cooktown

Mungana Mareeba CAIRNS
Almaden Atherton Innisfail
Ravenshoe Tully
Normanton
Croydon Ingham
Mt Surprise
Forsayth TOWNSVILLE
Ayr

Charters Towers Bowen
Pentland Collinsville
Richmond Netherdale MACKAY
Hughenden Etna Sarina
Julia Ck.

Rainbi
Cloncurry
Mount Isa Malbon Blair Clermont
Duchess Athol Capella Yeppoon
Selwyn Winton Emerald ROCKHAMPTON
Dajarra Aramac Barcaldine Jericho Alpha Blackwater Gladstone
Longreach Comet Mt Morgan
Springsure
Yaraka Biloela
Stockall NEW COAL RAILWAY Miriam Vale
Moura
Thargool Monto
Theodore Lawgi Bundaberg
Mundubbera
Maryborough
Charleville Wandoan Gympie
Michell Roma Proston Murgon
Quilpie Westgate Kingaroy Nanango Brooloo Nambour
Dalby Tell Yarraman Kilcoy
Glenmorgan Toowoomba Dakey CABOOLTURE
Cecil plains BRISBANE
Cunnamulla Millmerran Beenleigh
Inglewood Alom Ipswich Southport
Dirranbandi Warwick Beaudesert
Goondiwindi Texas Amiens
Wallangarra

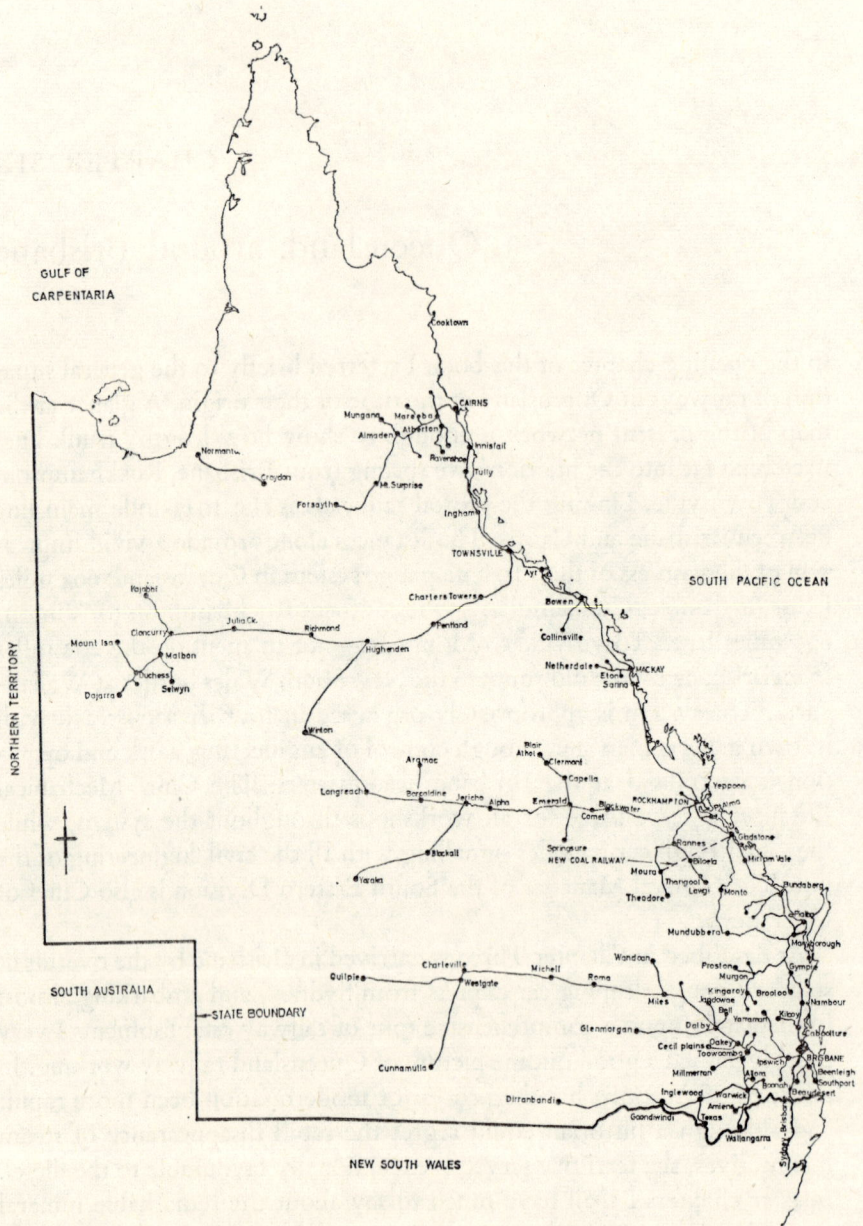

The railway network of Queensland

80

PLATE 11. Queensland steam power

(a) Sydney to Brisbane express via Wallangarra near Cambooya, hauled by a Class 'B' Pacific engine, No. 52

(b) Brisbane Central Station in 1964, with train for Petrie about to leave, with a Class 'B' Pacific

PLATE 12.

(a) Brisbane: the modern diesel depot at Mayne, showing (centre left) the new diesel servicing plant

(b) A heavy trainload of raw sugar from Proserpine to Mackay, hauled by one of the 90-ton '1300' class diesel-electric locomotives

Queensland than in any part of Australia. In pre-war days the need was less urgent. The vast mineral resources of the State were only just starting to be revealed, and with the onset of World War II it was very much a case of making do with the existing locomotive stock. The principal steam loco-motive classes then operating were 4–6–0 and 4–6–2 for long-distance passenger; 4–8–0 for mixed traffic and goods; and 4–6–4 for Brisbane suburban passenger. They were all characterised, and certainly not beauti-fied, by having sandboxes on top of the boiler; these were tall edifices shaped something like a cottage loaf. Originally one could detect some-thing of the Drummond influence, on the 4–6–0 and 4–8–0 engines of forty to fifty years ago, in their handsomely styled chimneys and domes with safety valves on the top; but in later years there was a change to a stove-pipe design.

Until the introduction of the 'Pacifics' in 1926 the most powerful variety was the 'B17' class 4–6–0 dating back to 1911, and having 17 in. by 23 in. outside cylinders, 4 ft. diameter coupled wheels and a tractive effort of 19,400 lb. The 4–8–0s, some of which were classified as 'passenger' and others as 'goods', also had 4 ft. diameter coupled wheels, but the 'C19' class of 1922 had cylinders 19 in. diameter by 23 in. stroke and a tractive effort of 23,600 lb. These 4–8–0s seem to have been used indiscriminately on passenger and goods trains until the introduction of the 'Pacifics'. The latter engines were very small by contemporary Australian standards, having cylinders $18\frac{1}{4}$ in. diameter by 24 in. stroke, and coupled wheels of 4 ft. 3 in. diameter. The tractive effort was no greater than 21,300 lb. They certainly met the needs of the day, and a total of 83 were built, 59 at Ipswich Works and 24 by Walkers. A further 55 were added to the stock in 1951, to help things out while the policy of dieselisation was being formulated. The 4–6–4 tanks used on the Brisbane suburban services were of generally similar proportions. The general size of these four standard classes can be appreciated from their total weights in working order:

Class 'B17':	4–6–0	81 tons
Class 'C19':	4–8–0	94 tons
Class 'B18$\frac{1}{4}$':	4–6–2	90 tons
Class 'D17':	4–6–4T	58 tons

It was the existence of so many locomotives of no more than moderate power that in years before World War II led to protagonists of road and air transport becoming vocal in their assertions that railways had outlived their usefulness. There was then a popular but a quite erroneous opinion that railways were outmoded. Some people even went so far as to urge that many sections of the railway in Queensland should be closed. Since the war, and with the knowledge of the herculean task performed by the railways during those years of the Pacific conflict, public opinion in Queensland performed a volte-face and it is universally recognised now by most thinking people that railways must continue to function as an important and integral part of the transport system of any country.

The damaging effect of the war traffic on the equipment and track of the Queensland railways was well known. There was no diminution in the pressure on the railways after the war ended, and the cumulative burdens of the war and post-war years created serious problems. Both the Government and the administration were fully aware of the obstacles to be overcome, not only to rehabilitate the railways, but to raise them to that standard of efficiency which would meet with the approbation of all Queenslanders and allow them to regard the railways with justifiable pride as the greatest and most valuable of the State's assets.

The outcome of this drive towards greater efficiency was the ordering of thirty new locomotives of the Beyer–Garratt articulated type from Beyer, Peacock and Company. Although a very powerful locomotive was required the specification was restrictive, limiting the maximum axle-load to $9\frac{3}{4}$ tons. At that time the immense mineral resources of the 'outback' regions of Queensland were largely undeveloped, and the new engines were primarily intended as a spectacular prestige job, hauling the then-'Sunshine Express' throughout over the 1043 miles between Brisbane and Cairns. The coupled wheel diameter was specified as 4 ft. 3 in., the same as on the 'B18$\frac{1}{4}$' class Pacifics; but use of the Garratt articulated principle and a wheel arrangement of 4–8–2+2–8–4 enabled a locomotive having a tractive effort of 32,770 lb. to be designed within the specified weight limits. It was intended that the locomotives should be used equally in freight service, just as the existing 4–8–0s of the 'C19' class were used. The latter engines were used on the Sydney mails, when the old 3 ft. 6 in. gauge route to the New South Wales border was still being operated.

The Garratts were required so urgently that Beyer, Peacocks sub-let part of their contract to the Société Franco-Belge de Matériel de Chemin de Fer, of Raismes, France, and of the thirty locomotives ordered nineteen were built in Manchester, and eleven in France. They were evidently intended to be the veritable 'flagships' of the modernisation programme, for unlike all previous Queensland locomotives, which were black with polished boiler bands, the Beyer–Garratts were finished in Midland red, and at first kept in magnificent condition. As it turned out however they were allocated mainly to Rockhampton, to work on the heavy coal trains from Callide to the coast. The traffic grew at such a phenomenal rate however that these splendid examples of steam locomotive practice were soon outdated, and today trains that require three 1980-horsepower diesels are now operated. Except for one engine that is now allocated to special workings, the Garratts, in common with the bulk of Queensland steam power, have now been withdrawn. In this same wave of rehabilitation some of the main line passenger engines, and the Brisbane suburban tank engines, were painted bright blue.

The modernisation plan began to take shape in 1950, and two years later delivery was taken of the first diesel-electric locomotives. Today, except for a few units engaged in shunting there is hardly a steam locomotive left in service. In the introduction of diesel traction the Queensland Railways adopted a policy of type-standardisation which has been of immense value in providing for efficient and fully rationalised service and maintenance facilities. When I was in Queensland, in August 1969, deliveries of new locomotives were bringing the total diesel fleet very near to the target of 400, which it is considered to be adequate to operate the entire main line traffic of the State. And these locomotives are of no more than *three* types. First of all there is a 90-ton Co+Co of 1500 to 2000 engine horsepower, for general-purpose haulages; secondly there is the 60-ton Co+Co of 840 to 975 engine horsepower, for the branch line passenger working, and lastly there are the 40-ton diesel-hydraulic locomotives used for shunting, and lighter work, particularly on branch lines where the limit of axle-loading does not permit the use of heavier units.

All these locomotives are of Queensland manufacture using imported power units. The 90-ton and the 60-ton engines are built by the English Electric Company of Australia, and, by the Clyde Engineering organisation, Queensland branch in Brisbane, while the 40-ton diesel-hydraulics are built by Walkers Ltd. of Maryborough, a rapidly-growing town on the coast roughly halfway between Brisbane and Rockhampton. The main line engines, both passenger and coal, are painted in a pleasing colour scheme of sky-blue and white, and unlike many diesel locomotives from which a very high utilisation is extracted they are kept in beautifully clean condition, even those engaged in the coal traffic. Their smart appearance reflects the clear blue skies and brilliant sunshine of the country through which they operate. The diesel-hydraulic shunting engines are finished in a quite distinctive livery of bright green and grey, with horizontal yellow stripes. The Clyde diesel-electric locomotives are extensively used in the Brisbane suburban area, where the traffic is now growing to such an extent as to promote urgent considerations towards electrification.

The introduction of diesel traction has been accompanied by the most careful regard to servicing facilities. Even before the first diesel locomotive took the road a special servicing depot was built, in 1951, at Mayne. There was no question of introducing diesel units at steam sheds, and trying to segregate the essentially 'dirty' and 'clean' operations as best one could. In 1968 Mayne depot was greatly enlarged and the new plant contains five roads on which roughly 100 locomotives and railcars are serviced daily. There is space to permit of four locomotives to be refuelled simultaneously, while ten others can be receiving attention on the inspection and servicing pits at the same time. Other depots exist at Rockhampton, which I was later able to see myself, Gladstone, Townsville, Cairns, and elsewhere. The very careful attention given to servicing has enabled the potentialities of the diesel locomotive for high utilisation to be fully realised in Queensland. On the main line up the coast, for example, one locomotive now works through over the 832 miles between Brisbane and Townsville, with only one intermediate refuelling, whereas in the days of steam haulage engines had to be changed roughly every 100 miles. The workshops for construction and repair of steam locomotives, and also for carriages and wagons, are at Ipswich, where the Queensland Railways had their origin; but the 'home base' of the entire diesel fleet is at the new plant at Redbank, between Ipswich and Brisbane, where any task between running repairs and major overhaul can be carried out.

I travelled into Brisbane in standard-gauge stock of the New South Wales Railways, but very early in the tour on which I was so enthusiastically conducted I was admiring the handsome stainless steel carriages of the suburban trains working into and out of Roma Street station. This is not only an important junction lying a little to the west of the city centre, but it is also the departure point of the long-distance express trains to the west and the north. The bulk of the commuter traffic is dealt with at Brisbane Central. There is still, of course, a considerable number of older carriages in use on the suburban trains, but the operation has been immeasurably smartened up by the introduction of the powerful Clyde diesel-electric locomotives. With a standard load of eight coaches a locomotive with an engine horsepower of 1650 can naturally produce quite a spectacular acceleration. At Roma Street also I had my first introduction to the modern signalling practice of the Queensland Railways. The station layout, although extremely spacious, is a complicated one. From the east a double-track line comes in from Brisbane Central, and then fans out into eight through lines. Immediately beyond the platform ends come a series of junctions, where the main quadruple-tracked route to the west makes a triangle with the main line to the north. The area is extremely busy in the morning and evening peak hours, and when I was there, at mid-morning, there was a considerable amount of freight movement.

Roma Street has recently been equipped with an installation of power signalling on the most modern lines. The signals themselves are colour light, with optical-type route indicators, and control is exercised from a console-type panel working in conjunction with a large illuminated diagram. The method of operation is on the one control-switch (O.C.S.) system greatly favoured in the United Kingdom in the early stages of the general modernisation of British Railways. It needs the operation of no more than a single thumb-switch to set up an entire route. Although strictly speaking the signalman does not need to see any trains in order to operate the station satisfactorily, with all movements so clearly displayed on the illuminated diagram, the signal box, strategically located in the centre of the triangular junctions to the west of the station, provides a splendid look-out over the entire area. Quite apart from the efficiency of operation, and the cleanliness of locomotives and carriages, I was charmed by the way in which the area, within railway property, was adorned by beautifully-kept gardens and lawns. It was more than reminiscent, and on a far more exotic scale, of the lawns planted at the lineside in the North Eastern Area of the London and North Eastern Railway, when the great John Miller was Engineer at York. At Brisbane the clear air and brilliant sunshine naturally contributed much to this very pleasing effect.

In addition to the locomotive-hauled trains for both main line and suburban traffic there are a number of very attractive stainless steel railcars, which can be operated either singly or as two-car assemblies. Although the development of mineral traffic is naturally forming such a major part of all Queensland Railway operating, very careful attention is being paid to the possibilities of tourist traffic, and particularly in fostering business to the centres of outstanding scenic attraction. For short-distance day travel a well-appointed and smooth-riding railcar has its points, but the Queensland Railway administration has been developing another aspect of this business. I have written already of the preponderance of night travel in journeying between the State capitals of Australia. In the long run up the coast from Brisbane to Cairns, which takes the best part of two days, there is of course a good deal of day travelling. Even so on a train like the 'Sunlander', which leaves Brisbane at 9.30 p.m. each evening, some of the choicest scenery is passed through in the dark. In 1962 a series of Daylight Rail Tours was inaugurated between Brisbane and Cairns so timed that the return journey is performed in five days, with four overnight stops, so that the entire route in both directions is seen in daylight. These tours have greatly increased in popularity since their first introduction, and upwards of twenty have been made during the cooler months of the Queensland year, that is between April and October.

I was very anxious to see something of the mineral traffic working in the north of Queensland, and yet time, in between other engagements, was very short; and our Australian friends were, I think, a little perturbed at our determination to travel north from Brisbane on the 'Rockhampton Mail' instead of by the beautiful air-conditioned 'Sunlander'. But the 'Rocky Mail', as it is popularly known, gave us an arrival in Rockhampton before 10 a.m., with the best part of the day ahead of us. Furthermore, in the beautiful temperate weather of a Queensland spring an air-conditioned train was not vital. Actually the 'Rocky Mail' turned out to be one of the most diverting and enjoyable night journeys we made in Australia. The sleeping cars, though old-fashioned by present standards, were most comfortable; massively built, with magnificent mahogany panelling and extremely spacious. As on the South African Railways there was not the slightest impression of travel on the 3 ft. 6 in. gauge. The berths are transverse, as in the United Kingdom, and except for such modern luxuries as private showers they lacked nothing in comfort. The train itself consisted of nine passenger vehicles and two vans, all of fairly light tare weight. The total load behind the locomotive was about 270 tons.

86

We slept well, but were called early to detrain briefly at Gladstone for breakfast in the station refreshment room. The scheduled halt of 25 minutes brought back thoughts of Swindon and Preston in nineteenth-century England—not that I am old enough to have experienced the reputed rigours of those celebrated meal stops! But meals on the station at Gladstone are one of the most highly organised things in Australia. Overnight the guard had ascertained the number of passengers requiring breakfast, and on arrival we found a pleasant room set out, and we were immediately offered a surprisingly wide variety of dishes. While things were no different for us than for the twenty or so other passengers taking breakfast, we also enjoyed the company of a young engineer of the signal department supervising the installation of centralised traffic control on the new coal-carrying line from Moura to Gladstone, and who joined us for that breakfast. The service in that railway restaurant was so swift and efficient, without the slightest impression of our being hustled, that we had ample time to enjoy the meal, and to relax for a few minutes afterwards before the warning shout 'All aboard' came from the platform.

For me that warning shout was the prelude to another early-morning run in the engine cab, and shortly before departure time I joined the driver and his mate on one of the Clyde '1503' series, 1650-horsepower diesel-electric locomotives for the run to Rockhampton. We had 68 miles to go, and with many intermediate stops and some stiff though not very long gradients, and the booked journey time is two and a half hours. As we pulled out of Gladstone, on a morning of cloudless sunshine, the country had already the unmistakable look of the tropics, although the railway does not cross Capricorn until just north of Rockhampton; but with the sight of the new 'Coal Railway' bearing away to the left it is time to make a pause in the story of our personal travels and tell something of the astonishing developments now in progress in this part of Queensland.

CHAPTER SEVEN

Queensland: major freight hauls

It is now necessary to take another look at the railway map of Queensland and to focus one's attention upon two points: Moura, lying some 110 miles due west of Gladstone, and Mount Isa, nearly 500 miles inland from Townsville. It is unusual in these days to read of the construction of lengthy new railways, especially through difficult mountain country; but the tremendous demand for Australian export coal, and the upsurge in the output of other basic minerals led to a re-appraisal of railway facilities for Moura mine. Coal is shipped from Gladstone, and prior to the year 1968 it was a long, roundabout haul of 195 miles from Moura, via Baralaba and Rockhampton. Even so, during the year 1967 some two million tons of coal for export was being conveyed by this route. In the years 1964–5, the owners of the Moura mine, the Theiss-Peabody-Mitsui Pty. Ltd., concluded an agreement with the Queensland Government for the construction of a new, short, direct line from Moura to Gladstone, which would shorten the haul by 83 miles. At that time the maximum train loads were 2000 tons, and it was predicted that this could be stepped up to some 3500 tons over the easier gradients of the new route. The first surveys began in 1965 and the line was opened in 1968. I was to learn later that it was not only over the new line that trains of vastly increased weight are now being worked. An enormous amount of mineral traffic is also being worked over the old route via Rockhampton, from the Blackwater coalfield.

The new line to Moura bears away to the left soon after Gladstone is left, and we headed out into thick bush country, through which the line is carried on an alignment that shows only too clearly how economy in first cost was a prime consideration when the line was first built. This is no route for making speed records. On many of the curves restrictions to 30 and even down to 20 m.p.h. are in force, and there are gradients, as in leaving Yarwan, that are 'heavy enough to get you stuck on a dewy morning', as the driver expressively put it. At many of the passing places the points are not interlocked, and a very simple and effective method of working has been designed by the signal engineers' department at Brisbane. At entry to the loops there are facing point locks, and these protect entry to the left-hand road in the loop. At the leaving end the train 'trails' the points. The mechanism is so designed that the action of the locomotive on entering upon the switch, which would be closed against it, is to cause withdrawal of the facing point lock and allow the switch to be trailed safely against the spring control. After the whole train has passed through and on to the single-line section ahead the mechanism is self-restoring, and the lock is re-inserted to protect the entry to the loop of the next train from the opposite direction. Single-line working is safeguarded, as in the United Kingdom, by the electric staff system.

The few signals, at intermediate loops, are mostly lower-quadrant semaphores, reminiscent of the English Great Eastern Railway, though of course one must recognise the strong influence of the firm of McKenzie and Holland, with its British ownership, and its works beside the main line on the outskirts of Brisbane. We were stopped in the approach to Aldoga loop, where a freight was arriving from the north, and after getting away again I was interested to see the arrangements for indicating a temporary speed restriction, with a flashing light surmounting a letter 'C', and a yellow sign indicating the speed to which we had to reduce. At the terminating point there was just a white board. To one used to British conditions the absence of illumination on some of the lineside notices is perplexing till one recalls that after dark all trains have powerful headlights. After clearing this area of restricted speed we had a pleasant spell at 50 m.p.h. over a fairly straight stretch through a mixture of grass land and bush. The track is excellent, and the locomotive rode very smoothly. Fifty miles per hour is the maximum permitted over this line, and from Aldoga onwards we were running near to this maximum for long spells between stations.

We were now approaching Mount Larcom, an interlocked station, and this was indicated on the approach station side by an inverted triangle sign by the lineside, painted with red and black horizontal stripes, alternately, in a phosphorescent paint that could readily be picked out in a locomotive headlight during hours of darkness. Another distinctive feature was the painting of the distant signal arm, in the approach to an interlocked station. The arm is red, with a fishtailed end as in the United Kingdom; but instead of the chevron band, the 'band' consisted of a device like a letter 'K' backwards. The outer profile was parallel to the fishtailed portion of the arm-end, but the inner end was vertical; the effect was thus ❯, with the triangular portion top and bottom filled in white. After leaving Mount Larcom at 8.22 a.m. we got along in fine style, over a countryside becoming more open, with views of distant mountain ranges. Stops were made at Epala, Raglan famed for its crabs, and Marmor, and then we came to another interlocked station, Bajool, where some of the points are electrically operated, and the distant signals are of the more modern painting, with yellow semaphore arms and a black chevron.

As we progressed northwards there was increasing evidence of the very serious drought conditions that were then being experienced in Central Queensland. We were running through an open country of parched grassland. Stops at intermediate loops were of the briefest: 20 seconds at Archer; 35 seconds at Midgee, and speed was worked rapidly up to 50 m.p.h. as soon as we were away. Through some incidental delays we were running a few minutes late, and our driver was anxious to make up time; but at Erinda we were stopped to cross an express fruit train. This is a specialised traffic that has shown a big increase in recent years. There are very large despatches of tomatoes and water melons from the Bowen district, and seasonal despatches of beans, bananas and pawpaws, all of which are conveyed in specially-equipped wagons, and worked at passenger train speed. The train we were to cross was a few minutes in coming, and with the sun now high in the sky it was blazing hot and I was glad to climb down from the cab for a few minutes and take some photographs. Then along came the fruit train with an engine of the same class as our own, and a seemingly endless rake of steel-louvred box wagons. She was running slowly to exchange staffs, and soon after her passing we were under way again, and a run of less than a quarter of an hour brought us into Rockhampton.

There, shortly after 10 a.m., there began one of the most intense days of sightseeing and note-taking that my wife and I experienced in all our Australian journeys. A fast car and some delightful hosts were waiting to whisk my wife away on a short whirlwind tour. She must see *everything*, before we returned to Brisbane that evening by the southbound 'Rocky Mail'. In the meantime I was taken to the traffic control to see the train graphs and gather some fascinating statistics on the running of the coal trains. At Rockhampton they are concerned with the old and the new route, and the great feature of the coal traffic on both routes is the working of the triple-headed trains. The trains from Moura take the new line, avoiding Rockhampton altogether, but they come under the surveillance of Rockhampton control: the trains from Utah come down the old line, through the outskirts of Rockhampton, and then down the main line we ourselves had traversed to Gladstone.

I was shown some of the statistics of this amazingly expanding traffic. In the week ending 16 August 1969, about a fortnight before my own visit, twenty-four triple-headers had been run from Moura to Gladstone over the new line, plus one double-header and one single-engined train. These twenty-six had between them conveyed 67,950 tons of export coal, and 7000 tons of aluminium ore for the Queensland Alumina plant at Gladstone. In the same week they had run thirteen triple-headers from Utah to Gladstone, nine double-headers, and nine single-engined trains, all carrying coal: a total of 51,496 tons for export from Gladstone. I must repeat, all this tonnage was conveyed over single-tracked railways in one week. This was no flash in the pan. A fortnight later the tonnage from Moura was no less than 82,900 tons of export coal, and again 7000 tons of coal for the alumina plant. This required twenty-six triple-headers, three double-headers, and six single-engined trains. The locomotives employed are exclusively the English Electric '1300' class, with an engine horse-power, on a triple-headed train, of 2940. The coal trains are composed of special hopper wagons each conveying a pay-load of 50 tons, and the gross tonnage to be hauled by the three locomotives, coupled in multiple unit, is around 4100 tons.

The new line from Moura to Gladstone, 112 miles in length, is being equipped for centralised traffic control operation from a single panel, while the line from Blackwater to Rockhampton, conveying traffic from the Utah mine, has been upgraded to render it suitable for these vast trains, roughly three-fifths of a mile long. Two-way radio between the engine crew and the guard is fitted on these trains, and the guards are using specially designed periscopes in their vans to watch over the running. They are run at little less than passenger train speed, and are fitted with the Westinghouse brake throughout. The old-fashioned chain and hook couplings have vanished from the modern express freight trains on the

Queensland Railways, and all wagons are equipped with massive centre couplers. The design of the wagons themselves has become a specialised activity in itself. In the handling of such freight tonnages as are involved on the Moura and Utah coal lines, and on the still longer hauls farther north, the indiscriminate use of general-purpose wagons would be inefficient and wholly uneconomic, and special wagons have been designed for each individual traffic, having regard not only to conditions while on the run but also to the most expeditious methods of loading and unloading at the terminal points.

It is not even a case of one wagon for one traffic. Separate designs of coal wagons have been developed for the differing conditions on the Moura, Utah and Mount Isa lines. Trains from the Moura mine are composed entirely of steel hopper wagons, arranged for bottom discharge at Gladstone on to a conveyor belt, by which the coal is transported to a stockpile ready for loading into the ships. Coal from the Blackwater district, Utah mines, is conveyed in huge aluminium coal hopper wagons, while the Mount Isa–Townsville traffic is worked with very large steel open wagons, with side doors. The large bogie aluminium wagons for the bulk transport of grain are also very interesting. The bodies are slightly elliptical in cross-section, and are designed for rapid overhead loading and for discharge through wells in the base into underground storage. One could write enthusiastically for page after page about the freight handling facilities of the Queensland Railways, though I should emphasise that by no means all of it is contained in special one-traffic trains. The bogie louvred steel wagons that I saw on the express fruit train we crossed at Erinda are general-purpose vehicles and used in the express goods services worked between Brisbane, Rockhampton, Townsville, Winton, and Mount Isa. It is remarkable that the journey time by express goods train over the 1435 miles from Brisbane to Mount Isa is now only 65 hours, an average speed of 22 m.p.h. My earlier reference to the running of the 'Rockhampton Mail' will have given some impression of the circumstances in which passenger trains are operated in Queensland. Our scheduled average speed over the 396 miles from Brisbane to Rockhampton was only $26\frac{3}{4}$ m.p.h. The express goods train speed over the same section is $24\frac{3}{4}$ m.p.h. In addition to the all-freight trains still faster delivery of smaller consignments is made by attaching the general-purpose steel bogie wagons to the Rockhampton mail trains.

In the Rockhampton control offices I was able to study the records of freight train workings on various lines and to talk to the controllers, and then we went out into the noonday heat of the tropics to see the station, yards, and the locomotive servicing plant. With diesel traction the one-time conception of a locomotive 'shed' has completely vanished, and the depots are now closely akin to roadside filling and servicing stations. It is true there was an old steam 4–6–0 in almost continuous shunting duty in the yard, but for train working out on the line the motive power was exclusively diesel. We were making our way round the yards, looking at signalling equipment, locomotives, and special-purpose wagons, when I was suddenly appraised of an unexpected duty it was hoped I would perform. The local newspaper, *The Morning Bulletin*, had learned of my presence in Rockhampton that day; a reporter would be at the station shortly and it was hoped I would grant an interview. A photographer arrived shortly afterwards at the diesel depot, and I was duly featured sitting at the controls of one of the new diesel-hydraulic shunting locomotives referred to in the previous chapter. The 'reporter' turned out to be a very charming young lady, who to my surprise seemed to take all her notes in longhand. Next day I had headlines in *The Morning Bulletin*: 'OVERSEAS PRAISE FOR STATE RAILWAY SYSTEM', and a meticulously accurate account of that interview was introduced thus: 'The Queensland railway system has, over the years, taken its fair share of knocks from a critical public. But in Rockhampton yesterday, a man who has been closely associated with the British railway industry for virtually a lifetime was loud in his praise for the much-maligned Queensland system. . . .'

I was still in the station yard talking to this young reporter when the northbound 'Sunlander' drew in, from Brisbane. This beautiful train, consisting of entirely modern air-conditioned stock, leaves Brisbane at 9.30 p.m. each evening, and arrives at Cairns, 1043 miles, at 2.45 p.m. on the second day. The overall average speed of $25\frac{1}{2}$ m.p.h. may seem very slow by European standards, but as I emphasised to that young reporter the Queensland railway system is most efficiently geared to the needs of the country, and to try and run fast expresses of the 'Southern Aurora' kind would impose great difficulties in operation and engineering for which there would be a very poor return. The through load of the 'Sunlander' is twelve coaches, to which a dining car is added for the daytime portion of the journey between Bundaberg and Mackay. There is first- and second-class sleeping accommodation of the most luxurious kind, and the train-consist includes a 'power car' marshalled immediately behind the locomotive, fitted with a diesel generating set to supply electric power to the whole train. Rockhampton station does not provide a heavy passenger traffic and a single platform face is enough for the through trains. Our Queensland friends had talked much of the beautiful coastline and inland country lying north of Rockhampton, and it was with something of wistfulness that I watched the 'Sunlander' depart, leaving the station, and at first making its cautious way down the main street of the town.

By this time my friends were urging an early lunch. A triple-header, returning empties from Gladstone to Utah, was due to pass in the early afternoon, and so far as my sightseeing was concerned this was a 'must'. There is a triangle junction just to the south of Rockhampton that provides direct access to the Blackwater line, so that these mighty coal trains do not actually enter Rockhampton. We went out by car to the point where road and railway together cross the Tropic of Capricorn, and then turned to follow the railway up the valley and 'pace' the train, so that I could observe the running of the splendid aluminium hopper wagons. It was making excellent speed, and when we finally decided to get ahead to find a suitable spot for photographing it was several miles before we gained sufficient advantage to be able to locate a vantage point, stop the car, and get ready. And I may add the majority of Australians are no laggards when it comes to driving a motor car! By that time we had sped so far up the line that I began to look at my watch; for we were due to catch the southbound 'Rockhampton Mail' back to Brisbane that night. But all was well, and we swung into the station yard just two minutes ahead of the other party bringing my wife from her equally lightning tour, and with about five minutes to catch the train!

We left Rockhampton determined that on our next visit to Australia we would go right up to Cairns. Back in Brisbane next day they told me of the tremendous Mount Isa project which involved the complete reconstruction of the 603-mile line to Townsville, in the years 1961 to 1965, and which has been generally recognised as one of the greatest railway works carried out anywhere in the world at that time. Although primarily intended to equip the railway for dealing with the greatly increased production at the Mount Isa mines the reconstruction of the line, to permit of working lengthy coal trains with two diesel-electric locomotives in

94

multiple, has brought all-round benefits in accelerated service for passengers, general merchandise and livestock. It was primarily the discovery of large reserves of copper, lead and zinc ores that led to the tremendous expansion programme at the mines themselves, with a rate of ore extraction increased from 4000 tons per day in 1954 to some 14,000 tons in 1965. Transport from the mines is entirely dependent upon the railway, and geological studies indicated that the reserves of ore are sufficient to ensure a continuance of maximum anticipated traffic for considerably more than twenty years. The cost of the reconstruction of the railway was estimated to be some 54 million dollars, and it was considered that this could be amortised in twenty years of traffic such as mentioned previously.

This was the first of several great projects that I was made aware of in Australia, in which the construction of new railways, or a complete modernisation of existing ones, formed a vital integral part of an enormous industrial expansion. In the United Kingdom, and in many other parts of the world, one is accustomed to seeing railways fighting a desperate rearguard action against the encroachment of other forms of transport, despite their inherent attributes for the bulk handling of heavy freight; but in Australia it was inspiring to find that railways are still regarded as the great and natural ally of industrial expansion. This is in some measure due to the vast distances to be covered, and the still-primitive state of some of the inland roads; but even so it makes good hearing. Before referring in some detail to what was done in the reconstruction of the Mount Isa line it is interesting to consider the several products of the mines, and their distribution and uses. First of all lead and blister copper ingots and zinc concentrates are conveyed to the coast, where the latter are stockpiled ready for shipment. The copper is refined at Stuart, at a plant adjacent to the junction of the Mount Isa line with the coastal route to and from Cairns. From this refinery copper in bar form is taken by road over the short distance to Townsville ready for shipment, but the slag is taken back to Mount Isa by train for further processing. Gold has been found in this residue, but this alone makes the heavy return load from Stuart to Mount Isa well worth while. There are other interesting details and side products of this great development; but I have written enough to indicate something of the background to the very extensive modernisation work done on the railway. I may add however that in the case of Mount Isa coal had to be hauled inland from Bowen to Collinsville to provide fuel for the new electric generating station, at the mines.

So far as railway reconstruction was concerned there was first the permanent way. The original line was in many ways a relic of pioneering days in Queensland. Much of the track was laid with rails no heavier than 42 lb. to the yard, and there were many bridges too light to carry the axle-loading of modern locomotives. In the hilly country traversed there were severe gradients of 1 in 50 and 1 in 33 combined with curvature as sharp as 5-chain radius. This restricted train loadings to as little as 325 tons between Townsville and Charters Towers. This of course was the critical section, being the final section leading to the coast. To cope with the projected increase in output from the mines, over a railway that would have to remain single-tracked, it was necessary to increase the train load to something like *ten times* its existing tonnage. To do this the track had to be relaid to provide 82-lb. rails throughout; the loops had to be greatly lengthened to permit long trains to cross without difficulty; underline bridges had to be strengthened, and finally a large amount of re-grading and re-alignment undertaken to provide a ruling gradient no steeper than 1 in 90 between Stuart where the Mount Isa line joins the main coastal route, at Hughenden, and 1 in 125 between Hughenden and Mount Isa. As a result of this work the maximum train load using the diesel-electric locomotives in multiple unit has been increased to 2600 tons.

To facilitate working of this greatly increased traffic a complete overhaul of the signalling was made between Stuart and Mount Isa. Previously the line was worked on the electric-staff system standard on the Queensland Railways, and the crossing loops were arranged for main line and loop working which involved a good deal of time in the crossing of opposing trains, or the overtaking of a slow one by another of higher priority travelling in the same direction. These time-consuming operations, while just tolerable under the older conditions of traffic, would have meant so much quite unacceptable delay nowadays that the use of trailable facing point locks, as referred to in connection with the running of the Rockhampton Mail between Gladstone and Rockhampton, was applied also to the Mount Isa line. It enabled many of the loops to be completely unattended. At the major centres other considerations made a degree of re-signalling necessary. At Charters Towers, Torrens Creek, Hughenden, Julia Creek, Cloncurry, and Mount Isa the governing factor in all cases

PLATE 13.

(a) A Brisbane-bound freight train crossing the scenic Stoney Creek trestle viaduct, on the line from Kuranda to Cairns, North Queensland

(b) On the re-graded Mount Isa line: a double-headed coal train of 2600 tons, passing through one of the new cuttings

PLATE 14. The new Moura–Gladstone Line

(a) A triple-headed coal train negotiating a spectacular 'S' curve in the Calliope Range

(b) A triple-headed train unloading at Auckland Point Jetty, Gladstone

was the great increase in the length of the tracks for berthing of the long trains; and whereas a single mechanical interlocking frame had in these instances controlled the whole yard, the lengthening of the loops put the further ends far beyond the limits of operation by mechanical rodding. Even the greatly increased traffic did not justify electric operation of these distant points, and so the use of trailable facing point locks was embodied in a revised method of working the yards as a whole.

The junction of the Mount Isa line with the main coastal route at Stuart constituted a special case. Previously a 52-lever mechanical interlocking had sufficed; but once again the addition of long refuge sidings, and a new yard, made mechanical working of the ordinary kind impossible from one signal box. The anticipated traffic was about 50 through train movements a day; but considerable shunting would also be involved, so it was decided to install colour light signalling throughout the area, controlled from a console type of panel. There is an illuminated diagram on which all train movements are indicated, and points and signals are operated from non-interlocked thumb-switches on the console. It is of course not possible to operate points or signals in such a way as to set up dangerous conditions, because although the switches themselves are not interlocked and are free to be moved at any time, the electric interlocking of the control circuits prevents any conflicting routes or movements being set up. The panel and illuminated diagram are attractively styled, making operating conditions vastly different from those of the old-time mechanically-operated signal boxes. As a signal engineer myself I was extremely impressed by the details of the installation at Stuart, and indeed on the whole of the Mount Isa line. There has been no mere following of practice developed elsewhere. A scheme has been worked out at Brisbane to suit the individual requirements of the various lines of the Queensland Railways, and the tremendous upsurge in traffic conveyed is an eloquent testimony to the efficiency with which this has been done.

The Mount Isa line, unlike that from Moura to Gladstone, is not entirely a freight line, though minerals from those great mines certainly provide its life-blood. This line also has its fully air-conditioned sleeping car train, the 'Inlander', which traverses the 603-mile route between Townsville and Mount Isa twice weekly. Nor must I omit to mention the special arrangements made recently for the movement of large numbers of live-stock. New trucking yards have been installed at Mount Isa and Julia

G

Creek to which roads for conveying beef cattle from as far distant as the Northern Territory have been constructed. On these roads the cattle are brought by road trains for transfer to the railway at Mount Isa or Julia Creek. Other major trucking yards, mainly concerned with sheep, have been built at Hughenden and other points on the line. It is not unusual to convey 900 head of cattle, or 3500 sheep, in a single train, worked by the ubiquitous diesel-electric locomotives.

CHAPTER EIGHT

New South Wales: the main south line

In the early history of railways in New South Wales it is remarkable to recall that there was considerable agitation in favour of horse traction. Some short-sighted men hankered after cheapness in construction and operation; but fortunately John Whitton had a resolute character to back up his firm convictions, and still more fortunately he was strongly supported by His Excellency the Governor, Sir John Young. In 1861 Sir John gave instructions for a line extending southwards from Campbelltown to Goulburn to be surveyed, and specified that it should be capable of carrying steam locomotives. The ensuing report was submitted to John Whitton, who supported the plan strongly, and concluded his comments by adding: 'The result for the colony would be greater expedition in means of transport, greater economy, greater comfort and regularity and above all, greater safety.' The outcome was that Parliament authorised not only the line to Goulburn, but an extension of the west line to Bathurst and to Murrurundi.

By the time of this report the line had been constructed from the main west line at Parramatta Junction, later changed to Granville in 1880, in a southward direction to Liverpool in 1858. I was interested to read that Liverpool is described as 'an old industrial town'. It is still no more than a wayside suburban station, and to an Englishman, with visions of Lime Street, the Edge Hill complex, to say nothing of the northern entrance to the Lancashire city over the former L. & Y.R. line, it was interesting to find 'Liverpool Signal Box' on the New South Wales Government Railways, the only one in the neighbourhood, to be a relatively small though busy mechanical interlocking. The through expresses to the south today do not follow the original line via Granville, but take the short cut from

99

Lidcombe to Cabramatta, joining the old line about three miles short of Liverpool.

During our stay in Australia we travelled twice over the historic and beautiful route south of Campbelltown, once on the Canberra–Monaro diesel-multiple-unit express, and then when we said farewell to New South Wales and travelled through to Melbourne by the 'Intercapital Daylight Express' operated jointly by the New South Wales and Victorian Railways. On both journeys I had the privilege of footplate passes, and so was able to see the country and the railway scene to the finest possible advantage. Before coming to a description of these interesting journeys I must refer to the history of the lines concerned, and to the build-up of train services to their present standard of excellence. The chief physical obstruction on the line south was the range of hills lying athwart the course beyond Picton. These did not provide so formidable an obstacle as the Blue Mountains, but the difference in altitude in the $31\frac{1}{2}$ miles between Picton and Bowral is nevertheless 1660 ft., making an average gradient of exactly 1 in 100. The earlier part of the ascent, when the railway is making its way up the steepest part of the escarpment, is more severe, and over the 25 miles between Picton and Aylmerton the average rate of ascent is 1 in 90.

It was on the 'Intercapital Daylight Express' that I was riding on the footplate over this section of the line, on one of the very comfortable '44' class diesel-electric locomotives, and even before we had passed Campbelltown some very interesting trains had passed, heading for Sydney. Among these were two that were steam-hauled, including a '38' class Pacific, but almost exactly at Liverpool we met the 'Spirit of Progress' express from Melbourne; this was followed at Macquarie Fields, by the luxury all-sleeper 'Southern Aurora'. Neither of these trains make quite such a fast overall time between the two cities as the 'Daylight'; but in the case of night trains it is convenience of departure and arrival times rather than fast overall average speed that count for most. Before coming to the mountain section a railway bridge of historic interest must be noticed, that over the Nepean River at Menangle. In the notes I took from the cab of the 'Intercapital Daylight Express' I find the comment 'fine river bridge'. I did not then realise that it was the oldest railway bridge in New South Wales, and moreover has a history all of its own.

Whitton decided that iron spans were necessary, and this proposal for the structure immediately attracted attention because it was to be the first iron bridge, or iron structure of any kind in the colony. This was before the general introduction of steel, and the wrought-iron girders were manufactured in England. They were duly shipped in 1861, and the load was such that two vessels were required. They left England in October 1861, but one was wrecked and its cargo lost shortly after leaving. The other one reached Sydney in April 1862—six months on the journey, but nothing unusual at that time. Replacements of the second cargo did not reach Sydney until December 1862, but once safely in Australia the bridge took only six months to erect, and the line was opened through to Picton shortly afterwards. Although a single-tracked railway was then constructed the bridge was made wide enough to carry a double line. The piers were built in the excellent stone available in the district; in fact the original name of Picton was Stonequarry. Since its original opening the bridge has been strengthened at various times, a most important addition being the building of new intermediate piers to halve the length of the spans and permit the use of heavier locomotives. There is certainly a vast difference between the McConnell 0–4–2s used on the line in its earliest days, and the massive '38' class Pacifics, which represented the final development of express passenger steam power in New South Wales.

At Picton, which lies in fine open country at the foot of the hills, the line actually approaches the town from the south, having made a considerable detour in working its way through an increasingly upland type of country. It reminded me very much of certain stretches of the Waverley route on the Scottish borders. Faced with the escarpment immediately to the south of Picton, John Whitton used a steeply-graded location in climbing the hill, to avoid the expense of extensive tunnelling; but now the railway doubles back on itself in a complete horseshoe bend, and climbs the escarpment on long gradients of 1 in 75 and five tunnels before the summit point is reached at Bowral. I had more than normal opportunity for observing the engineering features of this line, and of the surrounding country, because a freight train had been interposed between the 'Canberra–Monaro Express' and ourselves, and with three trains running over the line within the space of a quarter of an hour we were subjected to several checks by signal, though not enough to delay our running seriously. The country ahead for upwards of a hundred miles consists of a high tableland, all at around 2000 ft. above sea level, and while we were running slowly towards an adverse signal we met the Sydney-bound 'Southern Highlands Express' which is an excellent service from Goulburn. This was once a notable train for fast steam locomotive running.

Reverting once again to pioneer days, when the McConnell 0–4–2s were the star engines on this route, it is interesting to find that early Australian railway guides, like their contemporaries in England, threw a vivid light upon travelling conditions of the day. In 1886 for example, *The Railway Guide to New South Wales* has the following comments to make on the journey from Sydney to Goulburn:

On this route, as on all others, be sure you are at the station from which you intend to start (especially should it be the Sydney terminus) a full quarter of an hour before the train is to leave; more particularly so if you are not alone or have any luggage. Take the morning train if you wish to enjoy the varied scenery along the line. You will be able to dine at Mittagong, which you will reach about four hours after your train leaves the Sydney terminus. There is also a good refreshment room at Goulburn. Be sure you get into a carriage that is going to Goulburn, or to some place on the southern line, otherwise you will have to look out (sharply) at Granville, and change into a carriage going south. The guards, uniformly a civil, trustworthy and respectable class of men, always warn the passengers of every necessary change, and occasional stopping place, but passengers (especially ladies) are often inattentive and get 'carried on' in consequence—to the annoyance of themselves and the vexation and worry of everyone else.

Some idea of the prevailing speed in 1886 can be gathered from the fact that Mittagong, where there was a lunch interval, is less than 80 miles from Sydney, and reached in four hours, while the warning of a possible need to change at Granville is a reminder that trains left Sydney with portions for both the west and south lines, and were divided at Granville.

The original line from Picton, which quickly gained height by means of the original location, ran on higher ground until it rejoined the present route at Mittagong. It passed stations that mostly had a nostalgic British ring, such as Thirlmere, Buxton, Balmoral, and Braemar, though interspersed with these are names like Couridjah and Colo Vale. In the meantime, after crossing the Bargo River bridge and continuing on an almost continuous ascent of 1 in 75, the present finely-equipped main line is climbing into high bush country frequented by kangaroos and waratah.

102

The vertical-sided cuttings are blasted through solid rock, now pleasantly mellowed by profuse growth of a pretty red lichen. The speed with our modern diesel locomotive is a steady 30 m.p.h.; but as the driver said, we were going 'all-out'. There was no means, even if it were necessary, to get a little extra; one has got to sit back and take what the engine gives. It is not long since steam was superseded on this route. Our driver and his mate were both old steam men, and during the climb they recalled some of their work with the '36' class 4–6–0s and the Class '38' Pacifics: splendid engines on a bank and fast on the level, but now unfortunately outdated. Still travelling on the newer 'deviation' line we passed through the long Aylmerton tunnel, and by the time we passed Aylmerton itself, in fine upland country, we were nearing the top of the ascent.

The altitude was now 1931 ft. above sea level, and although still rising the gradients were easier and speed rose to 48 m.p.h. The track of the original line comes alongside at Mittagong, and here the likeness to hill country in the United Kingdom was heightened by a spell of rain, and cloud so low that we were almost running in fog. Near Bowral, on the left-hand side of the line is the old single-line tunnel, built when the line was first opened in 1867. It was only the second tunnel driven by the New South Wales Government Railways, and has a very handsome façade in heavy masonry. At Bowral, 82½ miles from Sydney, via the route now followed in the suburban area, the summit of the line is reached, at an altitude of 2210 ft., and from here onwards some real express speed is run. Before leaving the Picton–Bowral ascent however I must add that the deviation, avoiding the original incline and its gradients of 1 in 30, was brought into service in July 1919, and from that time onwards a gradual speed-up of train services on this line became possible. The Post Office required an overall average, on long-distance runs, of 30 m.p.h. with the mail trains. By the early 1920s, following consolidation of working over the deviation line, the time between Sydney and Albury, 401½ miles, was 12 hours, and by 1926 it was down to 10 hr. 54 min. The 'Intercapital Daylight Express', by which we travelled, takes 8 hr. 50 min., the respective average speeds at these three periods being 33½, 36½ and 45½ m.p.h.

From Bowral over the high plains, with distant hill ranges on both sides of the line, we had 55 miles of fast running. The track undulates, but there are many stretches where 70 m.p.h. can be run. There are rich farmlands, stretches of thick bush, and then miles of apple orchards. Everywhere the trees are the characteristic Australian blue gum, which when viewed from a distance look, to an Englishman, so like silver birches. The station names vary: Burradoo, Exeter, Penrose, Wingello; but the most appropriate of all is undoubtedly Carrick in a countryside that often looks so very like the south-westerly corner of Scotland. On this stretch I made many notes of speeds of 65, 67 and 70 m.p.h., and that our diesel was riding very smoothly. The track is splendid for the maximum speed of 70 m.p.h. now laid down. And so, after a run of just over three hours from Sydney, the line comes to Goulburn.

Even before the railway arrived here, in 1869, this city was a thriving place. Lying near the junction of the Mulwarree Ponds with the Wollondilly River it had been a natural settlement from the earliest days of inland colonisation, and when the railway era began it was the market centre of a large and influential district. The city was spaciously laid out in rectangular blocks, with wide roads and many fine buildings. The original railway station was in keeping with the general air of elegance in the place, and was considered the most handsome building on the south main line. Originally there was no more than a single platform, but early photographs show it to have been very smartly kept. It is interesting also to observe how the New South Wales Government Railways at that time followed contemporary British practice in the style of permanent-way maintenance. Both in station areas and on the open line the ballast was piled up to within an inch or so of the top of the rail, completely obscuring the sleepers and the rail fastenings. In England this was later found to hide the traditional 'multitude of sins' in the way of faulty packing under the sleepers, and in Australia as in the United Kingdom it is now the hall-mark of good track to have the top surface of the sleepers exposed.

Goulburn is the junction for the important branch line that runs southwards to Cooma. This had been completed before the turn of the century, but it derived a greatly additional importance when the open plains in the neighbourhood of Yass–Canberra were selected as the site of the future Federal capital after the formation of the Commonwealth of Australia in 1901. This now most gracious city is reached by a short branch line from Queanbeyan Junction, opened in 1914, and on its opening it was worked by the veteran '79' class 4-4-0 No. 210, later renumbered 1210. This engine (as previously mentioned in Chapter Four) is now enthroned on a plinth outside Canberra station. The journey over the sinuous branch line

'The Inter-City Express': Class C38 'Pacific' with train made up of vestibuled stock, between Sydney and Newcastle, New South Wales Railways

throughout from Goulburn is a delight, especially when made in the driver's compartment of the Canberra–Monaro Express. After leaving the main south line, at Joppa Junction, the branch at first runs on a very straight course over typical sheep-grazing country; there was a fine vista over Lake Bathurst, and then we began to enter rougher, rocky and more difficult country. The cutting sides were the colour of ochre, gradients as steep as 1 in 40 began to obtrude, but once on a stretch of straight track speed was soon up to 60 m.p.h. There was a backward sight of Lake George, stretching away towards the Mundoonen Range, and so we came to Bungendore, lately associated with the bandit Ned Kelly. Although he himself never operated in New South Wales, his exploits were fresh in mind at the time of our visit, for the making of the celebrated film was still in progress in this area. After Bungendore the going becomes more difficult than ever, with U-curves, 1 in 40 gradients, and equally steep descents. At Queanbeyan the eight-car train was divided, four coaches continuing on the main branch, and the other four diverging to Canberra. Although there is so much to see in this most beautiful capital city our first pilgrimage was naturally to see old '1210' on her plinth, and very fine she looked too, in her grey-green livery and stylish lining out.

Back to the main line at Goulburn, and to the journey southwards to the Victorian border, the general direction is south-west, and we head for the Cullerin Range, which lies completely abreast of the track. Past Breadalbane the going is fast, but the climb into the mountains involves gradients of 1 in 41 and 1 in 54 until the summit level of the whole route is reached at Cullerin station, 2395 ft. above sea level. In high rocky country, in continuous rain, in keeping with the Scottish Highlands names and the general lie of the land, we began the long descent to Fish River. The alignment is very winding, and speed had to be severely moderated; but the present route is nothing to what the original single line was like. At many places between Cullerin and Fish River the earthworks of the old line can be seen, and one can only imagine what it was like to fight one's way up such gradients on such an alignment with steam locomotives like old '1210' which now stands so serenely outside Canberra station. Fortunately the loads were not very heavy in early days, when less than a dozen four-wheelers constituted a main line express train. All the same it was not until the years 1913–16 that this part of the line was converted to double track, and the improved alignments made. By time that the 'P6' 4-6-0s were in their prime, and even they must have had a rare tussle going north where the gradient averages 1 in 75 for seven miles on end. Shades of Shap, but here it is a case of Shap with the fearsome curvature of the South Devon line between Newton Abbot and Totnes!

After Fish River the alignment becomes straighter, and down towards Jerrawa Creek we had a fine spell at 70 m.p.h. In passing I should mention that in Australia a creek is not necessarily a tidal inlet of the sea; it can be any small river or stream, and from this particular one there is another piece of stiff ascent to a summit level of 1953 ft. The gradients here are typical of what the original line was like before the improvements of 1913–16 with inclination constantly changing, and short strips of level intervening between lengths of 1 in 53, 42, 60, 41, and such like. It is rough sheep-grazing country, like some stretches of the Craven district in the West Riding of Yorkshire. I have a note in my travelling diary that it could be called 'anglo-bush'—in other words it was uncultivated virgin land, but with an English rather than an Australian look about it. From this summit point, at a distance of 187 miles from Sydney we had 12 miles of fast downhill running to our next stop, Yass Junction, 58 miles from Goulburn covered in 75 minutes.

From Goulburn I had been riding in the train rather than on the locomotive, and very pleasant it was. The open saloon cars ride well; they are beautifully appointed, and the walls are adorned with large coloured pictures that inevitably make the lover of fine country wish to travel far and wide in Australia. On the next stage of the journey the countryside still retains the same characteristics; pastoral, but in a mountain sense, with the rise and fall of the gradients on the railway reflecting the hills and dales of the terrain. As one progressed the vastness and the complete absence of any industrial concentration in the inland regions of Australia began to form a most vivid impression. Several freight trains going north were passed; activity at the larger stations was mostly concerned with sheep, and while we enjoyed lunch at the buffet counter of a restaurant car similar to that used on the night expresses between Sydney and Brisbane, we were running over a sharply undulating track with ruling gradients mostly around 1 in 75: Bowning, Goondah, Illalong Creek, Binalong, Galong, Rocky Ponds, passed in succession, and so we covered the 42 miles of hard going between Yass Junction and Harden in 62 minutes.

Back in the ordinary saloon on leaving Harden, after a good lunch, I must confess to falling asleep for nearly half an hour while we were running onwards to Cootamundra, a junction for branch lines running in several directions. The network spreading westwards including long routes extending to Griffith, to Lake Cargelligo, and a northbound fork that joins the west main line far beyond its passage through the Blue Mountains, at Parkes. Cootamundra, thanks to the transport facilities provided by the railway, has become the focus point of a great wheat-growing district, and its large flour mills can be seen from the train. Out in the plains its aspect, that of a big railway junction isolated in the heart of a vast rural area, is something like an Australian and much more cultivated version of De Aar, in South Africa. Out of Cootamundra there is a long climb in further hill country. Never before have I seen so many sheep properties! The gradients here are very broken, with an intermission of very severe if short lengths at 1 in 46, 1 in 60, with equally short lengths of level; and with a final sharp pull at 1 in 42, and the speed down to under 30 m.p.h. we come to another summit point 272 miles from Sydney.

There is some very rocky country in the next few miles, and skilful engineering work has been carried out to improve the gradients and alignment. The original single line, which now forms the southbound or down main line, has some exceedingly bad gradients in this area. From the summit point just mentioned there is a descent of nearly two miles at 1 in 40 to near Frampton, and an even worse one for nearly three miles at 1 in 49–40–45 to Bethungra. In the old single-line days these inclines were a tremendous handicap to the working of heavy northbound trains, and as there exists about three miles of favourable gradient between the two, where speed could rise to 60 m.p.h. or over, one could not use the simple expedient of local bank engines in rear, as on that fearsome first stage of the climb from Lithgow up the western escarpments of the Blue Mountains. Trains had to be double-headed over this stretch. When the time came to double the line entirely new locations were found for the up line, reducing the ruling gradient to 1 in 66 from Bethungra and to 1 in 75 from Frampton. On the latter stretch the down and up lines part company for a while and the deviation increases the mileage on the up line by just over one mile. The Bethungra deviation, which was brought into service in July 1946, involves a special location and tunnel that required some complicated surveying. On the new line the gradient on this sharply-curved stretch is compensated for the curvature, and is equivalent to 1 in 66 on straight line. This is severe enough but it is considerably better than the former precipitous ascent.

This fascinating piece of railway location is set in the most beautiful wooded hill country, strongly Scottish in its aspect; but very soon after passing Bethungra the line enters a level parkland country, and the driver of our diesel is soon piling on the speed. Just short of 19 miles farther on we are drawing into Junee, with the difficult 34½-mile run from Cootamundra completed in 45½ minutes. Junee is a locomotive centre of some importance. In steam days engines were changed here, and with gradients much easier from here over the remaining hundred miles of the run to the Victorian border, locomotives with a larger coupled wheel diameter were designed specially to suit the continuously fast running henceforth required. A large roundhouse and an elevated coaling stage remain as relics of the earlier days, though shunting work and occasional branch duties were still being performed by steam at the time of my visit. So far as the through Interstate expresses are concerned however Junee is now a place where engine crews are changed. The one diesel locomotive works through from Sydney to Albury and is remanned at Goulburn, as well as Junee. The original township was five miles away from the spot chosen for the railway junction, but a new township quickly grew up around the station. The important branch to Hay, opened in 1881, was built to command the trade of the Riverina district.

The Riverina is the name of the district lying to the south-west of the main line, and in the more inland reaches of the Murray River, which forms the State boundary between New South Wales and Victoria. Business interests in Melbourne sought to tap the trade of the Riverina, and as early as 1864 a railway was built on the Victorian side to a railhead at Echuca on the Murray River. The Victorians were thus first with railway communications into the area by nearly twenty years; but it must be remembered that the general line of the Murray River is no further from Melbourne than Goulburn is from Sydney, and in striking out from their respective capital cities the men of New South Wales had much further to go. Eventually there grew a series of branch lines from the N.S.W.G.R. main south line running to stations in the Riverina district.

From Junee the construction of the line was pushed on rapidly, but a considerable obstacle presented itself in the broad valley of the Murrumbidgee River in the approach to Wagga Wagga. Traffic was operated into

Bomen from September 1878, but the work of completing the line to Albury was complicated, in that constructional work on the section beyond the river could not be proceeded with until some means of getting material across had been established. To obviate this difficulty a temporary line was built from Bomen to the river bank, and a light temporary structure erected across the river itself. The line also enabled passengers and goods to be taken into Wagga Wagga, instead of transferring to road vehicles at Bomen and entering the town over an old toll bridge. The permanent access consisted of a long viaduct over the mud-flats of the Murrumbidgee River, and a handsome iron arched bridge over the main channel. On our run with the 'Daylight Express' the 22 miles from Junee to Wagga Wagga were covered in $26\frac{1}{2}$ minutes, and after a brief stop of only one-and-a-half minutes we set out on our non-stop run of 78 miles to Albury, the terminal point of the New South Wales Government Railways on this southern route. This final stretch is single-tracked, though the various passing places are laid out so that an express train can negotiate them at full speed.

This last stage of the long run through New South Wales provided the fastest sustained running of the whole journey. The gradients are relatively easy, the line straight, and the stations few and far between. There are a few quite isolated hills, but the country is fairly flat in nearly every direction. The sheep population must be enormous! A stretch of $63\frac{1}{2}$ miles from Kapooka to Table Top was covered in 61 minutes, and by then with hilly country appearing to the right of the line we were nearing the border, and the train was slowing down for the approach to Albury. The railway originally came to this important border town in 1881, and its arrival was signalised by the construction of one of the finest provincial stations in the colony. It is built in red and white bricks dressed with cement, and surmounted by a splendid clock tower. The main passenger platform, which was originally 400 ft. in length, was subsequently extended to no less than 1500 ft. to accommodate both main line trains involved in the change of gauge from the standard gauge of New South Wales to the 5 ft. 3 in. of Victoria. But having reached Albury, at 4.35 p.m., now in sight of the Murray River it is time to bring this chapter to a close.

CHAPTER NINE

Murray River to Melbourne

The railway came into Albury from the north in 1881, but eight years earlier concerted drive and planning in the much smaller and younger colony had resulted in the establishment of a Victoria railhead at Wodonga, on the opposite bank of the Murray River. For another two years the dissimilar and rival gauges faced each other. Connection there must inevitably be, but who should build the bridge over the river, and which of the two terminals should be the point of interchange? The outcome is briefly but succinctly described in Manning Clark's book: *A Short History of Australia:*

On the morning of 14 June 1883, a huge crowd gathered in Albury to witness the connexion between the railways of New South Wales and Victoria. The streets were gaily decorated with bunting: schoolchildren lined the streets to welcome the premiers of both colonies. That night a distinguished assembly sat down to a banquet at which the Governor of New South Wales congratulated those present on the auspicious union of the two colonies by the iron rail. These Australian colonies, he went on, were peopled by the same race, spoke the same language, possessed the same traditions and aspirations. The iron link they had forged that day should be the emblem of union. He hoped this would be the dawn of a fresh era of happiness and prosperity. His colleague the Governor of Victoria, expressed his confidence that the inevitable result of the rail union would be the union of the colonies themselves.

Yet union though that new link certainly was, it was also a confrontation. Nearly forty years after the ever-memorable 'Battle of the Gauges' in England, Australia made her first 'break of gauge' station an accomplished fact. That lengthy single platform face that lay behind the splendid outer façade of Albury station had eventually to be nearly quadrupled in

110

length, and there for nearly eighty years through passengers had to change trains. Our forebears were tolerant in their stoic acceptance of inconveniences in travel. One looks back to those grisly early-morning changes from train to boat on the Irish Mail service at Holyhead; those fantastic early-morning scrambles at the international station at Basle, after a night jogging half across Europe in a non-corridor six-wheeler! At Albury, on journeys between Sydney and Melbourne things were not quite so bad. On the south bound run one slept through New South Wales, and breakfasted after changing to the Victorian train; going north the transfer was before midnight. All the same it was no joke to change, taking all one's belongings from one end to the other of that long platform.

In our case, when travelling from Sydney to Melbourne, the only evidence of change was a change of locomotive, from the maroon of the New South Wales to the dark blue and gold of Victoria, and moreover, for the first time in my Australian travels, a named engine: *Sir Charles Gavan Duffy*. The name of an individual on the flanks of a diesel-electric locomotive is perhaps of even less significance than *Sir Gilbert Claughton* or *Sir Charles Cust* on the splashers of a London and North Western 4-6-0, or *Sir Watkin Wynn* or *Sir William Henry* on a Swindon 'Bulldog'. But at Albury the name of the diesel that took over haulage of the 'Intercapital Daylight' was highly significant so far as our own odyssey in Australia was concerned. We were entering upon the Victorian railway system at one of its extremities, and by the fact of our doing so on standard-gauge track we were in contact immediately with one of the very latest phases in Victorian railway development. The name Sir Charles Gavan Duffy on our locomotive however provides the clue for a different line of approach, for that gentleman, in his high office of President of the Board of Land and Works in the Victorian Government of 1858, was 'in' at the very dawn of railway enterprise in the colony.

On that stormy and lowering evening in late August, with darkness coming on earlier than usual, our fast non-stop run to Melbourne was likely to be a technical study of train operation rather than a chance to see something of the Victorian countryside, so in opening out a picture of the railways of Victoria as a whole in their most interesting origins we can go back to 29 March 1858 when Mr. Charles Gavan Duffy, as he then was, opened tenders for the construction for many railways in the colony. The Government had invited tenders for individual sections of a proposed line from Melbourne to the Murray River—not at Wodonga but at Echuca—and from Geelong to Ballarat. There was also an invitation to tender for the entire proposition, a route mileage of 207 in all. The opening of the tenders was made a semi-public ceremony, with the Governor, Sir Henry Barkly, the Executive Council, contractors, and press representatives all present. As briefly mentioned in the introductory chapter to this book, the Victorian Government Railways ran their first train in January 1859; but prior to that numerous private ventures had been proposed, and all except one had failed for lack of support, and very quickly the Government had stepped in. During the year 1855 extensive surveys for proposed Government railways were made, and in March 1856 the Victorian Railways Department was created by the then Legislative Council.

The planning of railways in the colony of Victoria took a decidedly different form from that in both New South Wales and Queensland. In the former, while Sydney was of course the main focal point a completely separate network originated from Newcastle, while in Queensland the lines originating from Brisbane, Rockhampton, and Townsville were unconnected until very many years later. In Victoria everything centred upon Melbourne, and the Government surveys provided for lines to connect with the gold-mining areas of Ballarat, and the rich farming districts of the Riverina, along the course of the Murray River. At the time the tenders for construction of the lines were invited in 1858 there did not seem to be any plan for direct connection with the railway system of New South Wales, and the trunk lines for which the tenders were opened in such ceremony by Mr. Gavan-Duffy are shown on the accompanying map. Ballarat was to be reached via Geelong, and the north line was to run via Castlemaine and Bendigo to its terminus on the Murray River at Echuca. Authorisation for the lines concerned had been made by Acts of Parliament dated 24 November 1857. In the event contracts were awarded for all except the section from Bendigo to Echuca. This came later; but a most important development so far as through connection with Sydney was concerned took place in 1859, when a private company, the Melbourne and Essendon Railway, was authorised to build a line to a point $4\frac{3}{4}$ miles out in the north-western suburbs of the city. The line had full Government blessing, and the story goes that when Sir Henry Barkly cut the first sod he did it so efficiently that the nearby labourers jocularly offered him a job on the line!

PLATE 15. Footplate work, large and small

(a) The author (right) with C. A. Cardew, on the New South Wales 'C38' Pacific No. 3827 at Gosford

(b) The driver (right) and fireman of 'Puffing Billy'

PLATE 16. New South Wales: Express for Sydney leaving Newcastle, with 'C38' class engine No. 3817

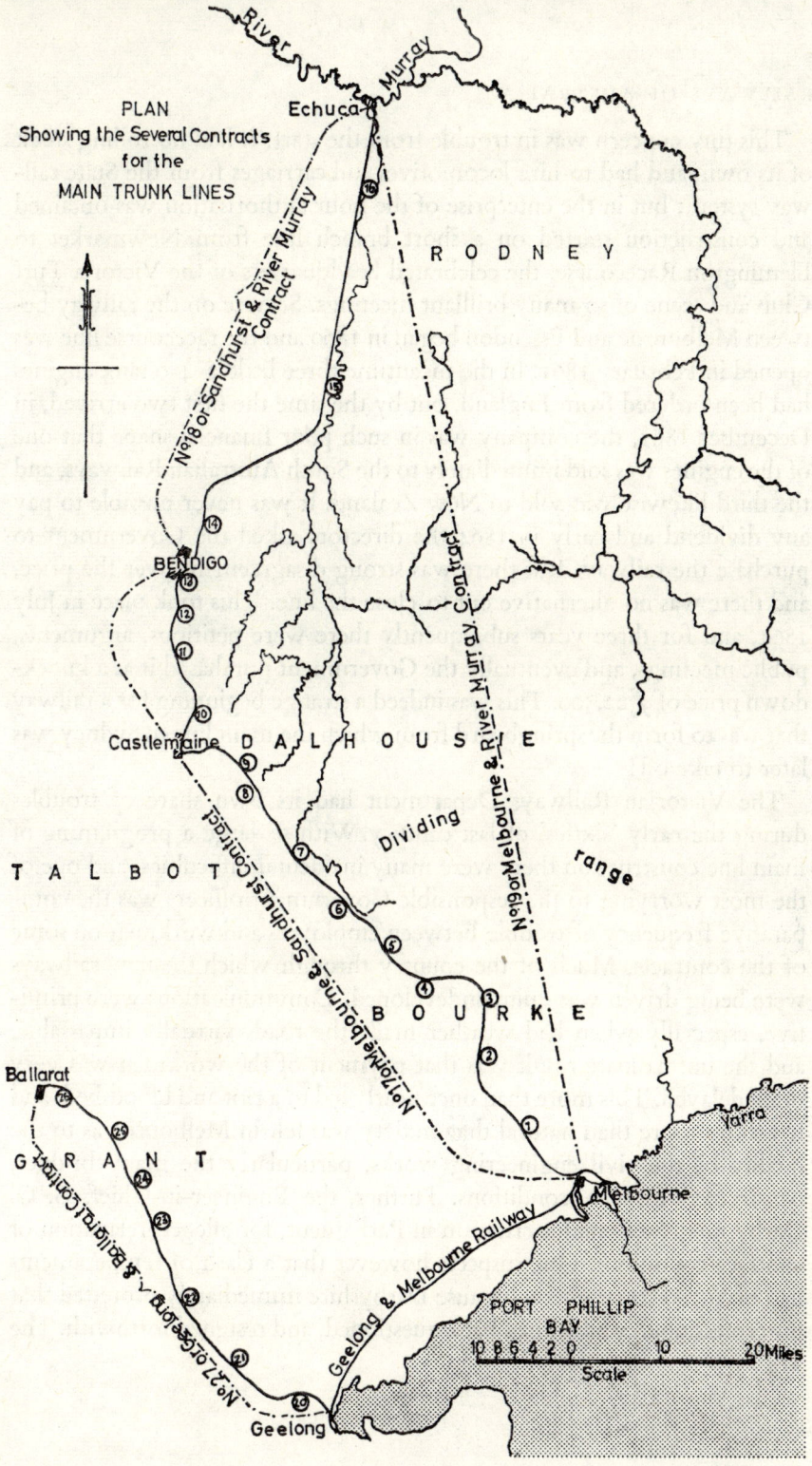

PLAN
Showing the Several Contracts
for the
MAIN TRUNK LINES

R O D N E Y

River Murray

Echuca

No.18 or Sandhurst & River Murray Contract

16

15

14
BENDIGO
13
12
11
10

Castlemaine   D A L H O U S E

9
8
7
6
5
4
3
2
1

No.19 or Melbourne & River Murray Contract

Dividing range

T A L B O T

B O U R K E

No.17 or Melbourne & Sandhurst Contract

Ballarat
26
25
24
23
22

G R A N T

No.27 or Geelong & Ballarat Contract

21

Geelong & Melbourne Railway

Yarra

Melbourne

20
Geelong

PORT   PHILLIP
BAY

10 8 6 4 2 0   10   20 Miles
Scale

Victoria: plan of the main trunk lines proposed in 1858

H

This tiny concern was in trouble from the start. It had no rolling stock of its own, and had to hire locomotives and carriages from the State railway system; but in the enterprise of the hour authorisation was obtained and construction started on a short branch line from Newmarket to Flemington Racecourse, the celebrated headquarters of the Victoria Turf Club and scene of so many brilliant meetings. Service on the railway between Melbourne and Essendon began in 1860 and the racecourse line was opened in February 1861. In the meantime three little 2–4–0 tank engines had been ordered from England, but by the time the first two arrived, in December 1861, the company was in such poor financial shape that one of the engines was sold immediately to the South Australian Railways, and the third likewise was sold to New Zealand. It was never possible to pay any dividend and early in 1864 the directors asked the Government to purchase the railway. But there was strong disagreement over the price, and there was no alternative but to close the line. This took place in July 1864, and for three years subsequently there were petitions, arguments, public meetings, and eventually the Government purchased it at a knockdown price of £22,500. This was indeed a strange beginning for a railway that was to form the springboard from which the main line to Sydney was later to take off!

The Victorian Railways Department had its own share of troubles during the early 'sixties' of last century. With so large a programme of main line construction there were many incidental difficulties, and one of the most worrying to the responsible Government officers was the comparative frequency of trouble between employers and workmen on some of the contracts. Much of the country through which the new railways were being driven was quite undeveloped. Communications were primitive, especially when bad weather made the roads virtually impassable, and the unfortunate result was that payment of the workmen was very often delayed. This more than once nearly led to a riot and bloodshed, and it was no more than natural that anxiety was felt in Melbourne as to the quality of the civil engineering works, particularly the many bridges, constructed in such conditions. Further, the Engineer-in-Chief, G. C. Darbyshire, came under criticism in Parliament, for alleged relaxation of contract conditions. One suspects however that a clash of temperaments had occurred somewhere, because Darbyshire immediately protested that his professional conduct had been questioned, and resigned forthwith. The new Engineer-in-Chief, Thomas Higginbotham, promptly made a thorough examination of all the works in question, and reported that everything was sound and satisfactory. How often, all over the world, is railway history repeated! One recalls inevitably the sad case of C. B. Vignoles in the construction of the Manchester, Sheffield and Lincolnshire Railway.

Whatever may have been the real causes for the agitation against Darbyshire, the Victorian Railways had certainly secured in his place a very energetic and efficient officer in Higginbotham, under whose direction the main lines to the State boundaries with both New South Wales and South Australia were planned and largely completed. He was often working under great difficulties. The Government was anxious to extend the railway system, but funds were low, and many were the directives that things must be done 'on the cheap'. Light rails, shallow road beds, and poor station accommodation were the order of the day, and it was in these prevailing conditions that in January 1869 the Commissioner of Railways directed Higginbotham to arrange for a survey of what was termed the Upper Murray, or north-eastern line. It was further stated that such a railway should be capable of carrying traffic at a maximum speed of 15 m.p.h. Essendon was to be the starting point of the proposed new line, and with such energy did Higginbotham deal with this assignment that contracts were let for the construction of the entire north-eastern line in 1870—a total of no less than 182 miles from Essendon to Wodonga. Fortunately this new trunk line was carried through relatively easy country, and the first section from Essendon to Longwood, 80 miles, was opened in 1872 and the remaining 102 miles to the riverside settlement of Wodonga in 1873. In such a way did one of the fastest and most important main lines in Australia originate.

The gradient profile of today shows clearly how Higginbotham achieved cheapness in the original construction. North of Longwood, in relatively easy and level country there are long stretches of comparatively uniform gradient; but in climbing over the coastal range to the summit point at the present Heathcote Junction there is scarcely a quarter of a mile at the same inclination over many miles of line. On the descent on the northern side of this summit point there are 97 changes of gradient in less than 17 miles. Whatever he was compelled to do in the matter of gradients, however, the terrain enabled Higginbotham to lay out a splendidly straight and direct route. For the most part it runs under the north-western slopes of the Australian Alps—a range that extends from Canberra to the Dandenongs, overlooking Port Phillip Bay and the city of Melbourne. Before darkness closed in on the wet and stormy evening of our journey I could see we were running along a level, broad valley something like the wider straths of the Scottish Highlands. This has indeed been a lengthy introduction to the north-eastern main line of the Victorian Railways, and when I climbed aboard the *Sir Charles Gavan-Duffy* in Albury station it was certainly a prelude to riding the highroad of the latest development in the Victorian Railways saga, the standard-gauge line into Melbourne.

It was in 1937 that the splendid new 'Spirit of Progress' train was put on, running non-stop between Melbourne and the break of gauge platform at Albury. The four handsome Pacific engines of the 'S' class, built in 1928, were streamlined for the job and finished in a new dark blue and gold livery to match the air-conditioned coaching stock. The journey of $190\frac{1}{2}$ miles between Spencer Street station, Melbourne and Albury was made in 3 hr. 50 min., an average speed of 52 m.p.h. The diesels took over in 1954, running to the same schedule. By that time however the great new project of building the standard-gauge line was passing beyond the stage of the drawing boards. The advantages to be derived from elimination of the break of gauge in traffic between the two neighbouring states had become a matter of national policy. In any case the increased efficiency in freight handling was immeasurably more than the ending of personal inconvenience to through passengers, in changing from one train to another at Albury. And so the new standard-gauge line was authorised, running beside Higginbotham's historic 5 ft. 3 in. gauge line for practically all its distance, and magnificently built so as to permit of continuous running at 70 m.p.h.

At Albury the very long platform is laid with standard-gauge track only, and the broad-gauge track coming in from the south leads into a long bay road that extends for 360 yards on the western platform face to a dead end just short of the original block of station buildings. Broad- and standard-gauge lines then run alongside each other to the crossing of the Murray River; both are arranged for both direction running. The working of the southbound 'Intercapital Daylight Express' was typical of present-day operation. The accompanying sketch plan shows the arrangement at the south end. Running in from the north the New South Wales engine

116

PLATE 17. New South Wales electric trains

(a) One of the new all-double-deck suburban trains, conveying 2250 passengers in an eight-car train

(b) A '46' class main line locomotive on arrival at Lithgow from Sydney with the 'Central West Express'

PLATE 18. Broadmeadow Running Sheds, near Newcastle (N.S.W.), showing the twin roundhouses

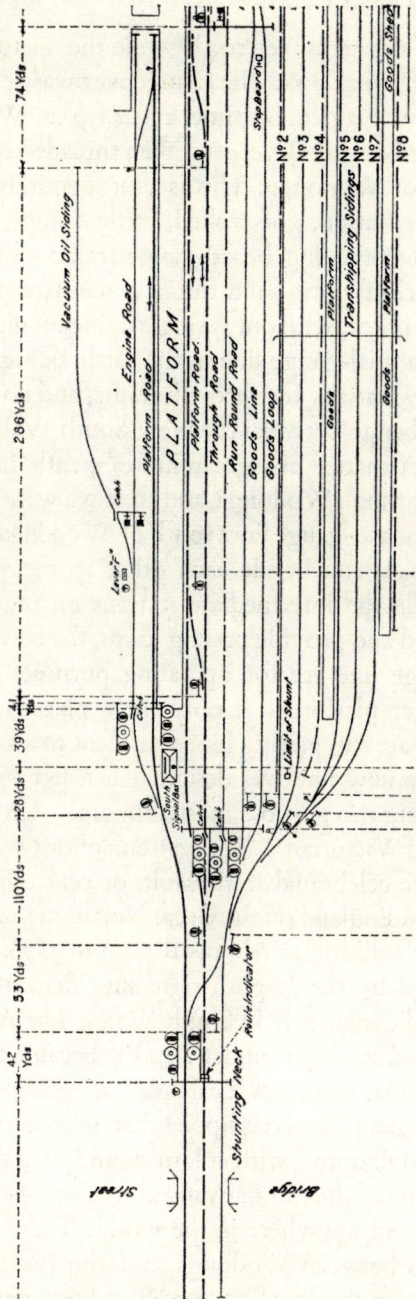

Albury: layout at south end of station

stopped just short of the crossover road, while the Victorian engine was waiting by the South Signal Box. The changeover was very quickly made and we were under way again, on time, at 4.48 p.m. We ran very cautiously out, across the Murray River, and then threaded our way through the fairly busy area of Wodonga. This is almost entirely a broad-gauge layout. The passenger station, goods shed, cattle sidings, and locomotive depot all deal with terminating broad-gauge traffic of which there is a good deal—particularly freight—and the new standard-gauge line passes outside the central complex, with only a single siding for diesel locomotives, and a connection to a dual-gauge line in the cattle sidings. The standard-gauge line was built essentially for through traffic, and it is across the river at Albury that interchange between the New South Wales and Victorian systems takes place. A matter of eight minutes' gentle running from the Albury start saw us through Wodonga, and then we were away in earnest.

The broad- and standard-gauge lines south of Wodonga are both single-tracked. The two roads run beside each other to the very outskirts of Melbourne, but while the intermediate stations on the original broad-gauge line are retained and provide passing loops, the corresponding loops on the standard-gauge line are for operating purposes only. There are intermediate passenger platforms at only three places on the standard-gauge line, and there are not passing loops adjacent to all the broad-gauge station locations. The new line was designed as a fast route for through traffic, and it is fulfilling this purpose most admirably. On the broad gauge the standard form of Victorian Railways semaphore signals are largely used. These are of the celebrated somersault, or centre-balanced, type of arm, that originated in England on the Great Northern Railway, following the disastrous double collision at Abbots Ripton in 1876. The design was adopted as a standard by the English signalling firm of McKenzie and Holland, and installed extensively in South Wales. The Australian branch of the firm introduced it 'down under', and it became standard in Victoria, Western Australia, and New Zealand.

The new standard-gauge line is equipped throughout from Wodonga to Dynon yards, West Melbourne, with colour light signals of the searchlight type, controlled by one of the most advanced systems of electronic remote interlocking to be found anywhere in the world. There is not one signal box in the 190 miles between Wodonga and the junction complex at Dynon. The working on this line between West Footscray and Wodonga is supervised and completely controlled from a small panel in one of the rooms in the railway headquarter offices in Spencer Street, Melbourne. There, the traffic controller can see from indication lights on the illuminated track diagram the exact whereabouts of every train on that 190 miles of single-tracked railway; from his experience he can judge the most advantageous positions for trains to be 'crossed', so that such crossings at one or another of the passing loops are made with the minimum delay to either of the trains concerned. The loop tracks on the new standard-gauge line are very long, mostly about 3000 ft., and where there is a close 'meet' it is often a matter of pride to both controller and train crews so to regulate matters that both get through without either train having to come to a dead stand. This, of course, is of considerable advantage if one of the opposing trains is a heavy freight.

We were soon bowling along in splendid style, with speed varying between 60 and 70 m.p.h. The gradients fluctuated, because there is little in the way of earthworks, the track following the lie of the land. But the line is now in magnificent shape, heavily ballasted and well aligned, and our diesel rode luxuriously. We passed a northbound freight train waiting in Chiltern loop, and on long stretches of straight track continued at a steady 70 m.p.h. Coming into distant sight of Alumatta loop signals—it was nearly dark now at 5.30 p.m.—we could see they were 'on'. My friends in the cab thought there would be a freight entering the loop, and so it turned out; but by easing down a little, and speed eventually reduced to a little under 40 m.p.h., it gave time for the freight to stow itself completely in the loop. The signals cleared for us, and with full power reapplied we accelerated so rapidly that our speed was over 50 m.p.h. when we took the points at the leaving end. It was a first-rate piece of modern railway operation. In the dusk it was not possible to judge if the freight had actually come to a stand, but the delay to her running cannot have been great. So far as we were concerned it was trifling.

From the cab it was not yet too dark outside to prevent my companions pointing out to me the skyline of the hill ranges where the Ned Kelly gang were finally rounded up. It was on this very stretch of line that they tore up a length of track to wreck the train on which the apprehending police were expected to be travelling; but a school-teacher managed to slip undetected from the hotel at Glenrowan which had been occupied by the gang, and the train was warned in time. The violent end of the gang and

119

the capture of Ned Kelly himself followed soon afterwards. The approach to Glenrowan provided one of the first noticeable pieces of adverse grading since leaving Wodonga, as the line ascends for $2\frac{1}{2}$ miles at 1 in 75. Had it not been for the check at Wangaratta however, and the fact that we had not recovered to more than 62 m.p.h. when we struck the incline, I should not imagine it would have made itself seriously felt. As it was it brought us down to 45 m.p.h. at Glenrowan station. After this, on long straight stretches of line where one could see the colour light signals at least three miles ahead, we ran at a steady 70 m.p.h. Another northbound freight we passed at Benalla loop, and by Violet Town, 85 miles from Albury, we were inside 'even time' from the start, 84 minutes exactly.

By this time the stormy day had developed into an evening of continuous deluge! It was extraordinary from the cab of the diesel to see the extent to which the headlight penetrated through the positive curtain of rain, and it certainly made no difference to the splendid speed of our running. 'Control' was not able to avoid bringing us to a stand for two minutes at Longwood loop. There was no 'opposing' train to cross, but presumably a preceding one was clearing the single-line section ahead. We had covered the 106 miles from Albury to Longwood in 105 minutes, start to stop, and once we got the road 70 m.p.h. running was quickly resumed. Up to this time I had not noted any traffic on the adjacent broad-gauge line, but when we drew nearer to Melbourne the night freights were following each other thick and fast. By Seymour, 129 miles in $128\frac{1}{4}$ minutes, we were back inside 'even time' despite the stop at Longwood. This line certainly provides the fastest long-sustained high-speed running in Australia; but from Seymour onwards the line begins to climb gradually to the range of hills encircling the city of Melbourne; and from an altitude of 464 ft. at Seymour the railway climbs to a summit point of 1145 ft. at Heathcote Junction, in a matter of 28 miles. This is the section where the changes in gradient are so frequent; in the aggregate however the rise did not trouble this competent and efficiently driven locomotive, and that 28 miles of rising track was covered in $28\frac{1}{2}$ minutes.

On the high ground on this stormy night it seemed for a little as though fog was coming on to add to the general unpleasantness outside the cab; but it was nothing more than some low cloud, and when we began the descent towards Melbourne the visibility became clear enough once again, despite the continuing downpour. Nearing Donnybrook, 170 miles passed in 169¼ minutes, we got a 'yellow'; Inspector Wallin remarked: 'That will be the "Spirit" in the loop.' We slowed to 40 m.p.h. before the signals cleared, and sure enough in Donnybrook loop the Sydney-bound 'Spirit of Progress' express was waiting for us to pass. Our speed was now being eased down for the outer approaches to Melbourne. We were running well on time, and so, at Broadmeadows, came the point where the new standard-gauge line parts company with the original North Eastern main line of the Victorian Railways. The 179½ miles of 'running alongside' had been covered in a few seconds over the even three hours, despite the several intervening checks, and one dead stop for two minutes. It had been a truly splendid exposition of modern single-line working under remote electronic control, and now we began the final approach to the complicated suburban area of Melbourne.

The original exit from Melbourne, as related earlier in this chapter, was made over the ill-starred Essendon railway. Broadmeadows, which we have just passed, is only 5½ miles from Essendon, and 10½ miles from Spencer Street. But the standard-gauge line is carried in something of a detour to the west, in order to make ready interchange with the lines from Bendigo, Ballarat and the west, and from Geelong, and traversing a section completely devoid of any stations in the 8¾ miles between Broadmeadows and Albion, where the line from Bendigo is joined. I have used the word 'joined', but there is no physical connection. The single-tracked standard-gauge line merely swings alongside. The increasing complexity of the lines in this approach to the heart of Melbourne is however not a thing to be appreciated in the gloom of a pouring wet night, and at this stage I will mention only one more incident of this deeply interesting journey. From Footscray our driver was 'crawling', slightly ahead of time, but knowing that any hurry would be fruitless and result in a dead stop for signals. The 'Southern Aurora' leaves Spencer Street for Sydney at 8 p.m. and the standard-gauge line is single-tracked from the terminus out to South Kensington. So through the long double-line loop from West Footscray Junction, over some dual-gauge track we felt our way until, round the curve beneath the underpass to the St. Albans lines, we saw her coming. The signals ahead quickly cleared, and the road was ours to enter Spencer Street station.

Thus, in the course of our journey through from Sydney we had passed the 'Southern Aurora' and the 'Spirit of Progress' twice. Early that same morning we had passed the trains that had left Melbourne the previous evening: the 'Spirit' at Liverpool, and the 'Aurora' at Macquarie Fields, at 8.20 and 8.26 a.m. respectively; and then in the evening our crossing times had been 7.38 for the 'Spirit of Progress', and 8.9 p.m. for the 'Aurora'. Such was yet another interesting sideline on long-distance travel in Australia. It only remains to add in concluding this chapter that we ran gently in to Spencer Street terminus to arrive on the very stroke of our booked time, 8.20 p.m.

CHAPTER TEN

The railways of Melbourne

The geographical situation of the city of Melbourne, lying just inland at the head of the fine, sheltered anchorage of Port Phillip Bay, on the tidal reaches of the Yarra River, is one of the world's natural sites for a great commercial, industrial, and cultural centre. From the earliest days of colonisation the small inner gulf of Hobson's Bay, with the promontory of Williamstown forming an additional shelter to the mouth of the Yarra River, formed a berthing area for ocean-going ships. It was indeed from Williamstown that the first railway in all Australia was built. But before delving into details of railway history it is advisable to take a broad look at the intricate group of lines that serves the city of Melbourne today. Otherwise one could well become lost in a welter of detail, and become confused and frustrated in trying to follow out the various routes. I hope the accompanying map will help to a general appreciation of the railway layout of the area.

The city centre, and all the more important centres of business and cultural activity, lie north and west of the winding course of the Yarra River, and it is the north bank of the river that has determined and con-strained the focal points of railway operation. But a glance at the map will show that the twin city stations of Flinders Street and Spencer Street have an association, and a strategic position quite unlike that of any of the major city stations elsewhere in Australia, in that both have a large number of through platforms, and that both are within a relatively short distance of each other. Spencer Street has a number of terminal platforms, dealing with long-distance and inter-state traffic; but Flinders Street, claimed as one of the busiest stations the world over, consists almost entirely of through platforms. Five busy passenger lines converge on Spencer Street from the west, and the through lines curving along the

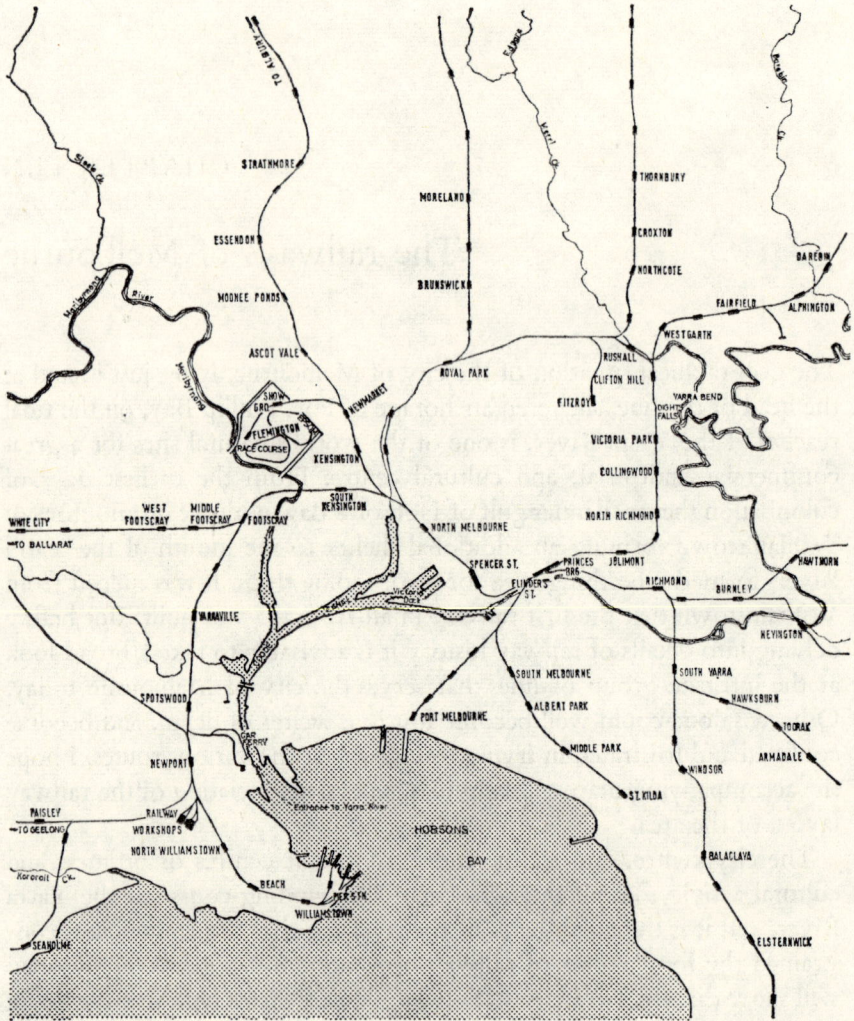

The Melbourne suburban area

northern bank of the Yarra are joined just before reaching Flinders Street by a line crossing from the south bank, which is itself a confluence of two suburban lines. From the east side of the Flinders Street station the great multiplicity of tracks leads a wide-spreading network of busy suburban lines. Assuming that our first concern shall be with commuters, Flinders Street station provides a natural starting point.

124

PLATE 19. Steam suburban trains

(a) Sydney outer suburban line, to Richmond; one of the veteran 4–6–4 tanks near Riverstone in 1968

(b) Another N.S.W. 4–6–4 tank, leaving Newcastle on suburban train to Toronto in 1965

(c) South Australian Railways: a Class 'F' 4–6–2 tank engine on down Semaphore local at North Adelaide

PLATE 20. On the Main South Line (N.S.W.)

(*a*) Picton station in the 1870s. The engine is 2–4–0 No. 10

(*b*) An early view of Goulburn station

Unlike so many great city stations—thinking, for example, of our own London Bridge, Waterloo, Paddington, and Victoria, where on arrival one has only completed part of the daily journey to business—Flinders Street is within a few minutes' walk of the very heart of Melbourne. The only comparable instances in London are Cannon Street and Liverpool Street. The railway visitor or sightseer who does not know the ropes would do well to keep clear of Flinders Street in the peak hours. It is a positive education to stand on the steps of St. Paul's Cathedral, diagonally across the road intersection opposite to the main exit from Flinders Street, and just watch! The people emerge in a solid mass of humanity, all in a bustling hurry, and should a stranger become involved in that irresistible stream, heaven knows to what part of the city he might be swept. This is written in no disparagement of the citizens of Melbourne; they use their railways, they know their city, and act accordingly.

Before proceeding too far however a word about the name of the station may be of interest. The street itself runs parallel to the railway, and forms the southernmost of the rectangular block of streets forming the city centre; but who, or what, was Flinders? Englishmen as a race are notoriously ignorant when it comes to history, and even more so when it is that of other countries, even those within the Commonwealth. I have even come across the man who thought Captain Cook was the founder of the present-day firm of travel agents! As to Flinders, I fancy that most people would confess that the name meant nothing more than little Polly of the nursery rhyme. Being a stamp collector I was familiar with the portrait of Matthew Flinders, and looked him up. He was the naval commander who virtually completed the discovery of Australia. There had been settlements, at Sydney Cove, on Port Phillip Bay, and in Western Australia which was first known as New Holland; but until Flinders sailed in a complete circumnavigation of the continent in a tall ship appropriately named *Investigator*, it was not known that these isolated settlements formed part of the same great land-mass. That circumnavigation took Flinders nearly two years to accomplish, in 1802-3. It was he also who suggested the name of Australia for this newly-determined continent.

My own exploration of the intricacies of Flinders Street station began at a quiet period, in early afternoon, and in very favourable circumstances. All the morning I had been in the neighbourhood of Spencer

Street, with a senior officer of the Signal Engineering Department. We lunched near the station, and then climbed into the driver's cab of an electric train bound for Flinders Street. I had already seen from the road-way beneath some very large gantries of semaphore signals spanning the tracks, and now I saw them again, to full advantage from the drivers' viewpoint. I am aware that today the semaphore signal, and particularly the lower-quadrant variety, is considered completely out of date, as obsolete, and yet in its way as picturesque as the steam locomotive; but the mere statistics of operation at Flinders Street are in themselves a resounding example of the way in which these tools of an earlier era have been maintained, and the skill with which they are being used. At three out of the four signal boxes concerned with the working of this vast traffic the interlocking frames are entirely mechanical. I had the privilege of meeting the signalmen who were on duty at these boxes, and it *was* a privilege; for it did not need more than a few minutes in each of those boxes for one to appreciate they were manned by men to whom railways and railway working were the very breath of life: dedicated railwaymen every one of them.

The signal gantries on the western approach to Flinders Street are some of the most picturesque I have seen outside the confines of the old North Eastern Railway, in England. There are no route indicators, and instead an arm for every possible route. And when I add that the line making its way round from Spencer Street is quadruple-tracked; that the line from Port Melbourne and St. Kilda that crosses the Yarra River is also quadruple, and that between them they lead into fourteen platforms it can well be imagined that there are quite a lot of semaphores in this area! The gantry carrying the home signals from the Spencer Street direction has nine posts for main signals and two for subsidiaries, while for outgoing trains there are fifteen posts, arranged variously on four gantries. All the main running signals are of the picturesque centre-balanced, or somersault type, and to add to the tremendous array the majority of the gantries spanning the tracks at the west end of the station platforms have a further series of arms relating to the opposite direction of running. To anyone interested in the history of signalling Flinders Street is a most fascinating period piece—but I hasten to emphasise once again, a plant that is coping punctually with an enormous traffic.

It is, of course, due for replacement; but on the Victorian Railways

126

there are priorities in everything, as indeed there are in all industrial concerns, large and small; and in recent years the priorities have been awarded to projects like the standard-gauge line from Melbourne to Albury, and more recently to the vast reconstruction of Melbourne Marshalling Yard, to which reference is made later in this chapter. It would have been another matter if the Flinders Street signalling was, through its age, leading to delays and difficulties in working. But it is not, and so despite its age it has had to carry on for a few years more. If the semaphore signals themselves are of much historical interest so equally are the interlocking frames. In the 'A', 'B', and 'C' boxes these are of the McKenzie and Holland 'cam and rocker' type, designed at Worcester, at a time when British signalling practice was circumscribed by a vast number of highly restrictive patents. Stevens and Sons, first in the field, naturally took the simplest course, with straight tappet locking. Saxby and Farmer followed with the 'rocker and grid' form of actuation, and McKenzie and Holland, faced with the prospect of designing something different or going out of business, produced the very celebrated cam and rocker type. It was a beautiful and ingenious, if complicated mechanism, and it was certainly significant of the attitude felt towards these alternatives in England that when the Stevens' patents expired both Saxby and Farmer, and McKenzie and Holland both adopted tappet locking, with their own form of drive. But in Australia the 'cam and rocker' mechanism of McKenzie and Holland remained to this day—ninety years after its first invention in England.

The station itself is a remarkable example of maximum utilisation of space, platforms area, and track capacity. The five island platforms are all nominated for definite suburban services, so that in the ordinary way regular travellers know from which platform not merely their usual train departs, but the entire service for their route will start, thus: Alamein and Box Hill, Sandringham, Essendon, Caulfield, Oakleigh, Mordialloc, and Williamstown, and so on. A visitor can only guess at the secret of success in working such a busy station, but the passengers seem to know their 'routes' as efficiently as the signalman, and entraining and detraining is slick, streamlined, and entirely devoid of confusion, even at the busiest times. But woe betide the stranger who gets in the way! Whereas on the western side of the station the platform roads converge into two quadruple-tracked routes, on the eastern side the layout spreads into an enormous nest of carriage sidings. At one point there are no fewer than sixty-six tracks abreast of each other. The aerial photograph facing page 176 conveys, perhaps more vividly than any amount of description, some impression of the railway complex just to the east of Flinders Street station.

What that aerial photograph cannot convey however is the ingenious alternation of running lines and sidings that has been devised in that amazing mass-demonstration of permanent way. Threading their way through the great areas of sidings are six pairs of running lines, in addition to the Clifton Hill lines which diverge immediately to the east of the station and do not pass through the siding area. The sidings are grouped, so that the very large quantities of rolling stock needed for the morning and evening peaks are berthed adjacent to the running lines on which they are used, and so in moving from sidings to the station platforms there is an absolute minimum of crossover movement, and no conflicting moves that could affect other services. Thus the Camberwell sidings are next to the Camberwell pair of running lines, and so on. The number of sidings interspersed between pairs of running lines is in proportion to the volume of traffic, and thus to the number of trains that require to be berthed. Taking a cross-section from the Burnley loop lines the sequence is, 5 sidings, Camberwell Lines; 10 sidings, Caulfield and Oakleigh Lines; 5 sidings, Sandringham Lines; 4 sidings, Special Lines; 4 sidings, Race Lines, and then 9 goods sidings.

Before the siding area, at Jolimont Junction the running lines converge to four pairs in the approach to Richmond station; but there again there are ten platform faces in the station, and immediately beyond the quadruple-tracked line to Camberwell diverges from the sextuple line leading to Caulfield and Sandringham. Through Richmond station, and on all the lines east of Flinders Street, each track is for the down or up direction as the case may be; but all the running lines through Flinders Street itself can be used in either direction, thus contributing very much to flexibility in operation. The enormous traffic worked into and out of Flinders Street is probably unique the world over in that the passenger accommodation is provided *entirely* in multiple-unit electric trains. For special passenger workings and freight passing through there are some locomotive-hauled trains; but the regular service is entirely worked with multiple-unit stock. The major suburban electrification around Melbourne had

PLATE 21. Tunnelling on the Main South Line

(a) Special train on the Bethungra Loop

(b) Bowral Tunnel, built 1866

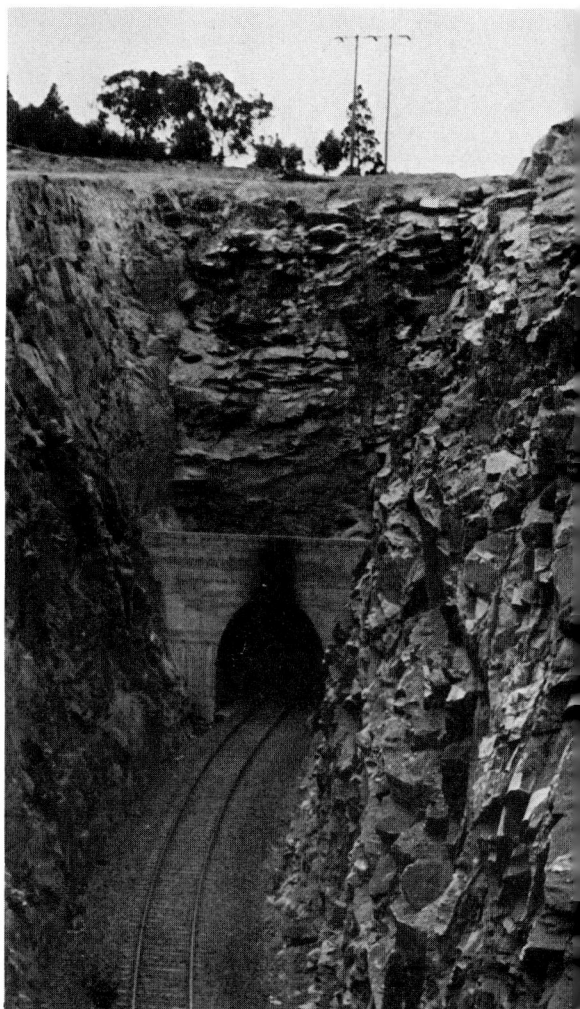

(c) Rock cutting entrance to Bethungra loop tunnel

been completed by 1930, though the rapid expansion of the population has required considerable extensions to the original electrification, and the conversion of some additional routes from steam traction.

The present traffic flowing in to the heart of Melbourne each day is strikingly demonstrated in the diagram reproduced herewith, which also shows that the distribution of passengers from the two principal stations is somewhat lopsided so far as the central area of the city itself is concerned.

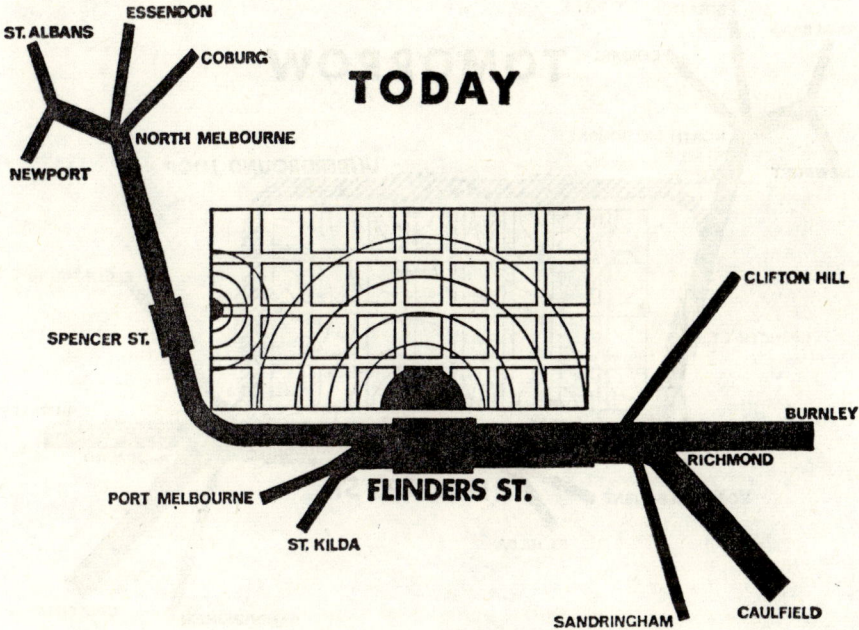

Traffic flow into Melbourne

The thickness of the flow lines indicate the volume of traffic on the various routes. Now however Parliament has authorised the building of an underground railway that will be quadruple-tracked, and which will encircle the central business area as shown in the second diagram reproduced. The provision of four additional stations in the central area will distribute the outflow of commuters more evenly, instead of disgorging the majority of them at Flinders Street. The quadruple-track system of the new underground loop will be constructed beneath existing streets and to keep within the width thus prescribed the underground tunnels

I

will be double-tiered—that is two at one level, as on most of the London Underground lines, and another two at a deeper level beneath them. Much preliminary work has already been done in sinking shafts and bores to examine the rock formations, and to ensure that no undue difficulties are encountered when the loop is built. Nevertheless tunnelling in any form can provide some surprises and shocks for the engineers. One would have thought, for example, that all the hazards of driving tube railways

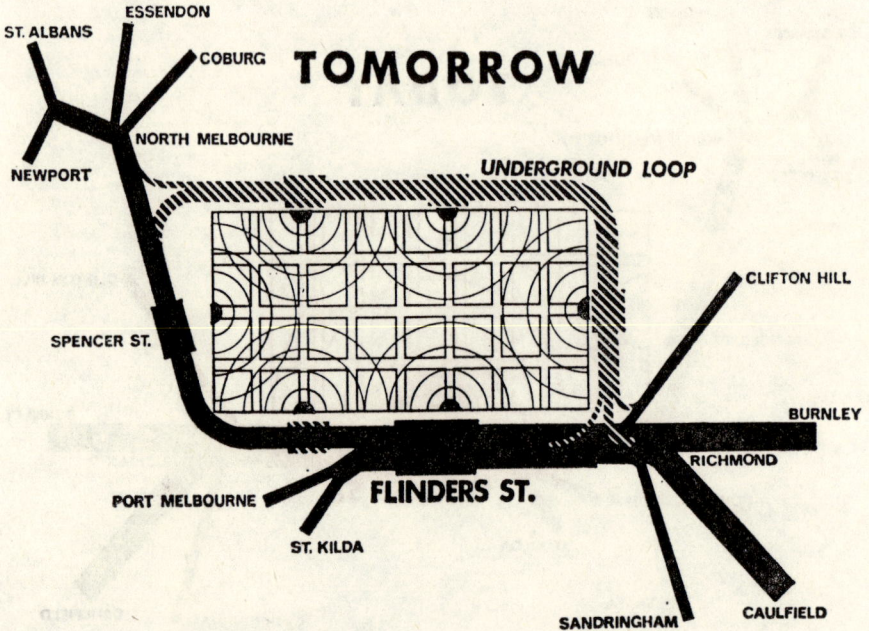

Traffic flow as planned with new underground loop

under Central London would have been discovered when the time came to drive the new Victoria Line which was completed in 1969; on the contrary, some quite unprecedented difficulties did arise. I have no doubt however that the work beneath the streets of Melbourne will be brought to a successful conclusion, come what may in the manner of unexpected troubles.

Moving now to Spencer Street, and the western approaches to the city, one meets a very different railway situation. The North and South Viaduct lines, as the quadruple-tracked section from Flinders Street is

130

known, spreads out into eight running lines at Viaduct Junction to traverse the through platforms at Spencer Street. Four of these lines with their associated platform faces, Nos. 11 to 14, deal with the ordinary suburban traffic; two are generally used for race traffic, and two are purely goods lines. But alongside this 'through' section and likewise forming a close counterpart of Sydney Central, is the large terminal station, having another nine platforms. Seven of these latter have only broad-gauge lines, but Nos. 1 and 2 are laid out with dual gauge to accommodate the through express passenger trains to Albury and New South Wales. The existence of the two gauges in the one station, and at two of the longest platforms, immediately brings to an Englishman thoughts of what Paddington and other large Great Western stations were like before that memorable May of 1892, when the *very* broad gauge of Brunel was finally abolished. As a signal engineer I have also had to cope with designs for point-operating equipment for certain South American lines where gauges of one metre and 1·6 metres were coincident. So it was with particular interest that I was taken to see some of the track-work at Spencer Street.

The great difference, and the associated difficulties, compared with situations I had already studied comes in the relatively small difference in these Australian gauges. It is only 6½ in., compared to nearly 2 ft. in South America, and 2 ft. 3½ in. on the old Great Western. The installing of point and crossing work at a place like Spencer Street is thus very much more restricted, and whereas true 'mixed-gauge' junctions abounded on the Great Western, in that both standard- and broad-gauge trains could be diverted, on the Victorian Railways the track layout has been so contrived that only one of the gauges is subjected to junction conditions at any one locality. In certain cases it has been possible to avoid using switches at all, as for example where the broad and standard gauges part company as in the diagrams Figs. 1 and 2, reproduced on page 132. Then there are instances where it is necessary to transfer the common rail from one side to the other, and the method of doing this, without the use of any switch tongues, is shown in Figs. 3 and 4. A complicated layout is shown in Fig. 5, where a transfer track is included within a turnout for the broad-gauge line. Nevertheless, one's admiration of the ingenuity in meeting problems arising out of the differing gauges is tempered with reflections upon how easily the differences could have been eliminated if

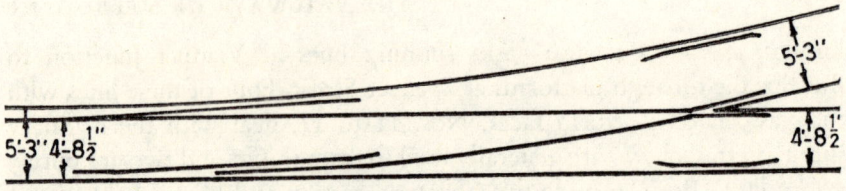

FIG.1 FIXED POINT TURNOUT TR4

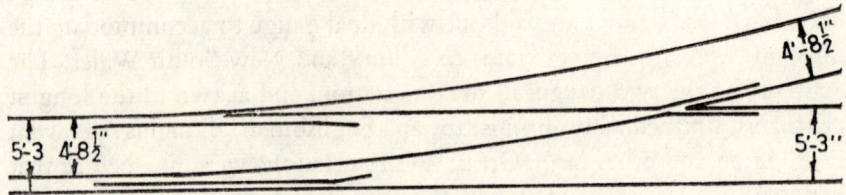

FIG.2 FIXED POINT TURNOUT TR1

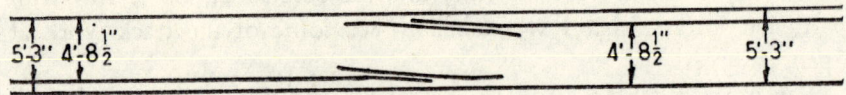

FIG.3 TRANSFER TR6

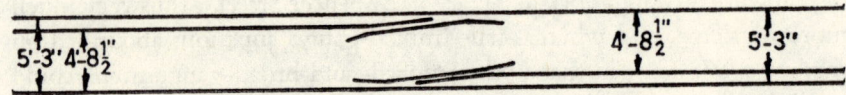

FIG.4 TRANSFER TR7

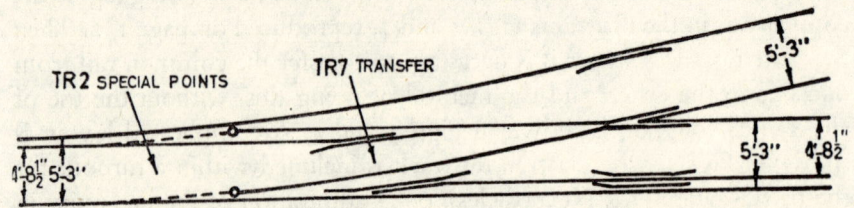

FIG.5 MOVEABLE SWITCH TURNOUT TR2

Diagrams showing arrangements for dual gauge point layouts

a little less individuality, and, shall I add, pigheadedness, had been evident in the now far-off pioneer days of Australian railways.

The outstanding new feature of the railway scene in Melbourne is of course the completely modernised marshalling yard. This is one of the most ingenious pieces of civil engineering planning I have ever seen. In the first phase of railway modernisation in the United Kingdom many new marshalling yards were constructed and most of these were at focus points of converging and diverging traffic such as Carlisle, Tyne Yard near Newcastle, Perth, and Millerhill (Edinburgh), where traffic from many origins comes together, and was sorted and re-marshalled for despatch to several divergent routes. At Melbourne the pattern of traffic is quite different. There is certainly convergence from many widespread origins, but the great bulk of such traffic is practically at journey's end. It is destined for road distribution within the city area, and only a relatively small proportion is routed to the docks for export. It is a case of sorting incoming traffic to bring similar loads into their appropriate sheds for cartage, and the huge goods station, adjacent to Spencer Street passenger station, is circumscribed by major city highways and the north bank of the Yarra River. A large yard already existed, but the sidings were not long enough to accommodate the freight trains of today; much cross-shunting was required, with consequent delay and congestion. Various physical conditions precluded a straightforward lengthening of the existing yard, and in any case full mechanisation was desired to increase the speed and efficiency of working and minimise damage to consignments.

British practice was studied closely and the experience with great yards like Carlisle duly noted; but when it was considered that full automation was desirable the physical conditions existing just to the west of Spencer Street imposed some very severe limitations. Serious thought was indeed given to the possibility of building an entirely new yard in the outer suburbs, where there was plenty of space; but all the available evidence pointed to the ultimate advantages of retaining the yard on its existing site, despite the difficulties likely to be experienced in the transition stage, and confined nature of the space available. To provide the automation required the yard would have to be constructed on the 'hump' principle, and the problem of securing the gradients necessary to provide the running of wagons under the action of gravity was accentuated

133

by the need for all the tracks in the automated part of the yard—where the gradients are critical—to cross the wide thoroughfare of Dudley Street, and that to secure the free flow of traffic the hump itself would have to be located either on, or near to, a 'flyover' crossing an intersecting track to the South Yard. This could not be moved because the limit of the South Yard itself was settled by the existence of Moonee Ponds Creek, immediately beyond.

In England, about a year before I actually visited Melbourne, I had been concerned with some of the preliminaries in connection with the supply of specialised equipment for this yard; but it was not until I had the privilege of walking over the site and seeing much of the heavy constructional work in progress that I fully appreciated the intricate nature of the civil engineering work involved to provide the gradients in the yard that were essential to a proper integration of gravity running of wagons with electronic control of their movements. The crest of the hump was located on the highest point of the 'flyover', and the first of the powerful wagon retarders is actually on the viaduct leading up to the 'flyover' crest. Even when a layout like this is planned on paper the difficulties of known physical conditions were quite exceptional in modern marshalling yard practice. But while the decision to construct the new yard on the site of the old one was unquestionably the correct one from the viewpoint of the final result and the benefits to be obtained therefrom, it was equally the most difficult when it came to carrying out the reconstruction work.

The heavy flow of freight traffic into and out of the city had to be kept moving, and moving with at least no appreciable diminution in efficiency. There would be no point in carrying out a vast reconstruction to provide improved service if during the process of reconstruction such dislocation, delay, and congestion prevailed as to cause traders to abandon the railway for other means of transport. On this account the most detailed attention was given to planning the stages in which the work of reconstruction would be carried out, to provide continued facilities for the handling of traffic when the civil engineering work was at its most intense. Commencing in 1966 the changeover work was planned to take place in no fewer than thirty-nine stages, with completion targeted for the end of the year 1970. It was considered that all concerned in the working of the yard should be kept fully informed as to what was going on at each stage, because a reconstruction on such a scale can be confusing to an onlooker to such a degree that those on whom reliance had to be placed for working in the interim period could well have felt that order could never emerge from such apparent chaos. Accordingly scale models were made, one depicting the yard as it would finally be, and another showing stage by stage how the reconstruction was progressing. These models were installed in a hut in the yard, and each successive stage was explained and depicted by the sequential alteration to the second model. Accordingly all concerned could appreciate the significance of each stage in the work, and in consequence the traffic had been operated with remarkable efficiency in the transition period.

Having 'walked' the yard, climbing the unfinished embankment leading to the flyover which will form the crest of the hump, and been fascinated by the models of the yard in its final and its transitional stages, I was taken finally to the West Tower, the great combined signal box and control centre from which operations in the entire area will be regulated. From its great height one looked out over the whole area, and I could see then the various geographical factors, such as the proximity of the Moonee Ponds Creek, that had been such a determining factor in the design of the yard. I saw also the second flyover, carrying the standard-gauge main line across the very middle of the entire marshalling yard complex. The working of the traffic will be controlled by a very large, and beautifully-designed panel instrument, in the latest electrical signalling style, with an operating console, and a large illuminated track diagram at the rear. The running signals are of the searchlight colour-light type, as now standard on all new power signalling installations on the Victorian Railways; but special signals are used, as in the United Kingdom, for indicating requirements to the drivers of locomotives propelling trains over the humps. These are of the so-called 'position light' type. Three white lights displayed horizontally means 'stop'; three white lights diagonally, is 'hump'; while three white lights vertically is the 'approach' signal. Taken all round the new Melbourne marshalling yard, of which the layout is shown diagrammatically in the accompanying sketch, is a magnificent piece of modern railway engineering in all its facets.

Flinders Street, Spencer Street, Melbourne Yard, are all features of the railway scene familiar enough to many regular travellers; but one little gem of modern Australian railroading will always remain overt from the

MELBOURNE YARD REARRANGEMENT

To Appleton Dock

East Coburg Lines

Moonee Ponds Creek

From West Footscray (connects to N.W., N., N.E. lines)

From Essendon (connects to N.E. lines)

To Dynon

WAGON SHOPS

SOUTH YARD

Entrance to Empty Returns Area

Entrance to Marshalling Yard via South Yard

Hump Engine Spur

OUTSIDE GOODS LINES

ARRIVAL SIDINGS

Coburg Goods Lines

Entrance to Arrival Sidings

GOODS LINES

To Canork shed & Eastern & Northern line loading

To Victoria Dock & Govt. cool stores

CEMENT SIDE

ROAD

Weigh Scale

loading.

FOOTSCRAY

To Victoria Dock

Entrance to 6&7 Sheds

No 7 SHED

No 6 SHED

WEST YARD

D BALLOON

C BALLOON

DEPARTURE TRACK

ST.

DUDLEY

No 5 SHED

Future Entrance

MELBOURNE GOODS DEPOT

Gantry crane

No 4 SHED

No 3 SHED

No 2 SHED

Rail Sale

CENTRE YARD

B BALLOON

A BALLOON

EAST YARD

No 1 SHED

FLINDERS ST. EXTN.

Entrance

Gantry crane

L.4 Entrance

Viaduct to Flinders St.

To Gippsland & south suburban lines

SPENCER STREET

Victorian Steam: An Australian Interstate Express, at the turn of the century, is headed by a class A 4-4-0 and an old class B 2-4-0

public gaze. And although it is located in the very heart of Melbourne it is not strictly a part of the railways of the city. I refer to that fascinating control panel in one of the ground floor rooms in the Spencer Street offices that regulates traffic working over the entire standard-gauge line between Dynon sidings and Wodonga on the Murray River. Many years ago when the art of applying the illuminated diagram to signalling control was first being developed a famous British railway engineer once said there were no technical difficulties in the way of controlling a signalling installation in York from a control office in London, 188 miles away. At that time the difficulties would have been financial, for there was then no way of exercising that long-range control other than by direct wire. But the technique of remote control has made immense strides since then, and by the use of electronic methods the entire standard-gauge line, from the point where it passes out of the inner suburban area of Melbourne, is controlled from that one panel.

In that basement room at Spencer Street I watched the running of the northbound 'Intercapital Daylight Express' from the indication lights on the panel. She was north of Wangaratta, and from clocking the lighting of successive lamps on the panel I could tell she was running at about 70 m.p.h. Other lights on that panel showed the whereabouts of freight trains. From one loop, where a freight train was halted, the driver rang up and asked the controller for information. The controller, from the beautifully displayed indication lights, had the whole working, from end to end of the standard-gauge line, verily at his fingertips, and could regulate movements to the best advantage, arranging 'meets' of opposing trains at loops where there would be a minimum of waiting time for either.

Such are a few of the railway operating 'sights' of Melbourne. So far I have written little about locomotives or rolling stock, nor of the interesting equipment that can change bogies of freight wagons to enable them to continue on a different gauged line. In operation however there can be few railway centres that can provide such a collection of superb examples of the different periods of signalling evolution as Melbourne, in the finely maintained mechanical plant at Flinders Street, the power signalling, and automated marshalling yard, and finally in the electronic centralised traffic control panel for the standard-gauge line.

CHAPTER ELEVEN

Victorian steam

Olivia my wife, like the understanding partner she has always been in all my work, has visited the scene of many of my adventures in signal boxes in the United Kingdom, and I shall always recall her becoming most excitedly concerned one night in a *contretemps* concerning 'The Leeds Fush' when we were together in a large power box in North-Eastern England. In Melbourne it was with difficulty that we got her away from the Dynon–Wodonga control panel; but outside the offices a car was waiting to take us to North Williamstown, and there the astonishing variety of the Melbourne railway scene was continued in full measure. For there is to be found the Railway Museum of Victoria, with a magnificent collection of representative steam locomotives, and in colours ranging from the bright greens of the nineteenth century, and the Tuscan red of the Tait era, to the unlined black of the final steam days, enlivened only by the scarlet of the running plate valances and the deflector shields on the 'R' class 4-6-4s. As with many railway museums however, some of the most interesting and important designs of the past had all disappeared before the Museum was set up. In Victoria, as on many of the pre-grouping railways in the United Kingdom, express passenger locomotives tend to be worn out and superseded long before the contemporary freight designs; so while there are some notable 0-6-0 goods engines and 2-4-2 suburban tanks in the collection at North Williamstown, the celebrated 'B' class 2-4-0s, and the 'A' class 4-4-0s are missing. One must therefore review Victorian railway steam power as a whole, rather than comment on what is now to be seen in the Museum—fine though that collection is.

A broad commentary upon the later nineteenth-century locomotives of the Victorian Railways could be that they were splendidly and unashamedly English in appearance, save for their very large cabs. The photographs reproduced facing pages 181 and 188 give some idea of the general 'look', much of which was preserved into the twentieth century in successive rebuildings. The cabs were large from the outset, not so much as a protection against inclement weather, which Australian engine-men were as tough to resist as any of their contemporaries in the United Kingdom, but in their extensive canopies a protection against the fierce and unrelenting sun of the Australian summer, when the 'shade' tempera-ture often soars well into the 'hundreds'. What these later photographs of old engines do not show however is the characteristic spark-arresting chimney, shaped like the ordinary domestic pouring funnel, and used on Victorian locomotives to minimise the risk of bush fires from spark-throwing steam engines. In a locomotive history of some complexity I have space to describe only a few of the more notable designs, and among the early ones the 'B' class 2–4–0 of 1862 was, for its size, one of the most successful designs ever to run the rails in Australia. It was certainly one of the most handsome. The original batches totalling 26 in all, were supplied from England by Beyer, Peacock's, and R. & W. Hawthorn, from 1862 to 1864. Another six came out in 1872, and two more were built in Australia in 1880 by the Phoenix Foundry, at Ballarat.

The design, with outside frames throughout, inside cylinders, and the picturesque outside coupling rods has been described as 'Old English'. It was certainly a very commonplace type on the home railways in mid-Victorian times. The 'B' class had a wealth of polished brass and copper work, and their appearance was greatly improved in later days when a handsomely styled cast-iron chimney of the orthodox type replaced the old 'Spark-arresters'. Despite their modest proportions they were so strongly built that they survived for over fifty years, and the colour plate facing page 136 shows one of them, about the turn of the century, assisting one of the 'New A' class 4–4–0s on an important inter-state express. The 'F' class 2–4–0, originating from 1873, and included among our pictures, was another long-lived Beyer, Peacock product dated from 1874. They, too, underwent various rebuildings, including conversion of some of them to 2–4–2 tank engines. The last of these latter was not scrapped until 1929. A contemporary 0–6–0 goods engine design of Beyer, Peacock origin is to be seen at North Williamstown in the 'T' class engine No. 94. This was actually one of a batch built in 1884 at the Phoenix Foundry, Ballarat. It has been finely restored, though not to the extent of having the original type of boiler, with raised firebox.

The most famous nineteenth-century passenger engines on the Victorian Railways were undoubtedly the two series of 'A' class 4-4-0s. The 'Old A', as the earlier series was known, dates from 1884 and was closely similar to the engines of similar type being introduced then on the New South Wales Government Railways, and referred to in Chapter Seven. They, like so many Australian locomotives of the period, came from Beyer, Peacock's; but the 'New A' class of generally larger proportions was built in 1889-91 at the Phoenix Foundry, Ballarat. The ten 'Old A' and the fifteen 'New A' 4-4-0s did the bulk of the main line long-distance passenger working, until the introduction of the still larger 'AA' class in 1900, but by that time the era of the 4-6-0s was approaching. Unfortunately no example of any of the 'A' series of 4-4-0s has been preserved. The last of the 'AA' class were scrapped in 1932. Before leaving engines of nineteenth-century vintage however, special mention must be made of the 'E' class 2-4-2 tanks, which bore the brunt of the Melbourne suburban service for many years. These splendid little engines, of which a fine example has been preserved, were perhaps the most English-looking of all Victorian Railways locomotives; they had no need of the large canopied cabs, and cow-catchers were not needed in the Melbourne suburbs. The engine now preserved at North Williamstown is virtually in its original condition, and is a most delightful 'period piece'. They had a monopoly of the suburban workings until 1908, when the 4-6-2 tanks were introduced.

Although the Victorian Railways continued to purchase many locomotives from overseas, and also from Australian manufacturers like the Phoenix Foundry, fine workshops had been set up at Newport, near North Williamstown, and others were in course of establishment at Ballarat and Bendigo. The first locomotive to be built new in the Williamstown railway shops was 2-4-0 No. 100, in 1871, and when the time came for the introduction of new and much larger locomotives the prototypes of new designs, as well as many subsequent members of the class, were built in Newport shops. Outstanding in the 'middle era' of Victorian Railways steam power were three outside-cylindered six-coupled classes, examples of all of which are fortunately preserved in the North Williamstown collection. These are the 'D' class mixed traffic

4–6–0 of 1902; the 'A2' class express passenger 4–6–0 of 1907 and the 4–6–2 suburban passenger tank engine of 1908. A high degree of stand-ardisation was achieved in these three classes, the eventual numerical strength of each being 261, 184, and 58. Construction of engines of one or another of these classes continued down to 1922. The 'A2' which is preserved at North Williamstown is in its final running condition, in plain black livery with stove-pipe chimneys and large smoke-deflecting shields; but the 'D2' and 'D3' 4–6–0s, and the 4–6–2 tank, are largely in their original condition.

In studying the design of the 'D' class 4–6–0 a degree of similarity to the New South Wales 'P6' class can be immediately detected in the spacing of the coupled wheels. While the stout individualism of the State of Victoria would undoubtedly have eschewed anything that looked like copying New South Wales, the great success of the 'P6' class was something that just could not be over-looked. Whatever influence there may have been however, Newport Works made a splendid job of their first 4–6–0, and engine No. 560, classed 'Dd', and put into traffic in 1902, looked extremely handsome in the full glory of the old green, gorgeously lined-out livery, with much polished brass and copper. The effect, on this fine 4–6–0, can be judged from a study of the colour plate facing page 136, where the livery is shown on a couple of older engines. In the following year how-ever, 1903, Thomas Tait, formerly of the Canadian Pacific Railway, became Chairman of Commissioners of Railways in Victoria, and it was generally thought to be at his instigation that the brilliant green livery was changed to one of Tuscan red, similar to that used on C.P.R. coaches, and on the tender panels and cab sides of the locomotives. Be that as it may the Victorian locomotives looked very well in the new livery, and examples of it are to be seen on the 4–6–2 tank engine, and on one of the 2–4–2 tanks on exhibition at North Williamstown.

The earliest engine of the 'D' class had straight running plates, as shown in the picture of the prototype engine No. 560 facing page 181; but in the later varieties the running plate was raised so as to expose the wheels completely, and continue straight above the outside cylinders and steam chests. All the various series of 'D' class engines, having 5 ft. 1 in. coupled wheels, had inside Stephenson link motion, and with a minimum of 'works' outside had a very English look, despite the raised running plate. This latter feature was nevertheless incorporated in the true express passenger 4–6–0s of the 'A2' class, first introduced in 1907, and certainly did not detract from their very stylish appearance. In their original form I have always thought they ranked among the most handsome of all Australian steam locomotives of the period. They had a striding, elegant air, set off by the splendour of the red livery, and in keeping with the traditions of the day they had a most artistically-shaped cast-iron chimney. At that time, too, there were no such things as smoke-deflecting plates. No fewer than 124 of these engines were built at Newport Works between 1907 and 1915, and all of these had inside Stephenson's link motion. It may surprise readers when I add that they were familiar to me from my early boyhood; but in the first edition of that beloved of books *The Wonder Book of Railways* there was a colour plate of one of these engines hauling an 'Interstate Express', presumably intended to be one running throughout on the 5 ft. 3 in. gauge between Melbourne and Adelaide.

This very fine range of six-coupled main line engines was introduced during the nineteen years when T. H. Woodroffe was Chief Mechanical Engineer, 1893–1912; he was succeeded by W. H. Shannon, and further engines of the 'A2' class built variously at the Newport, Ballarat, and Bendigo shops of the Victorian Railways had piston valves and outside Walschaerts radial valve gear. In their original form, I think these Walschaerts engines were in some ways even finer looking than the Stephenson batch. In the later ones the running plate was carried straight to the front end, whereas in the former lot it was dipped down to pass just clear over the outside cylinder. These 'A2' engines, whether of the Stephenson or Walschaerts variety, formed the absolute backbone of the Victorian Railways' passenger motive power for over thirty years, until, indeed, the arrival of the 'R' class 4–6–4s in 1951. It is true there were the 'S' class Pacifics, introduced in 1928, but there were only four of these latter, and they were reserved for special duties on the line to Albury. Reverting to the 'A2's', in due course they were modernised by the fitting of the highly utilitarian stove-pipe chimneys, smoke-deflecting plates, and improved valve setting. One of them has been preserved in its final working condition, painted in plain black, but still looking a thoroughbred.

The last of the Woodroffe engines to be specially mentioned are the 4–6–2 tanks designed for the Melbourne suburban service. These engines were a direct adaptation of the 'D' class 4–6–0s for short-distance working.

142

The Melbourne suburban lines mostly include gradients as steep as 1 in 50, and 1 in 40, climbing the hills that are ringed round the eastern outskirts of the city, and the introduction of new and heavy bogie coaching stock to provide for the ever-increasing commuter traffic needed engines of considerably greater power than the 2-4-2 tanks hitherto standard. At the same time electrification of the busiest routes was even then under consideration, and while providing large and powerful new steam loco-motives Mr. Woodroffe had also in mind their further utilisation in the event of their being displaced, because of electrification. Thus they were designed to include a high degree of interchangeability of parts with the 'D' class 4-6-0, and in fact to be readily convertible to a tender engine, if need be. Only two were actually done. A very neat and handsome design resulted, and the new engines in their dark red livery, at the head of the commodious new bogie coaches, were much admired by the travelling public. Even in the first decade of the twentieth century the Melbourne suburban services were worked at high intensity. As on most railways then using the Westinghouse brake, the drivers became expert at saving seconds. They approached the stations at comparatively high speed, and then made a rapid stop. Trains were rarely at rest for more than 15 seconds, and then off again in a thunderous acceleration.

The last locomotives of what may be termed the 'middle era' of Victorian steam motive power were the 'C' class 2-8-0s of 1918, intro-duced by Mr. Shannon. Good though the work of the Woodroffe 'D' class continued to be in general freight service, and examples of them were still being built new down to the year 1920, something considerably more powerful was becoming necessary for certain duties. The 'Dd' class 4-6-0s had a tractive effort of 22,800 lb., and Mr. Shannon took no half-measures in providing increased power. The coupled wheels were kept of the same diameter as in the 'D' class, but a much larger boiler was fitted, with higher boiler pressure, and the cylinders were increased from 19 in. diameter by 26 in. stroke to 22 in. diameter by 28 in. stroke. This put the tractive effort up to 38,400 lb.—considerably greater than that of any British 2-8-0 of the period. Of course the 'C' class was a much heavier unit, and its maximum axle-load of $18\frac{1}{2}$ tons, against the $13\frac{3}{4}$ tons of the 'D', placed a strict limitation upon the routes over which it would operate. But the 'C' class, of which 26 were built at Newport Works between 1918 and 1926, was a 'special-purpose' engine and it proved a great success. The earliest engines of the class had the handsomely-styled chimneys and red livery of the passenger engines of the day, but No. C10 which is now preserved at North Williamstown is in plain black with stove-pipe chimney and the continental-type of small smoke-deflecting plates which were fitted to the Gresley 'A3' Pacifics in the United Kingdom in their last years.

The 'K' class of light 2–8–0s followed in 1922, a standard design to provide enhanced tractive power over the 'D' on lines where the axle-load of $13\frac{3}{4}$ tons might not be exceeded. The fifty-three engines of this class were built at intervals between 1922 and 1946. The need was felt also for a locomotive of equal tractive power and route availability, but having a larger firebox that was better adapted to burn lower-grade fuel, and the 'N' class 2–8–2 was introduced in 1925. A relatively few examples of this excellent design were built prior to World War II, but it was later chosen for further production in the 'Operation Phoenix' to which reference is made later. The heavy 2–8–2s of the 'X' class, introduced in 1929, had the same relation to the light 'N' class as the 'C' class 2–8–0s had to Class 'K'. The 'X' class, as a study of the preserved example at Williamstown amply shows, is a truly massive job, with a huge boiler and firebox, high boiler pressure, and the same large cylinders as 'C' class. But the majority of the 'X' class are also fitted with boosters, which increase the tractive effort to no less than 48,360 lb. when that auxiliary is in operation. The 'X' class have a total weight of 103 tons, engine only, in working order, and a maximum axle-load of 19 tons. The tenders have a capacity of 8600 gallons of water and 9 tons of coal, and increase the all-up weight of engine and tender together to no less than $185\frac{1}{4}$ tons.

Even this monster design did not represent the ultimate in Victorian Railways' motive power. Construction of these engines continued at intervals between 1929 and 1947, but in the meantime an even vaster design was worked out and a prototype built at Newport Works in 1941, under the direction of A. C. Ahlston, Chief Mechanical Engineer from 1933 to 1955. This was the remarkable 'H' class 4–8–4 No. 220 aptly nicknamed 'Heavy Harry'. This enormous engine was intended for passenger working, and was provided with coupled wheels no less than 5 ft. 7 in. diameter; and whereas the 'C' and 'X' class engines had two cylinders 22 in. diameter by 28 in. stroke, the 'H 220' had *three* cylinders, $21\frac{1}{2}$ in. diameter by 28 in. stroke. The boiler and firebox was appropri-

PLATE 23. Diversity in special freight wagons
(a) Victorian Railways: motor car carriers

(d) Victorian Railways: double-decker sheep wagon.

(b) Queensland: dual-purpose wagon, used either for bulk cement, or copper ingots

(e) Victorian Railways: special quadruple-bogie 'well' wagon

(c) Western Australia: iron-ore wagon: Koolyanobbing–Kwinana traffic

(f) Western Australia: grain hopper wagon

PLATE 24.

(a) New South Wales: 'The Northern Tablelands Express', Sydney to Armidale, hauled by a 'C35' class 4–6–0 No. 3503, in 1960

(b) Victorian Railways: one of the 'S.300' class Pacifics, before streamlining, leaving Albury for Melbourne, with the 'Spirit of Progress' express in 1935

ately great, and while the grate area on the 'C' class was 32 sq. ft. 'Heavy Harry' had no less than 68 sq. ft. No fireman could be expected to supply such a firebox at a coal-rate designed for maximum haulage duties, and so a mechanical stoker was fitted. The tractive effort was 55,000 lb. and the total weight of engine and tender in working order was 260 tons— 'Heavy Harry' indeed! This magnificent example of steam locomotive design remained however the only one of its kind. After the war the changing trends of traffic diminished the need for engines of such vast power, and in due course 'he' was placed in the collection at North Williamstown. There one can be suitably impressed by his colossal size, but the only trouble is that 'he' is so big that one cannot secure a photograph that does justice to the fine proportions and immense length of the complete assembly of engine and tender. After all it measures 92 ft. $5\frac{3}{4}$ in. over buffers!

In dealing with successive developments of the freight locomotive stock of the Victorian Railways I have got somewhat out of strict chronological order, and must now go back to 1928, when the 'S' class express passenger Pacifics were first introduced. These four engines were originally of quite orthodox appearance, rather like a large 4–6–2 version of the Walschaerts 'A2' class 4–6–0, with a handsomely-fashioned non-stove-pipe chimney. They had 6 ft. diameter coupled wheels, and with three cylinders $20\frac{1}{2}$ in. diameter by 28 in. stroke a tractive effort of 41,670 lb. At the time there was no need for further engines of such power, but when the 'Spirit of Progress' train was introduced in 1937 these engines were fully streamlined, and finished in a new livery of dark blue, with gold lining to match the carriages. The original eight-wheeled bogie tender was replaced by a huge twelve-wheeler, that weighed $109\frac{1}{4}$ tons on its own. The combined weight of the streamlined engine and tender was $223\frac{3}{4}$ tons, with a maximum axle-load almost the same as 'Heavy Harry', namely $23\frac{1}{2}$ tons. As streamlined the four engines were named *Matthew Flinders; Sir Thomas Mitchell*, the Surveyor of New South Wales, who in exploring southwards to Port Phillip Bay was so enthusiastic about their newly-discovered area as to draw many settlers away from Sydney; *Edward Henty*, one of the famous English family who established the first permanent settlement in what is now Victoria; and lastly *C. J. Latrobe*, the first Lieutenant-Governor of the new Colony.

These four locomotives ran the 'Spirit of Progress' express from its inception until the time when it was changed over to diesel haulage, in 1954. As mentioned in Chapter Nine these engines maintained a schedule that demanded a non-stop average speed of 52 m.p.h. over the 190½ miles between Melbourne and Albury. The fact that there were only four 'Pacifics' on the railway showed how exceptional were the haulage demands on this specially luxurious night express to Sydney. The new 'B' class diesels were capable of working the majority of trains on the line single-handed. Since the completion of the standard-gauge line, and the inauguration of a second night train in each direction betweeen Melbourne and Sydney, the 'Spirit of Progress', like the 'Southern Aurora' and the 'Intercapital Daylight' is nearly always a single-engine job in Victoria.

The inauguration of the 'Spirit of Progress' train was a notable piece of railway enterprise in a period of deep industrial depression, which affected Australia as seriously as any part of the world. Very little money was available for replacements of rolling stock and this period was followed by the tremendous strain of World War II, when the railways of Australia generally had to carry unprecedented volumes of traffic with little in the way of additional locomotives and rolling stock. Systems of comparable size to the Victorian Railways needed yearly replacements of 20 to 25 locomotives to continue with efficiency, but during the period from 1929 right through to 1950 Victoria could only afford to provide *four* new locomotives per year. In 1949 however Sir John Elliot, then Chief Regional Officer of the Southern Region of British Railways, was invited by the Government to investigate and report, and he stated that

a very considerable programme of rehabilitation and re-equipment must be taken in hand without further delay, if a serious breakdown is to be avoided. The Commissioners have shown me their plans, and they seem to be sound and sufficiently far-reaching to serve the main purpose for which they are designed.

I can only confirm [he continued] that if these orders are not placed for steady delivery over the next 10 years, the ultimate price which the State and the people of Victoria will pay in transport inefficiency, delays, and in final breakdown of railway transport, will be still heavier.

The immediate outcome, so far as steam locomotive power was concerned, was the ordering of another fifty 'N' class 2–8–2s from the North British Locomotive Company, sixty light 2–8–0s of the new 'J' class, from the Vulcan Foundry, of Newton-le-Willows, Lancashire, and most interesting of all, no fewer than 70 of an entirely new class of express passenger engine, of the 4-6-4 type, known as Class 'R'. I shall have more to say about the 'J' class 2-8-0s in a later chapter, having spent nearly four hours on the footplate of one of them, between Corio and Ballarat. In this chapter I must conclude with some extended reference to the 'R' class. These were introduced as a general-purpose express passenger engine, of less power than the streamlined 'Pacifics' of the 'S' class. They clearly reflected the conditions of austerity for which they were designed, having two cylinders only; everything outside and readily accessible; a large boiler and firebox suitable for burning low-grade coal, and equipped with mechanical stokers. It was the heavy additional weight at the rear-end that led to the use of the 4-6-4 rather than the 4-6-2 wheel arrangement. Despite their considerable less tractive power, 32,080 lb. against 41,670, the total weight of engine alone is $107\frac{1}{2}$ tons, against $114\frac{1}{2}$ tons for the streamlined 'S' class. Everything was done, within a limited budget, to make the new engines look smart and attractive, and although the general finish was plain black the running plate valances and the small smoke-deflecting shields were scarlet. I had a short though excellent run on the footplate of one of these engines that will be mentioned in detail in Chapter Thirteen.

Although it was essentially a hard-slogging utility job the 'R' class 4-6-4 included many advanced features of design, intended to minimise maintenance costs and provide for long mileages between repairs. An important technical feature was the use of piston valves of very large diameter in relation to the cylinder volume. These were no less than 11 in. diameter for $21\frac{1}{2}$ in. diameter cylinders, and accordingly resulted in a very free-running engine. The mechanical stoker provided for a high coal-rate when the service demanded sustained high power, and rapid steaming was assisted by the use of two thermic siphons in the firebox. The mechanical and metallurgical details, of which very comprehensive accounts were published in the British technical press in 1951, reflect the careful attention given to every single item of equipment on these fine engines. All seventy engines of this class were built in Scotland by the North British Locomotive Company to the designs of Mr. A. C. Ahlston, who was Chief Mechanical Engineer of the Victorian Railways from 1933 to 1955. It must indeed have been a source of gratification to him that after having nursed the locomotive stock through the long, grim

147

years of depression, war, and then austerity, that he was able eventually to introduce a fine new design embodying all the fruits of the rather bitter experience gained in the earlier years of his chieftainship. Engine No. 704 of this class is preserved at North Williamstown.

CHAPTER TWELVE

Interlude with 'Puffing Billy'

A literary critic commenting on one of my books dealing with the history of British steam locomotives titled his piece, 'All Steamed up over the Killing of Puffing Billy'. It was a first-rate piece of creative journalism, creative because I had not become 'steamed up' at all, yet nevertheless capturing faithfully enough the sentiments of those neophytes who are loud in their assertion that steam traction on railways was a regrettable episode, best forgotten as soon as possible. In Australia, while there is just as much enthusiasm among historians and plain 'fans' as there is in the United Kingdom for the survivors of the steam engine, the official attitude is rather different. There are some, among my own circle of Australian railway friends, who would be ready enough to make an end with all steam haulage, even for special occasions. As a practical engineer I cannot blame them. I praised the remarkable degree of diesel standardisation that has been achieved in Queensland, and when running a railway whether from the viewpoint of organising workshops for repair and maintenance, or in the diagramming of locomotives to duties up and down the line, standardisation is an incalculable boon; and one can quite appreciate the feelings of a responsible engineer who has to keep under his wing not only different classes of locomotives but different forms of traction.

The volume of genuinely friendly interest in the historical aspects of railways is however something that has been most seriously taken into account in Australia, and in every State not only are Railway Museums already established, or the plans for them well advanced, but locomotives of important historical interest are being maintained in first-class condition and available for special trips by one or other of the 'enthusiast' societies. In so far as 'Puffing Billy' signifies steam traction as a whole,

149

there is no movement to kill him in Australia. He is being kept very much alive, and it is the gentleman himself, rather than any disillusioned admirers, who is being kept 'steamed up'. But in Australia, and particularly in the State of Victoria, the name 'Puffing Billy' means something far more than steam locomotion in general. At Belgrave, amid the exquisitely wooded foothills of the Dandenongs and only 25¾ miles from Flinders Street station, there begins a narrow-gauge steam railway that could be the dream of railway enthusiasts the world over. This splendidly managed concern is the Australian 'Puffing Billy'.

Before coming to describe how it came to attain the position of renown and affection it now occupies, something of the history of narrow-gauge railways in Victoria must first be told. In the latter part of the nineteenth century the construction of railways probing out radially from Melbourne was seen as a means of attracting settlers to the outback areas; but with the need for further lines and extensions to existing ones the high cost of construction was a serious handicap, and with contemporary developments in other parts of the Empire in view, Australian thoughts turned to the use of lighter, narrow-gauge railways. It was not a case of using the 3 ft. 6 in. gauge, as Queensland and Western Australia had done for their main trunk lines, but of adopting something still smaller, as was currently being done in India, and was proposed for many light railways in Ireland. There was also the outstandingly successful example of the Festiniog Railway in North Wales. In Australia however it was felt that the gauge of the latter railway was a little too narrow, and so when the first Victorian narrow-gauge line was laid down the gauge adopted was 2 ft. 6 in. This was opened in 1899 from Wangaratta, on the Melbourne–Albury main line, to Whitfield, a distance of 30½ miles. The territory through which this line ran was in open farming country, where a broad-gauge line would have presented no difficulties; but as an extension into the hilly country in the foothills of the Great Dividing Range was later envisaged the branch was built on the 2 ft. 6 in. gauge from the outset.

In the following year came the opening of the narrow-gauge line into the Dandenongs, that range of magnificently-wooded hills that lies little more than 20 miles distant from the heart of Melbourne. The broad-gauge line from Flinders Street then terminated at a place with the delightful name of Upper Ferntree Gully, and the narrow-gauge line was built from a new station alongside the broad-gauge terminus, through very hilly and difficult wooded country to a terminus high on the range that was called Gembrook. As the crow flies the distance between the two stations was less than 13 miles, but such were the twists and turns taken to avoid great rocky bluffs, and lessen the costs of construction by following the contours, that the distance by the 2 ft. 6 in. gauge line was 18 miles. The first train arrived at Gembrook on 18 December 1900, without any ceremony, in sweltering hot weather that caused the few lady spectators to use umbrellas for sunshades. The purpose of the railway was twofold, to carry timber and farm produce from the Dandenongs into Melbourne, and to attract excursionists for a day's outing in the hills. In this unobtrusive way the beloved 'Puffing Billy' of today was born.

The locomotives were of the same type as used on the Wangaratta–Whitfield line. Two came from Baldwin's in the United States and the rest were built at Newport Works. Three of them are in full commission today, exactly as they were delivered seventy years ago—to all outward appearances at any rate, and a fourth is awaiting possible restoration. Both the Wangaratta and the Gembrook lines were built by the Victorian Railways as feeders to the broad-gauge lines. As originally brought into service the Gembrook had two of the 'NA' class 2–6–2 tank engines, two passenger carriages, and a number of goods wagons mostly of open or flat type, on which farm produce could be loaded conveniently. The line very quickly became very popular with farmers and in the appropriate season vast loads of potatoes were sent into Melbourne. At other times there was heavy traffic in timber. Like the Festiniog Railway the loaded trains were worked in the downhill direction, thereby easing the problem of providing engine power. Like the broad-gauge trains all vehicles were fitted with the Westinghouse brake. At holiday times when excursionists in considerable numbers arrived at Upper Ferntree Gully seats were placed in the open trucks because the two small passenger carriages could not accommodate anything like the number of passengers who wished to travel. In the hot sunny weather that usually prevails in Melbourne at Christmas time a ride in the open trucks was to be preferred to the closed carriages. It was not until 1919 that the original two coaches were supplemented by some new carriages specially built for the excursion traffic.

I need hardly say that by the end of World War II the entire complexion of traffic in this area had changed. No longer was the little railway used for conveyance of farm produce. It could not compete, either for convenience or speed, with direct road haulage, and the excursion traffic on its own could not sustain the line in business. It only needed two landslips, in December 1952 and August 1953, to hasten the official closure of the line. But the second and much larger landslip had occurred near Selby, well up the grade. The section between Ferntree Gully and Belgrave was still clear, and the management of *The Sun* newspaper, prompted by motives that I have never been able to discover, arranged for thousands of Melbourne children to say 'Goodbye Puffing Billy' by providing free rides to Belgrave and back during December 1954. The public interest shown was terrific, so much so that despite the announced intention to close the line the Victorian Railways ran a number of tourist trips of their own during 1955. It became increasingly apparent that 'Puffing Billy' had a place in the affections of the community, quite apart from the more specialised interests of railway enthusiasts; and with an eye, no doubt, to what was currently happening in the United Kingdom, the 'Puffing Billy Preservation Society' was formed. Its aim was to keep the little train running by providing the necessary financial guarantee. The trips to Belgrave had shown clearly that there was need for railway communication, and far from closing the line the Victorian Railways decided to adopt a recommendation made by the Parliamentary Public Works Committee as long previously as 1944 and convert the $3\frac{1}{4}$ miles of line between Upper Ferntree Gully and Belgrave from 2 ft. 6 in. to 5 ft. 3 in. gauge, and electrify it.

This of course could have meant the end of 'Puffing Billy'. Indeed the Preservation Society was informed that narrow-gauge working must cease on 23 February 1958. Large crowds flocked to travel by the trains on this last day; thousands of people gathered along the $3\frac{1}{4}$ miles of line, and the tail end of each train bore a huge placard 'Goodbye Puffing Billy'. It could have been the last day of the Lynton and Barnstaple all over again, or the last days of many a standard-gauge line in England or Scotland, but for two vital factors. The first was that the interest created by *The Sun* trips, and the publicity accorded to them, had fairly 'started something'; and secondly, and even more important in my estimation, the line was a mere stone's throw from Melbourne. The official closure merely spurred the Preservation Society to redoubled efforts. The prospect of electric trains right into Belgrave was an added

152

incentive, for if the very picturesque mountain section could be re-opened the new broad-gauge trains would bring the excursionists in their thousands. In due course the Railway Commissioners agreed to an eight-mile section of the line between Belgrave and the site of the former station at Lakeside being reopened. The work was to be done by volunteer labour, but under the supervision of professional railwaymen from the Railways Department of the Victorian Government.

This, of course, is where 'Puffing Billy' had an immense advantage over some of the British railway preservation schemes. The Railways Department continued to take technical responsibility, and the proximity of Belgrave to the heart of Melbourne meant that the numerous volunteers could be readily organised on short-shift turns, if necessary. In the United Kingdom, volunteers working on the Talyllyn or the Festiniog railways had to make a positive expedition. It is much the same with the Dart Valley Railway. But the new station at Belgrave was no further from Flinders Street than Hemel Hempstead is from Euston, or Maiden-head from Paddington. This is not in any way to minimise the task so courageously undertaken by the Puffing Billy Preservation Society. They had a tremendous task. Much of the track had to be relaid and reballasted, and there was above all the small matter of that landslide beyond Selby. Men and women from all walks of life set resolutely about the task, and it was soon evident that with the professional supervision provided by the Victorian Railways the line was being successfully reconditioned by amateur labour. In November 1958 the Society had the invaluable help of the No. 3 Field Engineer Regiment, a unit of the Citizen Military Forces, who gave their services as a training exercise. They built a narrow-gauge engine shed, ash and inspection pits, and built the deviation line past the site of the 1953 landslip. The Victorian Railways provided second-hand permanent way material, and with astonishing rapidity in all the circumstances, the work of rehabilitation went forward. It was possible to forecast that by July 1962 the line would be reopened again as far as Menzies Creek.

There was to be no waiting for fine weather. The opening was tar-geted for a time in the Australian winter, which can be cold and miterable enough. The preliminaries took place in mist and rain on Sunday, 6 May 1962, when one of the little engines and some carriages were transferred from a broad-gauge transporter truck on to narrow-gauge rails, at

Belgrave. The event was appropriately publicised. The television newsreel men were there in force; hundreds of photographs were taken in weather so dark and lowering as to need flashbulbs. Public interest increased as the date of the official reopening drew near, and on 28 July 1962 it is estimated that more than a thousand people were thronging Belgrave station to see the first train leave. From that day 'Puffing Billy' has never looked back. Trains were made up to the maximum loads those little engines could take up the steep gradients and round the most severe curves; platforms had to be lengthened, but the work for the volunteers continued. Regular running of trains meant regular track maintenance, and all the time the Society had its 'sights' on the completion of their task of rehabilitation, the extension of the line from Menzies Creek to Emerald. The plan was evolved of working alternate weekends: the first on maintenance over the section open to traffic, the second on the restoration to Emerald. It was another colossal task for these indefatigable amateurs, and this second phase in the complete rehabilitation of the line took nearly three years to accomplish. When the first work-train steamed into Emerald in December 1964 it was the first time for eleven years that this upper part of the line had seen a locomotive in steam. Regular services began six months later.

One of the most pleasing things about 'Puffing Billy' is the support it has received from the Victorian Railways management. Our railway friends in Melbourne indicated that a visit to 'Puffing Billy' was a 'must'. A date was chosen, and I was duly issued with a footplate pass for the whole day; but we hardly guessed at the nature of our going. The normal way to Belgrave would have been to take a fast electric train from Flinders Street, but instead one of the Railway Commissioners, whom I had met in England in connection with preliminary work on the new Melbourne marshalling yard, took us out to Belgrave in his own car. As a former Chief Civil Engineer of the Victorian Railways he talked vividly of the work that had been involved in rehabilitation, for which he had been ultimately responsible. Then having reached Belgrave, and taken leave of us personally, the car and its cheery chauffeur were put at our disposal for the rest of the day, with the happy results later to be described. We sensed at once however that this was no formal, polite overseeing of a project operated by volunteers. Here was genuine, whole-hearted enthusiasm for it by one in very high authority, and it made a grand start to the day. And having passed on to the platform and walked the length of the long train, I had another big surprise. It was enough to defer detailed examination of the fascinating little engine on which I was to ride.

In the running of these trains only three railway employees are present, the driver, the fireman, and the guard. Railway employees indeed! Beside the engine I was met with broad grins and cheery handshakes from the same crew with whom I had ridden not a week earlier on an 'R' class 4-6-4 hauling a 510-ton enthusiasts' special between Melbourne and Corio! On the Victorian Railways it has always been the custom to set aside a crack senior crew for driving the Commissioners on special trips, inspections and such like, and this inimitable pair, Driver Haining and Fireman Greaves, are the present holders of this particularly important position. As well as ordinary main line work they are often called upon for special duties, as well as filling in the odd vacant day on 'Puffing Billy'. Having enjoyed all the chaff and back-chat of their congenial company on that big stoker-fired 4-6-4, it was a deeply interesting as well as amusing experience to squeeze into that narrow-gauge cab with them. The rail gauge may have been narrow, but the driver like his guest was of decidedly 'broad-gauge' proportions! Our engine was No. 6A, one of the three now working on the 'Puffing Billy' line. It is of the same design as the two original narrow-gauge locomotives of 1898 imported from the U.S.A.; but all subsequent engines, of which there were fifteen, were built at Newport Works.

For their size and weight they are remarkably powerful little jobs. The cylinders are 13 in. diameter by 18 in. stroke, and the coupled wheels 3 ft. in diameter. Their total weight in working order is $34\frac{1}{4}$ tons, but they have the very appreciable tractive effort of 12,515 lb. They certainly need it to haul the loads that now present themselves. We had a train of eight coaches and two vans, making a load of about 90 tons tare; but with nearly a hundred passengers on board the total load to be hauled would be around 115 tons. The open-sided coaches are unique in my experience of railway working. There are two horizontal bars to prevent children of all ages from falling out, and with the protection of these bars a high proportion of the younger passengers travel with their legs dangling outside. At first sight the approach of a crowded train reminds one of tragic pictures of trains conveying refugees from areas of earthquake or civil disturbance, when all normal travelling discipline is lost, and 'passengers' hang on where they can; but on 'Puffing Billy', although the travelling is perhaps a little unorthodox, everything is strictly in order. The Victorian Railways' guard sees to that. The whole train seems to be bursting with high spirits from end to end—and this did not exclude the footplate of the engine on my trip.

Away we went, climbing with a fierce, staccato exhaust on gradients that were mostly around 1 in 45. The curves are very sharp, and we were not far on our way before we came to the horseshoe bend at Monbulk Creek. Expressions such as horseshoe, when applied to the alignment of a railway, are usually picturesque exaggerations of the truth; but there is no exaggeration about the curve at Monbulk Creek. The colour plate facing page 168 has been prepared from a photograph I took from the rear van of a ten-coach train on the return trip to Belgrave later the same day. The location is made all the more attractive by the fine timber viaduct that spans the creek and the main road from Belgrave to Gembrook. The latter is a favourite stance for sightseers and photographers, so much so that 'no parking' areas have had to be prescribed to avoid congestion. There are places on the ascent where the gradient stiffens to 1 in 30, but the little engine went pounding away. It was hard work. The lever was only two notches from full forward gear, and although the regulator handle was only one-quarter of the way over on the quadrant plate I could sense that very little throttling of the steam was taking place. Haining and Greaves were skilled and highly experienced enginemen, and it was a pleasure to watch their management of this little engine in contrast to their hard main line running, of equal efficiency, with the big 'R' class 4-6-4.

We climbed into a very hilly, supremely beautiful region of virgin Australian bush. The gum trees, which one sees almost everywhere, grow to great heights, and in the brief clearings, as at Monbulk Creek, one can see range upon range of forested slopes rising high on all sides. Approaching the site of the 1953 landslide there is another horseshoe bend—an equally true horseshoe as that across Monbulk Creek—although the depth of it has been slightly lessened by the deviation that the army constructed to avoid the most seriously affected area. So, after more hard slogging we came to Menzies Creek, which was the temporary terminus of the line on its first reopening in 1962. Here, most appropriately, is situated the narrow-gauge railway Museum, but before describing some of the fascinating exhibits that are to be seen there I must say something of the signalling on the 'Puffing Billy' line. It is worked on the 'train staff and ticket system, exactly as on the single-line sections of the broad-gauge branch lines, and fullsize semaphore signals of the somersault type are used at the passing loops.

Menzies Creek, is now a crossing station. It is often the scene of great animation when two crowded trains are there at the same time, while to a railway enthusiast the sight of several preserved locomotives in the Museum adjacent to the station provides an irresistible incentive to breaking one's journey. For the moment we were continuing up to Emerald, the present terminus, through the most beautiful woodland country, with frequent vistas of far landscapes, all to the enlivening staccato bark of the little engine. The Victorian Railways had planned our programme right up to the minute. The car was waiting at Emerald to take us swiftly back to Menzies Creek, so that there would be ample time for a look round the Museum before taking the next down train to Belgrave. And having arrived in the Museum I must amplify a statement made earlier in this chapter about the standard motive power of the 2 ft. 6 in. gauge lines of the Victorian Railways. One of the most prominent exhibits at Menzies Creek, as yet not fully restored to an 'exhibition finish', is a splendid narrow-gauge example of the Beyer–Garratt type, No. G.42.

There were two of these engines, 2–6–0+0–6–2 type, purchased from England in 1926. Neither ever worked on the Ferntree Gully–Gembrook line, but they were originally allocated, one each, to the Colac–Beech Forest and to the Moe–Walhalla 2 ft. 6 in. gauge lines. The latter line was closed in 1954 and then G.42 was transferred to Colac, which latter thenceforward had both of the Garratts. After the closure of the latter line in 1962 the survivor G.42 was purchased by the Puffing Billy Preservation Society. She is a fine example of the high tractive power that can be built into a locomotive for the narrow gauge, where the maximum axle-load permitted is no more than $9\frac{1}{2}$ tons. The Garratts had rather more than twice the power of the little 2–6–2 tanks that are now working the 'Puffing Billy' line. These latter have also a maximum axle-load of $9\frac{1}{2}$ tons, and a tractive effort of 12,515 lb. The Garratts had a tractive effort of 27,630 lb.—a remarkable capacity for a small 2 ft. 6 in. gauge locomotive. One of the most striking exhibits in the narrow-gauge Museum is however not a 2 ft. 6 in. gauge locomotive at all, but a 3 ft. 6 in. gauge 4–8–2, splendidly turned out in green, with black and white lining from the Silvertown Tramway. This is of the same design as the Western Australian 'W' class, introduced in 1951, but it has a streamlined casing over the boiler mountings, and looks very striking in this guise. I was to meet 'W' class proper in full force when I paid a visit to Bunbury some weeks later. The Museum also includes certain steam locomotives from private railways, all having much interest to connoisseurs of the unusual in steam locomotive design and history. Further references to the Silvertown Tramway is made later in this book.

On the return journey to Belgrave my wife and I rode together in the rear van of a lengthy train, and I was then able to appreciate the good riding of the stock, providing a further testimony to the quality of the permanent way that has been relaid and maintained by volunteer labour. It was in rounding the curve over the trestle viaduct at Monbulk Creek that I took the photograph that Jack Hill used as the basis for his painting, facing page 168. On arrival at Belgrave we found the railway car waiting again, this time to take us for a comprehensive tour of the Dandenong Range. The scenic delights of this region, so near to Melbourne yet so remarkably unspoiled, form no part of the present story, except that from some of the highest points, admirably arrayed with look-out terraces and vantage points, we could see the circle of hills that encompasses Melbourne on every side, except that of the sea, and then one could appreciate how all the main railway lines radiating from the city have to climb hard before they reach the inland plains. I had already experienced something of this on an excursion to Ballarat, and with mention of this it is time to commence the next chapter.

CHAPTER THIRTEEN

Melbourne—Geelong—Ballarat

The early plans for railway development in Victoria, although conceived on a most comprehensive plan, followed the pattern of railway development elsewhere, in that lines connecting important centres of activity were not necessarily constructed by the most direct routes. The cities of Melbourne and Ballarat provide an almost classic instance of this. The level line along the north-western shores of Port Phillip Bay was the very first country line in Victoria. It originated in a private enterprise at Geelong as early as the year 1850; but this first project collapsed for lack of funds, and it was not until February 1853, when the Geelong and Melbourne Railway Company received its Act of Incorporation, that things began to move. This railway was planned to connect with the Government line from Williamstown, referred to in Chapter Ten, and to exercise running powers over the $6\frac{1}{2}$ miles of that line between Newport and Spencer Street. The Geelong railway got away to a good start. The Lieutenant Governor, C. J. LaTrobe, travelled by steamer from Melbourne to Geelong to cut the first turf on 20 September 1853, and construction proceeded from the Geelong end. It was there that the railway had been enterprised, and it was from there that all activity proceeded.

The independent part of the line, 39 miles of it, was completed long before the Williamstown railway was ready, and so that a service could be operated between Geelong and Melbourne the company built an additional halfmile of line at Greenwich, as the neighbourhood of Newport was then known, to a jetty on the River Yarra. The journey into Melbourne was then completed by steamer. It is strange on reflection that these railway enterprises did not start in Melbourne itself, and that the most metropolitan sections were the last to be completed. Be that as it may a train service was operated between Geelong and Greenwich from 26 June 1857. At first there were four intermediate stations, and their picturesque names are worth recalling. Starting from the Geelong end one came to Cowie's Creek, Duck Ponds, Little River, and lastly Werribee, but 'Cowie's Creek', is now 'North Shore', and 'Duck Ponds' is 'Lara'. Many more intermediate stations have since been constructed. When the Government line was finally completed through train service between Geelong and Melbourne was inaugurated in January 1859. There were originally three passenger trains in each direction daily, and the journey time for the 45 miles was two hours. A competing steamer service between Melbourne and Geelong caused much loss of traffic; funds were low, receipts very disappointing, and eventually in June 1860 the line was sold to the Government.

Some weeks before our own departure from England I had been advised by the two very efficient enthusiast societies, the Australian Railway Historical Society, and the Association of Railway Enthusiasts, that they were combining in the promoting and organising of a rail tour during the time we should be in Melbourne, and I was not only invited to join the tour but favoured by the Victorian Railway authorities with footplate passes for the most interesting parts of the journey. So it was that I had the pleasure of riding practically the entire length of the historic Geelong and Melbourne Railway at express speed on a 4–6–4 locomotive of the 'R' class. Arriving at Spencer Street station on a rather wet and windy August morning I quickly found that rail tours in Australia are very much the same as at home. Nearly every seat was taken in the heavy twelve-car express train, and enthusiasts of all ages and both sexes were armed with ciné and still cameras, tape recorders, and well provided with knapsacks bulging no doubt with ample sustenance for a long day's railway sightseeing. The tour could not have been more fortunately planned from my point of view, for not only was it to provide me with a fine example of Victorian steam locomotive performance, but we were later to follow the original route to Ballarat.

Climbing aboard the big 4–6–4 No. R.707, I met for the first time the irrepressibly good-humoured driver and fireman with whom I rode on the 'Puffing Billy' line. Here they had a big modern engine, and it was the first time I had ridden on a locomotive equipped with a mechanical stoker.

160

PLATE 25. Heavy freight working

(a) Three-cylinder 4–8–2 (N.S.W. Class 'D57') with dynamometer car, leaving Cootamundra for Sydney

(b) A 'D57' leaving Junee, with a 1000-ton load

PLATE 26. In the heart of the country

(a) A New South Wales 'mixed' train on the Gilmore–Batlow branch line, hauled by a '19' class 0–6–0 of 1877

(b) South Australia: a Class 'T' 4–8–0 (3 ft. 6 in. gauge) on a down Quorn freight near Orroroo

The coal is brought forward through a large tube from the tender, and in this tube there is a worm, exactly like a much-extended version of the worm-screw in a domestic mincing machine. The coal is delivered into the firebox by this worm-screw, and feeds its own way down the grate. I have always noticed how on modern well-designed steam locomotives there is very little need for the fireman to 'place' the coal on the grate. Sir William Stanier's 'Duchess' class on the London, Midland and Scottish Railway were an outstanding example of this; you just feed the coal through the door, and the shape of the firebox, the slope of the grate, and the slight 'action' of the engine at speed did the rest. They had an even bigger grate than the Victorian 'R' class, 50 sq. ft. against 42 sq. ft. So far as long-sustained running was concerned No. R.707 was not seriously extended on the trip to Geelong; but while I was on the footplate she steamed very freely.

The twelve coaches of our train weighed 510 tons empty, and with such a load of passengers it would have meant a gross tonnage of about 550 behind the tender. Even though the day was a Saturday the suburban area was very busy with commuter trains, and on starting away, and following at first a track parallel to the standard-gauge line, and beside the new Melbourne marshalling yard, we were checked by signals from another train running so closely ahead that we could see it on the open stretch between Yarraville and Spotswood. But it was taking the line down to Williamstown, and after slowing to 20 m.p.h. at Newport to take the junction on to the Geelong line proper we got going in fine style. Once again, as in New South Wales north of Gosford, I had the thrilling experience of being on a big steam locomotive working hard and fast, an experience that I had so often at home in years gone by, but which is now no more than a memory. On a fine, straight and level track, with the inclement weather of Melbourne clearing pleasantly, 'R.707' soon whipped that big train into speed. Laverton was passed at 64 m.p.h., and we continued at a general average of 60 to 65 m.p.h. except where a very short length of 1 in 94 brought us down to 56 m.p.h. A slack to 60 m.p.h. is prescribed through Werribee, but we were soon back at our former speed, with the engine riding steadily, and all the familiar noises, smells, and taste of coal dust on your tongue that invariably accompany the experience of riding steam. At Little River, $29\frac{1}{2}$ miles from Melbourne, passed in 41 minutes, we were just comfortably inside the schedule laid down for this special train, and entering then upon a section of single line continued at 60 m.p.h. until nearing Lara.

Now the complications of the rail tour programme began to enter into the proceedings, and on reaching Corio the train was to be divided. The leading six coaches were to take the old main line to Ballarat, while the remaining six were continuing along the main line beyond Geelong as far as Colac. From Corio the Ballarat train was worked by a 'J' class 2-8-0 No. 512, and to this I transferred. We were not quite finished with 'R.707' and her cheery crew, for arrangements had been made for the two trains to run parallel to each other between Corio and North Geelong for photographic purposes. Plenty of time was allowed in the schedules for such passengers as desired to detrain to walk along to their chosen stances and photograph the two trains running exactly abreast. As can well be imagined there was some lively badinage between the two engine crews while this particular operation was in progress. On reaching the junction at North Geelong, we, on engine 'J.512', turned away from the coastal route, and once assured that all our passengers had rejoined the train we started away for Ballarat. But I must first of all make a few notes about the engine itself. The 'J' class is a hard-slogging general utility 2-8-0, with a maximum axle-load of $14\frac{1}{2}$ tons and a tractive effort of 28,650 lb. This is rather below that of the familiar varieties of 2-8-0 on British railways, but the latter were not so restricted in the matter of axle-loading. Of the sixty engines of the class, all built by the Vulcan Foundry, in England, in 1953-4, thirty are coal-burners and thirty oil-burners. Another restriction in design was in length, for to suit various branch-line duties they were required to be accommodated on 53 ft. turntables.

The history of the line from Geelong to Ballarat is closely interlinked with the Government plan for the main trunk lines of the State, as embodied in the map dated 24 March 1858, and indicated on the sketch map on page 113. The construction of the line was subjected to much the same difficulties as those experienced by contractors and Government in the building of lines to the north and north-east of Melbourne. The original contractors failed financially, and a new contract had to be drawn up in 1860. In general the country traversed was not difficult, though prolonged wet weather added to the troubles in construction and greatly retarded the work. In the 48·7 miles between North Geelong and Warrenheip the altitude increases from only 57 ft. above sea level to 1723 ft., though from that summit point a very steep gradient leads down into Ballarat. It is not a route of dramatic mountainous country, but rather of fine open uplands, with broad vistas extending for many miles. The biggest engineering work was the Moorabool Viaduct, some five miles from Geelong. The Moorabool river is one of the largest in the neighbourhood, and from two branches in the Great Dividing Range flows not directly into Port Phillip Bay, but into Lake Conniwarre, that punctuates the Queenscliff isthmus to the south of Geelong. The Moorabool Viaduct is 1300 ft. long, with ten spans, and having a maximum height of 115 ft. It is a splendid example of early railway construction in Victoria.

The completion of the viaduct was the last link in the line between Ballarat and Geelong. As the time approached there was considerable hustle and excitement to get the job finished. After the delays and difficulties that had hindered early proceedings a tremendous sense of urgency developed, and on Saturday, 29 March 1862, track laying on the viaduct had reached such a stage that the contractors worked on long after darkness had fallen. Government and contractors' officials had gathered at the site, and in the light of flares the platelayers toiled on, until just before midnight the last spike was driven. Amid cheers, a waiting engine steamed over from the Ballarat side and the railway was finished. Less than a fortnight later the line was finally opened by the Governor, Sir Henry Barkly, in a great ceremony and banquet at Ballarat, and public traffic began the next day, 11 April 1862, with a service of four passenger trains each way between Melbourne, Geelong, and Ballarat. At first only a single track was laid, although the formation and all the bridges were of sufficient width to carry two. This, however, was no more than a temporary stage, and double tracks were in operation throughout from August 1862, and from that time freight traffic also was carried. In such wise was the first link in the main line to the State boundary with South Australia forged.

There is no vantage point to match the engine footplate when making an assessment of any railway route, and although the Geelong–Ballarat line has now reverted to single-line track there is no mistaking its quality, and its status as a one-time inter-state main line. Of course this status was only remotely in view at the time of its original construction. The main thing was to secure railway communication between Melbourne and

Ballarat. I was to appreciate the difficulties of working in full measure on this trip. Engine No. 'J.512' was not steaming too well, and although we now had only half of the huge train that 'R.707' had brought out of Melbourne, a gross load of 275 tons was no light weight for an engine of 28,650 lb. tractive effort to work over a route including long gradients as steep as Shap. Furthermore, in Victoria as in the United Kingdom, the number of firemen who are fully experienced in working steam under arduous conditions is growing ever less, and this makes all the more inspiriting the attitude of the Australian railways in general, in their readiness to keep selected engines in good mechanical condition and to run trips for enthusiasts. There was a remarkable instance of this when the standard-gauge line between Melbourne and Albury was completed, and the 'Spirit of Progress' train was to make its last journey on the 5 ft. 3 in. gauge. Greatly daring, the enthusiast societies approached the Victorian Railways suggesting that the last 5 ft. 3 in. gauge run might be made with steam haulage, although the train had been diesel-hauled for the previous eight years. The Railways Department agreed, and put a couple of 'A2' class 4-6-0s on to the job.

On leaving North Geelong it was clear that No. 'J.512' was going to need some expert management on this heavy road. We stopped at Moorabool to take water, and after mounting the short incline that follows the famous viaduct, we got away into pleasant upland country. As we accelerated on easier gradients past Gheringhap I could see that the engine had an insatiable appetite for coal, and the demands for steam were taking their toll. The driver and fireman between them worked like Trojans, but in climbing the 3-mile rise to Bannockburn the speed dropped to 21 m.p.h., and the boiler pressure from the rated 200 lb. per sq. in. to 110. It is always difficult to judge just what is making a steam locomotive so temperamental. I have seen it many times over at home, but in this case there was nothing for it but to stop for a 'blow-up', and this we did at Lethbridge. The worst of the climbing lay immediately beyond that station, and we could not afford to tackle nearly nine miles at an average inclination of 1 in 75 with such a deficiency in boiler pressure. While we stood opportunity was taken to clean the fire thoroughly. These engines are fitted with rocking grates, and the bars were 'rocked' extensively; and in the meantime clinker was cleared away, while under the continuous action of the blower the pressure steadily rose. So with the fire clean and bright once more and the gauge needle only just below the 200 lb. per sq. in. mark, we restarted.

Now I began to see the real quality of this engine. Pressure was nicely held at the 170 to 180 mark, and we pounded up the heaviest part of the bank on gradients of 1 in 66, and 1 in 71, at 22 to 26 m.p.h. The country-side was very reminiscent of the English north country, with its dry-point stone walls and wide landscapes, with intermissions of the characteristic Australian bush, full of thickly-growing blue gums. Meanwhile we were gradually mounting higher and higher. At Meredith the altitude is 1126 ft; at Elaine 1270, and following that there came a particularly tough piece with three miles continuously at 1 in 72, through a beautifully wooded stretch where the speed fell to 18 m.p.h. and the boiler pressure to 150. There is no respite on this line, and we were now coming into the region of the gold diggings. The stations were Lal Lal, Yendon, and Navigator, and by that time we were up to over 1600 ft.; and so we came ultimately to Warrenheip, where at 1723 ft. above sea level we made a trailing junction with the present main line from Melbourne. By the route we had travelled the distance was 92·4 miles; by the present direct route it is only 69·5, though there were certainly reasons why this latter route was not built earlier. And so finally from Warrenheip on a steep descending gradient of 1 in 52 for two miles, we came into Ballarat.

There was plenty of the 'wild west' atmosphere about Ballarat when the line from Geelong was completed in 1862. No elaborate mining equip-ment was needed to dig for gold; a pick and shovel, and powers of endurance were the prime requisites, plus—needless to say—a good deal of luck in choosing one's site. In the early days the diggings consisted very largely of innumerable one-man concerns, and much difficulty was experienced in the enforcement of such legislation as was passed by the State Parliament. Injustices and grievances led to evasion of licence pay-ments; adventurers 'cashed in' on the disorder, and less than eight years before the completion of the railway there had occurred the open revolt of a large body of 'diggers' involving the deliberate burning to the ground of the Eureka Hotel, the mass burning of licences, and the assembly within a hastily-constructed stockade of some 150 intrepid men, who defied the forces of law and order until their 'fortress' was attacked and demolished by a detachment of fully-armed troops. The establishment of railway communication with Melbourne had a pronounced effect upon the general tempo of life in the Ballarat goldfields, and the station itself in its imposing exterior was a visible sign of the advance of law and order into what had largely been a 'shack' community until then.

Today Ballarat station is a period-piece of the finest order. Its general *ensemble* can be viewed to advantage from the level crossing immediately to the west of the platforms. There are four running lines passing through, with two centre roads between the platform lines. An all-over roof in the best Brunellian style spans the entire layout. This is not a sumptuous arch in the style of Bristol Temple Meads, but rather an enlarged version of the design of roof to be seen at Exeter St. Thomas's. Controlling movement through the station is a fine example of a Victorian Railways semaphore signal gantry, and from the photograph facing page 193 it will be appreciated that all four roads are now signalled for both-direction running. The level crossing by which a main road intersects the railway is entirely English in its design and equipment, being fully gated, and gate gear interlocked with the signals. But it is above all the exterior that provides so magnificent an appearance. The style is grandly classical, in the fashion adopted for many public buildings in Australia in the latter part of the nineteenth century. Above the main entrance is a finely pillared portico surmounted by a tall clock-tower crowned with the cupola so greatly favoured in contemporary Australian architecture.

For twelve years Ballarat marked the westernmost extent of the line. At the same time it was realised that great benefits were to be derived from the provision of railway communication with the extensive western areas of the State, quite apart from any consideration of a trunk line through to the border of South Australia. The developing township of Hamilton, some 200 miles to the west of Melbourne, was then considered the immediate goal, and a great scheme-making ensued, with rival proposals of routes proceeding from the three nearest points on the existing railway system, namely Ballarat, Castlemaine on the north line to Echuca, and Geelong. A glance at the map is enough to show that a line running direct from Geelong was likely to produce the shortest route, and the easiest to operate; but it was not generally favoured because it was thought to be most susceptible to competition from seaborne traffic. At that time also, it must be borne in mind that the principal means of communication between Melbourne and Adelaide was by sea. In the event, all three routes to Hamilton were authorised, and the line westwards from Ballarat, which today forms part of the inter-state main line, was opened as far as Beaufort in 1874, and to Ararat in 1875. Subsequent extensions took this first-class main line north-westwards to Stawell, 76 miles beyond Ballarat by 1876; to Murtoa, $111\frac{1}{2}$ miles by 1878; and to Horsham, $129\frac{1}{2}$ miles by 1879. Ultimately the border station of Serviceton was reached in 1887, and through communication was then established between Melbourne and Adelaide. The South Australian Railways had

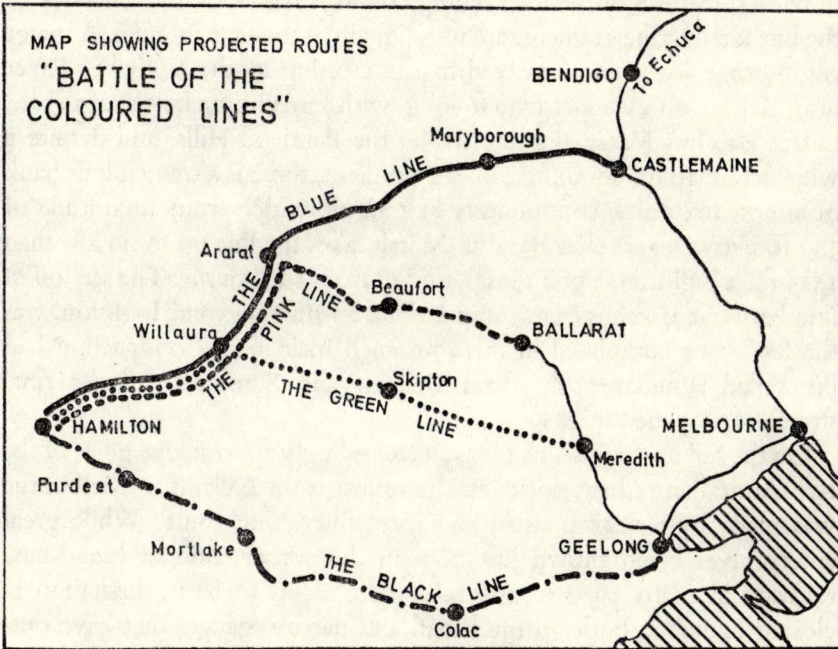

MAP SHOWING PROJECTED ROUTES "BATTLE OF THE COLOURED LINES"

Victoria: projected lines westwards from Ballarat and Geelong

adopted the 5 ft. 3 in. gauge for their main lines, and there was thus no 'break-of-gauge' problem at Serviceton. The route followed was via Geelong, and the length of run on the Victorian Railways, from Melbourne to Serviceton, was 308 miles.

For some time prior to the establishment of through railway communication to the South Australian border it had been realised that use of the original route between Melbourne and Ballarat would be a considerable handicap. The coastal route to Geelong was increasing in busyness, and with the addition of inter-state traffic congestion could well begin to

167

develop on this line. It was in many ways an analogous case to that of the original Great Western route to the West of England, via Bristol. So, in Victoria a new direct route was planned, running in virtually a straight line from Melbourne to Ballarat. From Melbourne itself the Bendigo–Echuca line was used as far as Sunshine, and then it traversed virgin country. While the general direction was certainly straight from one city to the other, some considerable deviations were necessary in negotiation of natural features of the intervening country. Although the tendency of the line is rising the gradients are not difficult in the first 30 miles. A major engineering work was involved in the crossing of the Werribee River near Melton, on a viaduct 1230 ft. long, with a maximum height of 125 ft.; but at Bacchus Marsh the line strikes the Pentland Hills, and despite a wide detour to the south, to ease the gradient, there is a tremendous bank of almost ten miles, continuously at 1 in 48, which from an altitude of 340 ft. above sea level at Bacchus Marsh takes the line up to no less than 1513 ft. at Ingliston, a point just 45 miles from Melbourne. The section of line between Bacchus Marsh and Ballan, $4\frac{1}{2}$ miles beyond Ingliston, was the last to be completed in this shortened main line. Construction had proceeded simultaneously from Ballarat and Sunshine and the final stretch was opened in 1889.

On the rail tour on which I was an exceedingly appreciative guest of the two Australian railway societies, the return from Ballarat to Melbourne was made by a very unusual and most interesting route. While great enterprise is being shown just now in the construction of brand-new railways in many parts of Australia there seems to be no hesitation in closing branches, both on the broad and narrow gauge, that have out-lived their usefulness and profitability. One of these was part of a cross-country line that ran almost due south from Ballarat to a junction with the Geelong–Port Fairy line at Irrewarra, near Colac. It is a noticeable characteristic of the Victorian Railway system that practically all lines feed ultimately towards Melbourne. The numerous branches converge towards the larger centres, such as Hamilton, Ararat, Bendigo, and so on, and from such the main lines themselves converge towards the capital. The line the route of which we were to trace was an exception. It made a cross-country connection between one radiating line and another, and it withered and died. In approaching this route however the tour-train, still hauled by the 'J' class engine No. 512, travelled by a branch line that

The Joy Ride: Puffing Billy crosses the Monbulk Creek trestle, near Belgrave, in 1969

is still very much alive, namely that which leaves the inter-state main line to Serviceton at Linton Junction about 2½ miles to the west of Ballarat.

Linton Junction is the beginning of the existing branch that extends for 34 miles to the south-west to Skipton, though a passenger service is now operated only as far as Newtown. This branch was an early development of railways in the Ballarat district; it was opened as far as Scarsdale, 14¼ miles from Linton Junction, in 1883, and at that time the junction was known as 'Scarsdale Junction'. This nomenclature provides an interesting parallel case to Great Western practice in England, where in many cases the originating point of branch lines were named after the terminus of the branch, rather than after some local association. Ashburton Junction and Tavistock Junction are instances that come to mind. The extension to Linton was completed in 1890, and this remained the terminus of the line for twenty-six years. It is a very pleasant run to Newtown, through the same kind of open upland country that we had traversed on the heavy climb up to Warrenheip, from Lethbridge; a mixture of bush and grasslands with much evidence in places of worked-out gold diggings.

Newtown was, until 1953, the junction for the cross-country line to Irrewarra, which we were to follow by road; but the tour train continued to Linton, to provide opportunity for an inspection of Smythe's Creek Viaduct, just over a mile beyond Newtown. This is a timber trestle in the American rather than the Brunellian style. The original structure was destroyed by fire in 1956, and in other circumstances this could have led to the closing of the line beyond Newtown; but such was the nature of the freight business conveyed from Skipton that the viaduct was quickly rebuilt, to the original design, and the line reopened. Arrangements had been made for participants on the tour to view the viaduct to the best advantage. The train crossed it, and then stopped, allowing those who wished to climb down, and scramble down the steep embankment to the creek below. In the meantime the train had been propelled back to the far side. After an appropriate time to allow the ciné and camera folk to choose their stances the train drew forward again, giving a splendid picture as it crossed the lofty viaduct. This was a typical example of the manner in which the Victorian Railways cooperates with the enthusiastic societies by the display, to the best advantage, of historical features of the system. So eventually we came to Linton, the present passenger terminus of the line. The extension of some 13 miles, to Skipton, was opened in 1916.

The cross-country branch line from Irrewarra to Newtown is now completely dismantled, though evidences of its route remain, in the earthworks and relics of station buildings, buffer stops, mileposts and such like. It began as no more than a branch from the Geelong–Colac line, extending only from its southern end at Irrewarra to Becac, $8\frac{3}{4}$ miles. This short length was opened in 1889. It was extended northwards to Cressy in 1910, a further $11\frac{1}{4}$ miles, and provided Cressy with its first railway communication, $111\frac{3}{4}$ miles, with Melbourne. The final link in this cross-country route, from Cressy to Newtown, was completed in 1911. Then however the railway strategy of this part of Victoria was completely changed by the construction, in 1913, of a new radiating feeder line, leaving the Geelong–Ballarat line at Gheringhap and running due west to intersect the Irrewarra line at Cressy and continue westwards for a further 66 miles to Maroona. The entire line from Gheringhap to Maroona was built in a single year, and from that time it can be said that the ultimate fate of the Irrewarra–Newtown line was sealed. As showing the piecemeal build-up it is interesting to recall that on the southern part of the line from Irrewarra the mileposts indicate the mileage from Melbourne via Geelong, while from Newtown, the mileage was via Bacchus Marsh and Ballarat. The two sets come together at Cressy, $111\frac{3}{4}$ miles via Irrewarra, and $117\frac{1}{4}$ via Ballarat. Against these two was the significant $85\frac{1}{2}$ miles via Gheringhap; and this latter, since 1953, has been the only way to go to Melbourne by train from Cressy.

CHAPTER FOURTEEN

'The Overland'

On a cold blustering Sunday night in early September, the climatic equivalent of an English March, a group of Australian friends foregathered
with our son and daughter-in-law at Spencer Street station to bid us
farewell from the eastern states; for now we were bound for Adelaide on
the first stage of our long railway journey right across Australia. We were
travelling by 'The Overland' express, which makes the run of 483 miles
between the two capital cities in an actual time of 12 hr. 50 min., though
because of the difference of half an hour between South Australia time and
that of the eastern States the journey time by the clocks at either end is
only 12 hr. 20 min. going west, though 13 hr. 45 min. going east. At the
moment there is evidently no traffic to demand a daylight service between
the two cities, as a counterpart to the 'Intercapital Daylight' on the Sydney–
Melbourne run. All the same 'The Overland' is an exceedingly heavy
train, and the collective enterprise of the various Australian railways is
such that a 'Daylight Overland' could easily be a possibility of the future
—particularly as the current slogan is 'See Australia by rail'.

Before leaving Melbourne some mention must be made of the connections between 'The Overland' and the Sydney expresses. It is certainly
indicative of the punctuality expected and achieved by Australian long-
distance trains that only 20 minutes is allowed between the arrival at
Spencer Street of the 'Intercapital Daylight' from Sydney, at 8.20 p.m.,
and the departure of 'The Overland' at 8.40 p.m. Clearly the 'Daylight' is not expected to be late! Eastbound, 'The Overland' also connects with the northbound 'Daylight', but at Sunshine, not the Spencer
Street terminus. At Sunshine there is a single platform on the standard-
gauge line to Albury, used specially for interchange traffic with the broad-
gauge line to Ballarat and the South Australian border. On the night of
our journey 'The Overland' was a very heavy train of sixteen coaches, and

171

weighing some 820 tons, was hauled by a pair of 'S' class diesel-electric locomotives coupled in multiple-unit. Prior to the introduction of the diesels the train was frequently run in two portions. Even so, it was nearly always double-headed. The sleeping cars, like those of the 'Brisbane Limited' by which we had travelled earlier in our tour, are beautifully appointed, and rode most comfortably.

One great disadvantage of air-conditioned carriages, to the railway enthusiast, which I was to experience in full measure at a later stage in our journey across Australia, is that one cannot open the windows. I can recall long hours of enjoyment spent with a camera at the open windows of South African trains. I must admit there would have been no inducement to open any windows during the early stages of our run with 'The Overland', or even to look out. It was a miserably wet night, and we learned afterwards that there was snow in Melbourne on the following day. So the late evening run to Ballarat, and our ascent of the Ingliston bank, went unrecorded. But this stretch of line is definitely one of those noted down as a 'must' in daylight for any future trip to Australia, like the mineral routes of Queensland, inland from Gladstone, Rockhampton, and Townsville, the coastal route up to Cairns and the westward continuation of the New South Wales main line beyond Lithgow. Country like that around Bacchus Marsh, that involves such a wide detour and a gradient of 1 in 48, must inevitably involve some splendid scenery. We were turning in for the night by the time 'The Overland' stopped at Ballarat, and after that we were conscious of nothing more than the vague incidentals of a good night journey until it was daylight next morning; and by then we were far into South Australia.

The first through passenger train service was inaugurated between Melbourne and Adelaide on 19 January 1887 as soon as the line to Service-ton was completed. Westbound it was known as the 'Adelaide Express' and eastbound the 'Melbourne Express', and for the first two years it ran via Geelong. It provided the first intercapital journey in Australia on which a change of train was not required at the State boundary, and indeed it remained the only one until as recently as 1930, when the standard-gauge line into South Brisbane was brought into service. It was in 1926 that the night service between Melbourne and Adelaide was named 'The Overland', as an historic reminder of the epoch-marking change that came over Australian intercapital communications when the overland route by rail between Melbourne and Adelaide was established, and completely superseded the previous methods, either by sea or by coach over the most primitive of country roads. Despite the establishment of through railway communication the boundary point between Victoria and South Australia remained very much of a 'frontier' for many years.

For one thing nobody then could be quite sure where the State boundary was! It had been agreed many years previously that the 141st meridian of longitude should mark the boundary, and a surveyor by the name of Tyers marked out what he thought to be the border in 1839. He had used three different methods of calculation to establish the actual position on the ground and got three different results! Two other surveyors marked new lines, but a check of their surveys in the 1860s revealed a discrepancy of two miles. Thus there arose a point of great dispute between the two colonies. Both claimed the two-mile strip of land running north and south, and this quarrel had many repercussions that came to affect the railway working at the border. In the disputed territory neither colony could legitimately assert authority. A man arrested by the Victorian police, for example, could claim he lived in South Australia. The two colonies imposed customs duties, and this of course led the colonists who felt so disposed to indulge in diverse brands of smuggling. The hard carefree life of the Australian 'outback' was ideal for the development of countless runs of contraband goods!

In the disputed territory was built the railway station of Serviceton. There was certainly cooperation in the design and layout of a station that was to be a major exchange point. The Victorian Railways placed the contract, and paid for the work; but then South Australia claimed that as the station was in the 'disputed territory' there was no certainty to whom it belonged, and they refused to pay any share of the cost until the border dispute was settled. Believe it or not, the matter was not settled until the year 1914, when the Privy Council found in Victoria's favour. Even then, it was not until 1917 that Victoria was reimbursed, by payment to her of South Australia's share of the original cost of the station. Today the cost of operating and maintaining the station and yard is met jointly by the two railways in the proportion of 56 per cent to Victoria and 44 per cent to South Australia. The actual border is now about $1\frac{1}{4}$ miles west of the station. Passed in the middle of the night Serviceton must be virtually unknown to the majority of present-day travellers, particularly those riding in air-conditioned coaches. Here, of course, engines and train crews are changed. The imposition of inter-state customs activities ended with the establishment of the Commonwealth of Australia in 1901, but conditions prior to that must have been pretty exciting at times.

An article in the *Victorian Railways Newsletter* of August 1969 was shown to me when I was in Melbourne, and in referring to Serviceton as 'The Station with Dungeons' the following vivid description of the underground premises, which are still accessible, is worth quoting in full:

They're musty, cobwebby, dusty; there are no windows and little natural light, and the only air comes from small metal ventilators. A section is propped up with wooden bearers to prevent cave-in.

In the cells area, a double row of little cubicles, separated by a passage way, is beneath and parallel to the Melbourne end of the railway platform. At the entrance are two small sections built as guard-houses.

Iron rings were once fastened to the brick walls so that prisoners could be secured, presumably by chains or handcuffs. The rings have long been removed by souvenir-hunters but the space they previously occupied can be seen.

Local opinion is that this unique jail held miscreants travelling interstate under guard. While most passengers had a meal in the refreshment rooms, prisoners were secured below, until train departure time.

Another suggestion is that the area was for solitary confinement that was necessary from time to time for the convicts that worked on the station buildings.

But it seems more likely that the prison was intended for smugglers caught in the act, because Serviceton was a border settlement where custom duties had to be paid in the 'eighties and nineties'.

Close to the cells area is a section believed to be the mortuary. It is an eerie chamber with pieces of wood on the stone floor, and cobwebs hanging from the rafters of the low ceiling.

A customs inspector had a section under Serviceton platform in another area. His duties were to prevent smuggling and to collect duties. Anyone caught evading payment was arrested and locked up to await trial.

Even the 11 South Australian Railways employees and their families had to pay customs duties to Victoria, up to 1890, after which business at the station was conducted by Victoria.

Such is the solid, typically nineteenth-century station by which 'The Overland' says farewell to Victoria, and starts away on the long run across the level coastal plain that extends practically from Bordertown to Tailem Bend, and the approach to the crossing of the Murray River.

Until reaching the disputed 141st meridian the Murray River, which we crossed between Albury and Wodonga, forms the northern boundary of the State of Victoria. It rises in the Snowy Mountains and flows westward for nearly 800 miles till it ceases to be the boundary between New South Wales and Victoria, and becomes a wholly South Australian river. And it is at Murray Bridge that this main line of the South Australian Railways begins to partake of a mountain character. In this direction of running too it is fortunately daylight by this time, so that the traveller who is astir can enjoy the beautiful scenery as the train makes its laborious and winding way through the Adelaide Hills. It is just over 60 miles from Murray Bridge to Adelaide, but it is mighty hard going for the locomotives, especially with such a load as 820 tons.

To appreciate something of the railway that I awoke in time to enjoy, a reference is first of all needed to the gradient profile. At Murray Bridge the line is only 53 ft. above sea level, whereas in the ensuing 60 miles it rises to 1613 ft. and then descends again to 78 ft. before its final gentle rise over the last $1\frac{1}{4}$ miles to 101 ft. in the Adelaide terminus. Although there is some heavy climbing facing westbound trains, the ascent to the summit point at Mount Lofty is spread over nearly 40 miles. Whereas on the western side of the hills in the 17·1 miles between Mount Lofty and Keswick there is a difference in altitude of 1526 ft.—an average inclination of 1 in 59. On both western and eastern slopes however the ruling gradient is 1 in 45, and although the climb from the Murray Bridge side includes two appreciable breaks, with lengths of steeply-falling gradient, these are of little use for increasing speed to rush the ensuing ascents as the curves preclude anything in the nature of normal express speed. The section throughout from Murray Bridge to Adelaide is thus a slow grind, requiring expert enginemanship both uphill and down. The line was built to synchronise with the extension of the Victorian Railways to Serviceton. The first $34\frac{1}{2}$ miles from Adelaide to Nairne were completed in 1883, and the continuation to Murray Bridge in 1886, ready for the inauguration of the through service to Melbourne in 1887. Originally it was single-track throughout, but the line was doubled as far as Mitcham, $5\frac{1}{4}$ miles in 1908; to Sleeps Hill, 7·4 miles in 1915; to Eden, 9·1 miles in 1919, and to Belair, 15·7 miles in 1928. The last-mentioned station marks the easternmost extent of the 'hill' suburbs of Adelaide.

From the sleeper, while the long train wound its way round curve after curve, I looked out on a fresh spring-like morning to a countryside that seemed largely given over to sheep farming. It was rough and upland, strongly reminiscent to me of the Craven district of the West Riding of Yorkshire, where so much of my boyhood was spent. From Callington, where we crossed the Bremer River, our twin-diesels seemed to be making heavy weather of it, but it was not until later that I discovered they were climbing on 1 in 45. After all, 820 tons is a mighty load, even when you have nearly 4000 horsepower to haul it, on such a gradient. Furthermore, on these gradients there is no compensation for curvature, and there were times when the long train was strung out round a full half-circle. The enormous 4-8-4 steam locomotives of the '500' class that preceded the diesels, and which had a tractive effort of 51,000 lb., were allowed a maximum load of 500 tons on this gruelling section through the Adelaide Hills. This section indeed led to the production of the most powerful steam passenger locomotives ever to take the road in Australia, and travelling over it behind 4000 horsepower of diesels I can well appreciate the reason why.

We passed Nairne near an intermediate summit point of more than 1200 ft. altitude, in country well befitting the Scottish name, and then came Mount Barker, the junction for a long branch line leading to the wide coastal lagoon of Lake Alexandrina, and to a terminus on Encounter Bay at Victor Harbor. We were running downhill for a time, on a stretch with a ruling grade of 1 in 50, and at 7.45 a.m. made a brief stop at Balhannah, which is the junction for another branch line that runs north-eastwards through the very heart of the Adelaide Hills to Mount Pleasant. Balhannah is the site of an interesting development in signalling on the South Australian Railways that I had an opportunity of inspecting thoroughly at a later stage of our tour. The countryside is very beautiful hereabouts, with pine forests in addition to the ubiquitous blue gum. One delighted in the variety of the station names, for the next one after Balhannah was Ambleside. A very severe climb follows through a mixture of orchard country and forest land. At one time the whole lengthy train seemed strung out round a long left-hand curve, and in a countryside very Scottish in its appearance, with the rough hillsides clothed with dead bracken in its beautiful golden colouring, the speed at one time fell to 10 m.p.h. So at 8 a.m. we drew into Bridgewater, where many passengers alighted.

We were now at an altitude of about 1300 ft., and on restarting entered

PLATE 27. The City of Melbourne: aerial view showing the extensive carriage sidings on the eastern approach to Flinders Street

PLATE 28. The Victorian 'R' class at work

(a) Engine No. 748 leaving Stawell, with a passenger train for Dimboola

(b) No. 748 leaving Flinders Street, Melbourne, with an A.R.E. tour special

upon the final stage of the climb. The distance was no more than 23 miles from Adelaide, yet nearly an hour's running still lay ahead of us. The country was delightful. Masses of yellow gorse in bloom coloured brilliantly the gum tree bush; we passed a most inappropriately named station —to an Englishman at any rate—Aldgate (!), and the diesels ground on up the 1 in 45, through a countryside of willow trees and daffodils blooming into profusion, till we came finally to Mount Lofty, where we stopped to set down passengers and to cross a three-car multiple-unit diesel train proceeding eastwards. Then at last we were turning downhill, when only 19½ miles from Adelaide and up at an altitude of 1613 ft. The hills are so thickly clothed with woodlands that no broad vistas are to be seen in the early stages of the steep descent. The speed was constantly being checked, as we rounded curve after curve; sometimes we came down as low as 10 m.p.h. negotiating rocky glens, and stretches where the virgin bush was interspersed with orchards and open common land golden with gorse.

At Belair the line becomes double-tracked and the hillsides are dotted with handsome villas. The altitude is still as much as 1000 ft. above sea level, but at less than 14 miles from the centre of Adelaide this lofty 'suburb' is becoming extremely popular. As yet however there are no more than glimpses of the plains below; the trees are still thickly clustered and tall growing. In making a way down this wooded hillside however one can quite well imagine how, for many years, it constituted a barrier against the westward extension of South Australian activities from Adelaide, and its railway development was in keeping with the development itself. It had been the fourth of the early settlements to be established as a colony following five years after Western Australia, in 1834, and preceding the establishment of Victoria as a colony independent of New South Wales by a full sixteen years. But to a remarkable extent South Australia remained isolated in its early days, and many attempts to establish communications to both east and west had been abandoned. In 1830 Charles Sturt, with a small party in a whaleboat, made their way down the Murray River in conditions of great privation, and eventually came to the lagoon near the sea which Sturt named Alexandrina Reservoir. But the country was then entirely devoid of white settlements; the natives though few in number were hostile, and the only way to make a safe return was by the way they had come, by rowing up the river. But Sturt had seen enough in the region of Alexandrina Lake to realise that there was a place suitable for a settlement, and only four years later the 'colony' was established.

Having got thus far, and settled upon the site of the future capital city, and named it Adelaide, in 1836, the settlers began to look towards development, and the natural course was to try and establish contact with their nearest colonial neighbours in Western Australia. Little did they then realise what lay between! In 1840 an expedition was fitted out to try and discover a route for stock between the two colonies. The explorer John Eyre searched for pastoral lands to the north, but finding none turned to the west. After suffering great hardship he returned to report that a desert, rather than land suitable for farming, divided South Australia from Western Australia. Three years later Charles Sturt set out to explore the centre of Australia. He found nothing but large tracts of virtual desert, where, as he expressed it, 'sandy undulations' succeeded each other like waves of the sea! His companion's comment was even more forceful: 'Good Heaven, did man ever see such country!' So the colonists of South Australia found themselves encompassed on all sides, by desert to the north and west, and by a densely-wooded and inpenetrable mountain to the east, and elsewhere by the sea. Beyond the mountains little was known of the country stretching eastwards, and in those early days the free settlers of South Australia had little desire to associate with colonies like New South Wales and Van Diemen's Land, which had grown out of convict settlements. So South Australia settled down as a tight little community of its own, and its early railway development clearly reflected this situation.

It was in July 1852 that the 5 ft. 3 in. gauge was adopted as the standard for New South Wales, and Victoria and South Australia were not only informed, but warned that any departure from this standard would incur severe penalties! I have told earlier in this book what happened in New South Wales, but South Australia played to the rules, and her first railway, a seven-mile line along the coast between Goolwa and Port Elliott, was duly laid to the 5 ft. 3 in. gauge even though the motive power was by horse. This was in May 1854. The first steam railway was opened between Adelaide and Port Adelaide in 1856, a distance of no more than $7\frac{1}{2}$ miles. This little line, similar to the Williamstown railway on the outskirts of Melbourne, and the Sydney and Parramatta Railway, was typical of the modest beginnings of railways in the Australian colonies; but in Adelaide it was symbolical of the hopes and subsequent disappointments of the early days of the colony. It was in 1852 that the Peninsular and Oriental Steamship line first operated a mail service between England and Australia, and on the first homeward journey in September of that year the *Chusan* called in at Adelaide, on her way from Sydney and Melbourne back to Singapore. This caused great satisfaction at the time, because certain people had averred that the anchorage at Port Adelaide was not suitable for the ocean-going ships, even though the *Chusan* was an armed merchantman of no more than 699 tons. Satisfaction nevertheless gave place to deep disappointment, because Adelaide was not continued as a port of call in the first mail contracts, despite the establishment of railway communication between the port and the city in 1856. It was not until 1874 that Adelaide was included in the regular mail-run schedules.

Thus South Australia remained isolated by land and sea. The mail service was maintained by a seaborne connection between Adelaide and Albany, in Western Australia, and railway communication began to extend through the pastoral lands to the north of Adelaide towards the mining centre of Broken Hill, just across the New South Wales border. All this early history could well be most vividly in mind as 'The Overland' made its cautious way down the steep descent from Mount Lofty, and one could reflect upon the astonishing change that has come over communications in considerably less than a hundred years. In a single night, in the luxurious comfort of a 'roomette' cabin, we had made the journey over what was virtually an unknown land; and when it comes to sheer speed only a week earlier our daughter-in-law, returning from an inter-state hockey festival, had left Adelaide after a comfortably late breakfast, and arrived in plenty of time for lunch with us at Essendon Airport, Melbourne. Nevertheless, to the business man, or to folk like ourselves who had a big programme of daytime engagements and sightseeing, 'The Overland' has a great advantage, in its relatively late departure from Melbourne, and arrival in Adelaide at 9 a.m. We certainly found a very full round of activities awaiting us on our arrival.

In the meantime the train was working its way down the gradient. At Blackwood, passed at 8.43 a.m., the station yard was full of commuters' cars parked for the day. As at home, parking is an immense problem in the heart of Australian cities, and the majority of regular travellers leave their cars at the local stations. At Eden Hills, where the altitude is down to 595 ft., we had our first glimpse of Adelaide, remarkable in that we were

179

now only nine miles from journey's end. We were still in very rough and hilly country however; deep cuttings and a tunnel cut off the view, and then at last we came fully into the open. The suburban stations now came in rapid succession and how familiar to us from the United Kingdom were many of the names! Lynton, Clapham, Torrens Park, Mitcham, Hawthorn, Goodwood. At the latter station we made a junction with the main line from the north, and the track is quadrupled over the last few miles. Keswick and Mile End followed—strange neighbours to an Englishman—and so we eased gently into Adelaide to arrive dead on time at 9 a.m.

PLATE 29. Victorian railway viaducts

(a) A freight train crossing Melton Reservoir Viaduct

(b) A typical trestle viaduct, on the Ballarat–Linton branch, Smythe's Creek

(a) 'F' class 2–4–0, originally of 1873, as running in 1914

(b) 'R' class 0–6–0 goods, as running in 1914

(c) 'D' class small-wheeled 4–4–0 of 1887, as rebuilt in 1912

(d) 'Dd' class 4–6–0, express engine of 1902

(e) 'M' class 4–4–2, originally 4–4–0s introduced 1878–86, as later rebuilt

(f) 'Y' class 0–6–0 of 1888

(g) 'New A' class express passenger 4–4–0 of 1889

(h) 'V' class 2–8–0 Vauclain compound goods

PLATE 30. Vintage Victorian steam

CHAPTER FIFTEEN

South Australian steam power

From what I have written in the previous chapter it can well be imagined that the steam locomotive did not undergo any very rapid development in South Australia during the latter part of the nineteenth century. Before the line to Serviceton was built there had been no more than 106 locomotives on the 5 ft. 3 in. gauge, of twenty-one different classes. Many had been picked up second-hand. Two came from the ill-starred Melbourne and Essendon Railway, and others from the Canterbury Railway in New Zealand. Down to the year 1884 by far the most numerous was the 'K' class 0-6-4 tank, designed and built by Beyer, Peacock and Company in 1879, and incorporating that firm's characteristic shapes of chimney and dome cover. Connoisseurs of Irish locomotive practice will however immediately notice the likeness between these engines and the 0-6-4 tanks of the Sligo Leitrim and Northern Counties Railway, introduced in 1882. The Irish engines were indeed a direct adaptation of the original design for South Australia, easily practicable because both had the same gauge. The S.A.R. 'K' class had coupled wheels 4 ft. diameter, whereas in the Irish development this diameter was increased to 4 ft. 9 in. There were eighteen of the S.A.R. 'K' class. They were used on mixed duties, including a fair amount of local passenger service around Adelaide.

In view of the construction of the line across the Mount Lofty range, and its opening in 1883, it is remarkable to find that no new locomotives were immediately purchased. It seems evident that very little traffic was expected until the link-up with the Victorian Railways at Serviceton was established. The only appreciable addition to the stock in the intervening years was the Class 'P' 2-4-0 suburban tank engine. Six of these came from Beyer, Peacock's in 1884, and a further fourteen were built in South Australia, by Martins. New power for the inter-state traffic was introduced

in 1885-6 in the form of two new classes: an inside cylinder 4-4-0 with
16½ in. by 20 in. cylinders and 5 ft. 1 in. coupled wheels, known as
Class 'Q'; and an outside cylindered 4-6-0, Class 'R', with 18 in. by 24 in.
cylinders and 4 ft. 6 in. coupled wheels. The original examples of both
these classes came from Dübs, in Glasgow, though subsequent additions
were built by Martins, in South Australia. There were eventually 22 of the
4-4-0s and 30 of the 4-6-0s. The latter engines worked on the mountain
section between Adelaide and Murray Bridge, and the 4-4-0s from there
onwards to Serviceton. Both were tiny little things, even by contemporary standards. The 4-4-0s had a tractive effort of no more than 11,800 lb.
and the 4-6-0s of 17,700 lb., but they were no doubt adequate to deal
with the light loads then prevailing.

In 1894 a much larger and more powerful 4-4-0 design was introduced,
known as Class 'S'. This had 18 in. by 24 in. cylinders, and coupled wheels
as large as 6 ft. 6 in. diameter. It was intended to make considerably faster
running on the north main line between Adelaide and the break-of-gauge
station at Terowie, and also on the inter-state main line between Murray
Bridge and Serviceton. These new engines, which were entirely a South
Australian product, were of typically British appearance, with straight
running plates, large, deep coupled wheel splashers, finely-proportioned
boiler mountings and a large bogie tender, that had a strong likeness to
that of the Caledonian Dunalastair class 4-4-0s of the second, third, and
fourth series. A distinctive Australian feature was the cab, the roof of
which was extended forward almost to touch the safety-valve lever, and
backwards to provide shelter from the fierce noonday sun over the footplate of both engine and tender. They were smart working, as well as
smart looking engines, and frequently exceeded 60 m.p.h. in passenger
service. The 4-6-0s were rebuilt in 1899 as Class 'RX' with improved
boilers carrying a much higher pressure, of 175 lb. instead of 145. The
tractive effort was thereby increased to the more useful figure of 21,420 lb.
A further 54 engines of this design were added to the stock between 1909
and 1915; but these, and the 18 'S' class 4-4-0s of 1894, were the *only*
broad-gauge main line engines possessed by the South Australian Government Railways until the arrival of Mr. W. A. Webb as Chief Commissioner of Railways from 1922 onwards.

Before describing the astonishing transformation that was wrought in
a very short time, I must mention the handsome 'F' class 4-6-2 tank

engines introduced in 1902 for the Adelaide suburban services. It would not be true to describe these engines as a tank engine version of the 'R' class 4–6–0, because they had considerably larger coupled wheels, 5 ft. 3 in. diameter, and a different wheel spacing. They were neat and workman-like engines, and put in many years of hard work. At the time of writing none of the original total of forty-three remain on the register. In addition to these however it is good to record that a number of locomotives are preserved in the Museum of the Australian Historical Railway Society at Mile End, including one of the 'P' class 2–4–0 tanks of 1884, a 4–6–2 tank, and one of the 'RX' class 4–6–0s. There are of course a number of more modern engines the remarkable story of which must now be told.

In the middle of the year 1922 a new Railway Commissioner was appointed in South Australia. His name was W. A. Webb, and he came from the U.S.A. It is no exaggeration to say that in Australia the name of Webb became as widely known, honoured, and respected as that of his namesake in the British railway world of the nineteenth century. Railwaymen and enthusiasts alike speak of the 'Webb era' in South Australia and discuss its points as freely and frequently as their counter-parts in the United Kingdom talk of the 'Webb era' on the London and North Western Railway at Crewe. W. A. Webb was a colossus among Australian railwaymen. He found the South Australian Railways run down, under-equipped, with its management in a mood of resigned complacency. The motto then could well have been: 'It can't be done.' But Webb was as astute a diplomatist as he was an experienced and dynamic administrator. He did not stamp around saying that everything and everybody was wrong, and that they had better change their ways—or else——! He studied the railway and its running in all its aspects for the best part of six months, and then he acted, swiftly and incisively. Here, of course, I am concerned only with his impact on the locomotive stock; but his action there was symbolical of his general attitude towards modernisation.

The 'RX' class 4–6–0s were rated to a maximum load of 190 tons on the severe gradients through the Mount Lofty ranges. This was no mean tonnage for an elderly 4–6–0 seeing that the uncompensated gradients of 1 in 45 were equivalent to 1 in 37 on the worst curves. The Chief Mechanical Engineer who had held office during the war years, B. J. Rushton, had been asked to provide a locomotive that would take double that load. This was a very tough assignment, seeing that there was then no prospect of using heavier axle-loading than the 18 tons previously laid down as a maximum on main lines. Rushton did a lot of exploratory work, including consideration of a Garratt. The last-mentioned system of articulation had its origin in Tasmania, and Australian men in general regarded it much more favourably than their contemporaries in South Africa, for example. But whatever was considered Rushton eventually came out with the answer that it could not be done. How seriously the management pressed it, and how seriously the challenge was taken, one cannot say now; but so far as doubling the tractive power was concerned, nothing more enterprising, nor modern than two 'RX' engine units built into the Garratt style would have provided the necessary tractive power. The simple outcome however was that nothing was done, and when Webb arrived from the U.S.A. the Melbourne express was taken over the mountains by a pair of 'RX' class 4-6-os. The standard of performance on the easier stretches may be judged from the caption to a picture in *The Railway Magazine* in 1909, which showed 'The Melbourne Express at full speed (about 40 m.p.h.)' Rushton was due for retirement in 1922, and in his place there was appointed a young engineer of thirty-two, F. J. Shea, who took office early in 1923.

About the turn of the year Webb announced to the press that vast new engines were to be introduced in South Australia, and, laying down the conditions of working between Adelaide and Murray Bridge, he wrote to a number of firms in England and Scotland, as well as in Australia, inviting suggestions for five new types. The result of these early investigations narrowed the projected new types down to three, 4-8-2, 2-8-2, and 4-6-2, and Shea set about the detailed designing. It was a tremendous step for a railway that had previously run nothing bigger than 4-6-os with a tractive effort of little more than 20,000 lb. to embark on the design of new types with tractive efforts varying between 35,000 and 55,000 lb. It is true that Shea had visited Canada and the U.S.A. at the end of World War I, and had seen for himself the size and power of contemporary American locomotives; but it is one thing to see, and to ride on large locomotives, though quite another to work out the detail design and take full responsibility for the working of such a vast change from previous practice. With the designs completed tenders were called for from British, Canadian, United States, French, Belgian, Czecho-

184

slovakian, as well as Australian firms. There was local concern, even at this stage, that the contracts might go outside Australia; but in the event all the original offers were rejected, as their prices asked were considered by Mr. Webb to be much too high.

Webb and Shea together went through the various tenders, and picked out a short list of firms, who were asked to re-quote, it being pointed out to each the highly competitive nature of the business. Again the local press voiced its concern, and when a contract for ten of each type, 4-8-2, 2-8-2, and 4-6-2, was placed with Sir W. G. Armstrong-Whitworth and Co. of Newcastle-on-Tyne, England, a perfect storm of protest blew up. Among the trade unions and in Parliament, supporters of South Australian firms raised the proverbial 'hell'. The press, ever ready to take a knock at the Government and always violently critical of the railways, joined in with the utmost zest. It seemed of little concern to these opponents of Mr. Webb that the best local price was *seventy-three per cent* higher than that of Armstrong-Whitworth, and that in reality the local firms had neither the plant nor the capacity to build engines of such size —let alone in the time required by Mr. Webb. The character of the new Commissioner was never shown to finer effect than these critical days. Ignoring all the fuss he confidently recommended the Government to confirm his acceptance of the English tender, and on Tyneside the thirty huge engines were duly built.

It is indeed interesting that the contract *did* go to Armstrong-Whitworth's. The firm had embarked on locomotive construction after World War I, when the sudden end to munition production and of big guns left the Elswick factory desperately short of work. It was a venturesome move to go in for locomotives against such highly experienced competitors as the North British, Vulcan, and Beyer, Peacock's, to say nothing of near neighbours like R. & W. Hawthorn Leslie, and Robert Stephenson's; but at that stage the enterprise of Armstrong-Whitworth's was boundless, and they went so far as to announce that they intended to make their Elswick plant the largest locomotive manufactory in the world. Hearing of this ambition I remember a British railwayman asking if 'A.W.' had heard of Baldwin's in the U.S.A.; and if they indeed intended to grow bigger than that vast plant they were presumably making plans to move the River Tyne in order to get the necessary space! Size of the works apart however, Shea's 4-8-2s were among the largest and heaviest non-articulated engines ever built in the United Kingdom, and even though public opinion had to some extent been prepared for them by Webb's carefully organised publicity campaign, when they did arrive they created an absolute sensation.

Just imagine on the one hand a little 4–6–0 with two 18 in. by 24 in. cylinders, of 1899 vintage, with an all-up weight of 89 tons, including its tender, and on the other the first of the enormous '500' class 4–8–2s, with cylinders 26 in. diameter by 28 in. stroke, 84 ft. long from buffer to buffer, and weighing 213 tons. The tractive effort was 51,000 lb.—nearly two and a half times that of an 'RX' 4–6–0. Never, surely, in all railway history had there been such a staggering step-up in power. One can think of many instances where locomotive engineers have advanced from the 4–4–0 type to the 4–6–0; from the 4–4–2 to the 'Pacific', and similar enlargements where the tractive effort has gone up 50 per cent or there-abouts. In the English idiom, it was as though Doncaster had gone straight from a Stirling 2–2–2 to a Gresley 'Pacific', or Crewe had jumped from a Webb Precedent 2–4–0 to a Stanier 'Duchess'. It goes almost without saying that Shea had some teething troubles with his great new engines. It would have been little short of a miracle if he had not done, and need-less to say exaggerated accounts of some of these troubles appeared in the press. But taken all round the new locomotives were an outstanding success.

Although designed by an Australian engineer, and built in England, their characteristics were almost entirely American, both in their general appearance and in major details of the design. To accommodate them on the line much relaying of track had been necessary. The maximum axle-load had been increased to $22\frac{1}{2}$ tons, while the cross-sectional profile of the locomotives had been enlarged, over the vintage 'RX' class, to such an extent that they fitted the single-line tunnels 'like a glove'—as one critic expressed it. The confined space around them in the tunnels was one cause of complaint from the enginemen; exhaust fumes, which previously passed freely past the cab, came seeping in, and making things unpleasant on the footplate. The 4–8–2s of the '500' class had enormous grates of 66 sq. ft., and they were equipped with mechanical stokers. I believe that these engines were the first ever to be built in the United Kingdom with mechanical stokers. The apparatus installed was of Ameri-can manufacture, particularly specified by Mr. Shea. Although so profoundly different from anything they had handled before, the South Australian drivers and firemen took them readily, and they were soon justifying all that was hoped for by taking 500-ton loads over the mountains without assistance. This was an increased tonnage in rough proportion to the increase in tractive effort, and it virtually abolished double-heading—for some time at any rate.

The original contract placed with Armstrong-Whitworth also included ten freight engines of the 2-8-2 type, with a maximum axle-load of 18½ tons—as in the 'RX' 4-6-0—and a tractive effort of 40,400 lb., and ten 'Pacifics'. These latter were designed for the relatively level run onwards to Serviceton. In Webb's day the locomotive divisional point was at Tailem Bend rather than Murray Bridge, and over this eastern section the new 'Pacifics' were rostered to haul trains of 575 tons without assistance. Over the mountains the maximum Pacific load was only 270 tons. But with locomotives in the form of the new 4-8-2s capable of taking 500 tons between Adelaide and Tailem Bend, and 'Pacifics' for the easier run, the South Australian Railways had, through the enterprise of Commissioner Webb and the designing skill of Mr. Shea, leapt into the very forefront of maximum Australian steam power. That all the new engines looked highly American in outward appearance was no matter. In the design and construction they were a first rate Anglo-Australian job.

The mastery they showed over the earliest tasks given to them was however not enough for the South Australian Railways. Mr. Webb wanted to work still bigger loads over the mountains, and Mr. Shea set to work to make provision for boosters on both the 4-8-2s and the 2-8-2s. The booster engine chosen was contained in a four-wheeled truck, and the experimental application to one of the 2-8-2s having been successful the 4-8-2s became 4-8-4s, and the 2-8-2s were developed into 2-8-4s. In the case of the 4-8-4s the tractive effort with the booster in operation became no less than 59,000 lb. and this enabled the train load over the mountain section to be increased from 500 to 540 tons. On the more level stretches of the Northern Line, between Adelaide and Gawler, the booster-fitted 4-8-4s were now able to haul trains of 2500 tons. The English-built 2-8-2s also did very good work, and when more heavy freight engines were needed, in 1927, authority was given for the construction of ten more. It was a matter of the utmost gratification in

Adelaide that these new engines, Nos. 710 to 719, were built at the workshops at Islington. With a tractive effort of 40,400 lb., they were the most powerful engines that had been built in Australia up to that time. The booster was applied in this design to the two-wheel trailing truck, and when operating increased the tractive effort by 8000 lb.

These engines were designed to operate on rails weighing no more than 60 lb. per yard, and the effect of the heavy axle-loading on the booster-fitted trailing truck was such that the civil engineer stipulated that in further heavy freight engines something must be done to reduce the axle-loading if operation over 60 lb. rails was to be continued. Mr. Shea then produced the really amazing '720' class, with the 2-8-4 wheel arrangement, a maximum axle-load of $19\frac{3}{4}$ tons, and a tractive effort with the booster in operation of 52,000 lb. The '720' class, with a wheel-arrangement known in the U.S.A. as the 'Berkshire', could at first glance have easily been mistaken for the mammoth power of some American railroad, so completely American was their appearance, and so vast their bulk. They too were built at the Islington Works under the direction of Mr. Shea, and their success, coupled with his development of the English-built 4-8-2s into the booster 4-8-4s, certainly puts Fred Shea among the very top rank of Chief Mechanical Engineers of the steam era, not only in Australia, or even in the British Commonwealth, but anywhere in the world. The 'Berkshires' with their lighter axle-loading had not the same haulage capacity as the booster-fitted 4-8-4s over the mountain section, being limited to 450 tons; but they were permitted to work onwards to Serviceton, and over that section their load was no less than 1100 tons. The first five of the 'Berkshires' were built in 1930-1; six more in 1938-9, and the remaining six in 1942-3.

The year 1936, centenary of the foundation of Adelaide and of South Australia itself, was marked by the appearance of F. J. Shea's last locomotive design, and the decking of the 'Overland Express' in new colours. All over the world the craze for streamlining was spreading to the most unlikely locomotives and trains. American locomotives, long characterised by plain black painting and a plethora of gadgets hung on outside, were being smartened up and painted in bright colours. The Victorian and South Australian Railways jointly agreed for the coaching stock of the 'Overland' on a livery of bright green, with thin parallel stripes of black and gold at the top and bottom, and in hauling such a smart turn-out it

PLATE 31. Victorian and South Australian steam

(a) S.A.R. 'S' class 6 ft. 6 in. 4–4–0 of 1894, with a huge tender heavier than the engine

(b) V.R. One of the famous 'A2' class 4–6–0s now at North Williamstown Museum

(c) S.A.R. 'RX' class 4–6–0, at Mount Lofty in 1935

PLATE 32. Victorian signalling

(a) Control Panel at Melbourne Yard, West Tower

(b) Installing the new relay-interlocking console (right) at Camberwell, alongside the pistol-grip power frame previously in use

was realised that monster all-black engines, however impressive to the railway enthusiast, would hardly be in keeping with the coaches. It is true that booster 4–8–4s were not nearly so festooned as the majority of their American contemporaries; but they were plain all over. That was enough.

In the brightening-up appearances the South Australian Railways once again followed American styles, and in particular that of the Southern Pacifics on the large 4–8–4 locomotives used for hauling the 'Daylight Express' between San Francisco and Los Angeles. The Southern Pacific in applying a degree of streamlining, accompanied it with a garish array of crimson and yellow paint, which, although eye-catching to the last degree, was not very dignified. The South Australian Railways also adopted the deep, stylishly-curved valance, but merely put a false cladding over the boiler to hide all the pipes, leaving the chimney, dome, safety-valves and sandboxes exposed. In outline the engines looked neater, and as though having slightly larger boilers. The basic colour remained black, but the newly added valances were painted a handsome shade of green, and the smokebox fronts were treated with aluminium paint, in the manner of the Southern Pacific 'Daylight' engines. On the South Australian Railways the 4–8–4s henceforth became known as the 'Palefaces'. It was with these dressed-up locomotives that naming began in earnest on the S.A.R., adopting the titles of leading personalities in railway and transportation circles. In their final form the 4–8–4 engines of the '500' class continued to bear the brunt of the work on the mountain section between Adelaide and Tailem Bend for a further sixteen years, including the gruelling period of World War II. Their retirement and withdrawal began in 1956, after the introduction of diesel traction, though fortunately one of these splendid and historic locomotives is preserved in the Museum of the Australian Railway Historical Society at Mile End.

On the outbreak of war in 1939 Shea was asked to undertake Government work in connection with the management of aircraft production, and F. H. Harrison became Acting Chief Mechanical Engineer. He was later confirmed in this appointment, and it fell to him to design an entirely new class of 4–8–4 locomotive. While the 'Webb era' had provided a limited number of locomotives of outstanding power, and capability for the heaviest main line working, reliance was still being placed to a re-markable extent on the very elderly 'RX' 4–6–0s for much intermediate working, and towards the end of World War II these were run down to almost the limit of useful service. In considering the design of Harrison's new 4–8–4s a characteristic of steam locomotives that is diametrically opposite to that of diesels must be borne in mind. The latter are at their most efficient when worked at full power. It therefore pays to have units of no more than moderate power, and couple them in multiple when heavier work is needed, when the combined unit can still be operated by a single crew. A steam locomotive however loses little of its efficiency when it is under-run, so in many circumstances it is advantageous to have large locomotives capable of high maximum power output, which can still be used with reasonable efficiency on lighter duties. I have felt it was necessary to expand a little on this point, because many photographs of the Harrison 4–8–4s in action show them hauling quite light trains.

The new engines were designed for running at 70 m.p.h. on track laid with 80 lb. rails and 45 m.p.h. on 60 lb. rails. A tractive effort of 32,000 lb. was required, and to achieve a satisfactory ratio of tractive effort to adhesion weight, within the limitation of axle-load to a maximum of $15\frac{3}{4}$ tons, eight coupled wheels were essential. Harrison had taken a leading part in the designing and production of the giant locomotives of the Webb–Shea era; he was a first-rate mechanical engineer, and the '520' class, as the new engines were known, was a beautifully-balanced design making clever use, amid the strictures of wartime conditions, of modern materials and techniques to secure maximum tractive effort for a minimum of weight. In conformity with popular trends in styling, the new engines had to receive a degree of streamlining. As first schemed out the smokebox front was to be 'bullet-nosed', after the style of the New York Central 4–6–4s then used on the 'Twentieth Century Limited'; but before the design of the '520' class was finalised the highly distinctive Pennsylvania 4–4–4–4s of the '6100' class appeared, and the styling of the '520' class was closely modelled on these latest American mammoths.

The first of the new S.A.R. 4–8–4s was completed at Islington Works in 1943, and was named '*Sir Malcolm Barclay-Harvey*,' after the Governor of South Australia. The name will be familiar to students of Scottish railway history, for Sir Malcolm was the author of a very interesting pre-war book on the Great North of Scotland Railway. In Australia he took the greatest personal interest in the production of the '520' class, and this interest was once the underlying cause of a very amusing *contretemps* in the C.M.E.'s office. In South Australia the naming of locomotives was a

190

fairly new departure, and the attitude of the staff appears to have been quite different from that which had prevailed in the United Kingdom for generations past. Here, on the majority of railways little notice was taken of individual names, particularly when the process became so systematised as it did on the Great Western in the Castle—Hall—Manor—Grange days. A running man might have at his fingertips the merits or foibles of '5098' or '4933', but ask him about *Earl of Eldon* or *Caradoc Grange* and he would almost certainly have to check their numbers before replying. In South Australia apparently it was different, and I quote the following story from one of the fine publications of the A.R.H.S.

One day Frank Harrison called in his clerk and said, 'Find out for me where Barclay-Harvey is.' The clerk replied 'Yes, Sir' and returned to his office. About an hour later he returned to Harrison's office and said, 'Sir, I have rung up Government House and Parliament House and made other enquiries but nobody seems to know where Sir Malcolm is.' 'Stone the lizards, Jack,' replied Harrison, 'I meant the b—— engine *Sir Malcolm Barclay-Harvey*.'

Continuing in a slight digression I must add that the reverse process can equally have its pitfalls, as the Southern Railway of England once learned to their intense embarrassment. The Spanish Ambassador of the day was something of a locomotive enthusiast, and when he was travelling, either officially or otherwise, he always made a point of going forward to see the engine. On this occasion the Southern received advance notice that he would be travelling up from Dover by one of the boat trains. An engine in specially good condition was allocated to the job, but until the train arrived in Victoria no one thought to check up on the name. It was *Sir Francis Drake!*

In South Australia the '520' class were very successful, and twelve of them were built between November 1943 and December 1947. Their most usual run was between Adelaide and Port Pirie. In their heyday the prospect of conversion of some non-standard gauge lines to the 4 ft. 8½ in. gauge was actively in consideration, while the provision of enhanced power for the Commonwealth Railway crossing the waterless Nullarbor Plain was also in hand. Harrison was Technical Assistant to the Commonwealth Railways and was responsible for maintenance and operation of locomotives and rolling stock on that line during the war. His 4 ft. 8½ in. gauge version of the S.A.R. '520' class was a most interesting project, but it never materialised. In contrast to the actual '520' class built at Islington the Commonwealth variety would have had 6 ft. diameter coupled wheels, instead of 5 ft. 6 in., a boiler pressure of 250 lb. per sq. in. against 215, and an engine weight of 138 tons against $111\frac{1}{4}$. To provide for running across the 'Plain' enormous tenders carrying 17 tons of coal and 18,000 gallons of water were proposed. For the 60 lb. rail stretches of the S.A.R. the corresponding loadings were 5 tons of coal and 8200 gallons of water. The estimated weight of these tremendous engines was 298 tons. With mention of these engines however the story of the 'giant era' of steam motive power in South Australia is already ended, and it is time to look at the lines leading north towards that remarkable system, the Commonwealth Railways.

PLATE 33. Famous Australian stations

(a) Spencer Street, Melbourne, in 1872

(b) The border station at Serviceton, today

(c) Albury: the imposing exterior at time of first opening

PLATE 34. Ballarat, Victorian Railways

(a) The classical exterior

(b) View from level crossing, showing signal bridge, gates, and all-over roof to station

CHAPTER SIXTEEN

Adelaide and lines north

At the close of a long journey, especially when much of it has been made in hours of darkness, no one except perhaps the most dedicated, perfervid railway enthusiast is in much of a mood to study track configuration and general railway layout at his place of arrival. I must admit to sentiments of this kind when we first came to Adelaide, though I was vaguely conscious that we were rather boxing the compass in the last few miles. But then, when travelling anywhere south of the Equator my sense of direction never seems to become fully attuned to the fact that the sun 'moves the wrong way' across the sky, and at noon stands due north! It was only on making closer acquaintance with the fine terminal station that I realised in coming from Melbourne we had made a clockwise half-circle round the city of Adelaide and when we coasted up to the buffer stops we were travelling due east. Boxing the compass indeed! But then of course the line up to Mount Lofty and onwards to the Victorian State boundary was one of the later lines to be built in South Australia, and it used the terminus built to serve older railways, heading west and northwards from the city. This also explains why of the six running lines curving northwards at first from the terminus the left-hand pair are the 'south lines'; the centre pair are for Port Adelaide, and the right-hand pair are the 'main north' lines.

There is surely no group of lines in the whole of Australia that has undergone greater changes in its relative importance, or more rapid evolution in the last seventy years than the network that began to fan out from the junction of Salisbury ten miles to the north of Adelaide. Three maps have been prepared, showing the situation in 1905, 1925, and 1970. Referring to the first of these the broad-gauge system north of Adelaide was of very limited extent, consisting only of the main line to Terowie, $139\frac{3}{4}$

SOUTH AUSTRALIA   NEW SOUTH WALES

OODNADATTA

MARREE

SILVERTON   BROKEN HILL
COCKBURN

PORT AUGUSTA   QUORN

PETERBOROUGH
PORT PIRIE   TEROWIE
GLADSTONE

BRINKWORTH
WALLAROO
MOONTA BALAKLAVA   MORGAN
PORT WAKEFIELD

VICTORIA

ADELAIDE
MURRAY BRIDGE

SERVICETON

KINGSTON

3' 6" GAUGE

4' 8½" GAUGE

5' 3" GAUGE

MOUNT GAMBIER

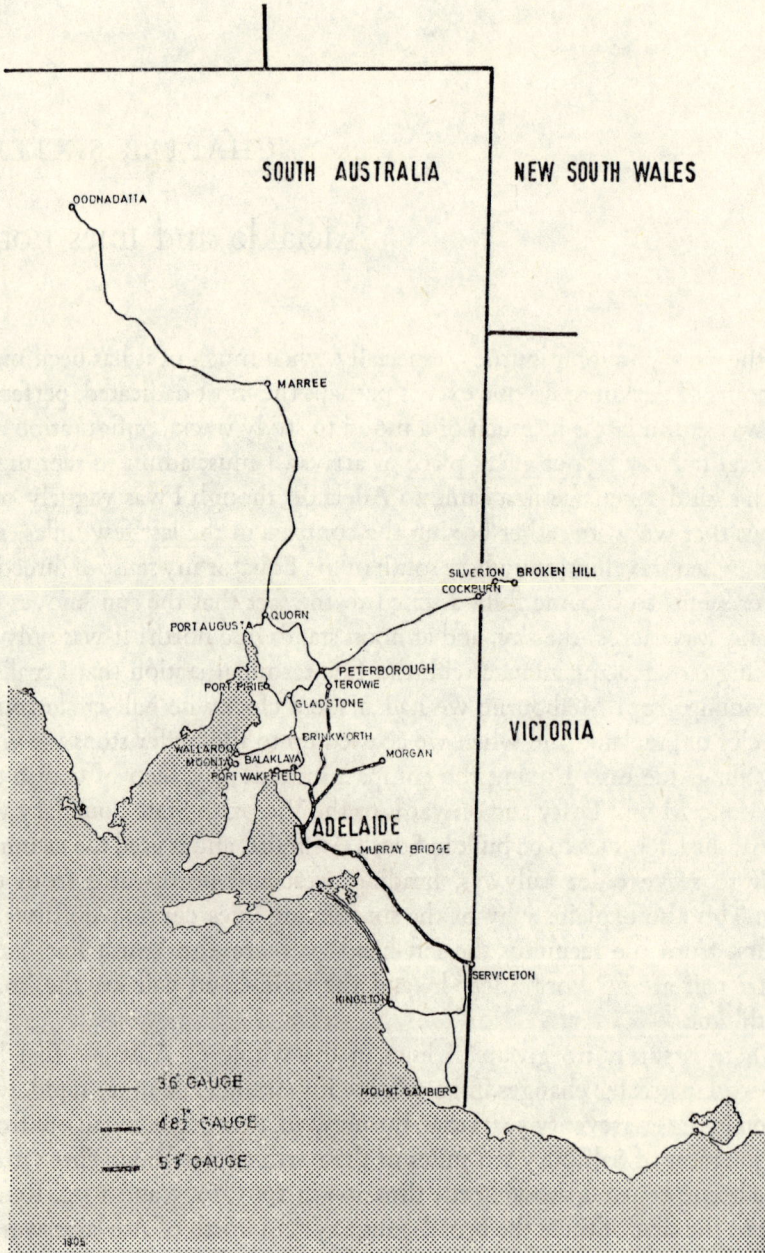

Adelaide and lines north—1905

194

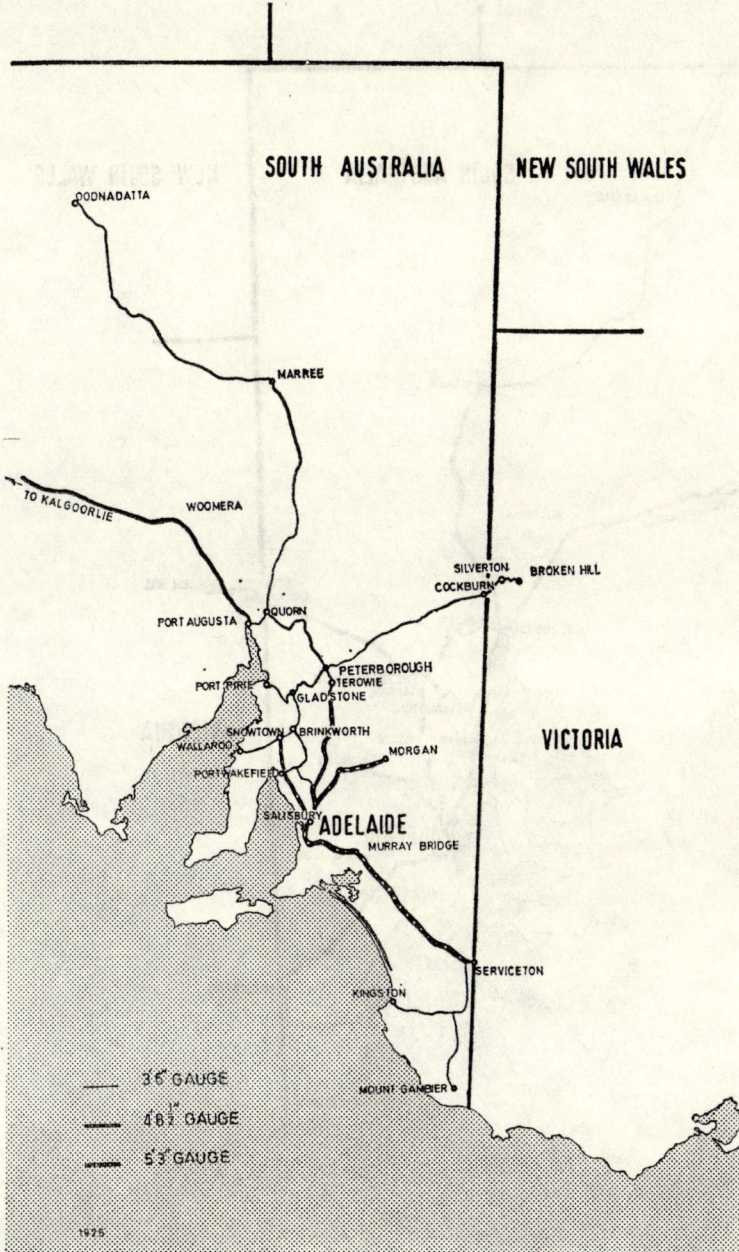

Adelaide and lines north—1925

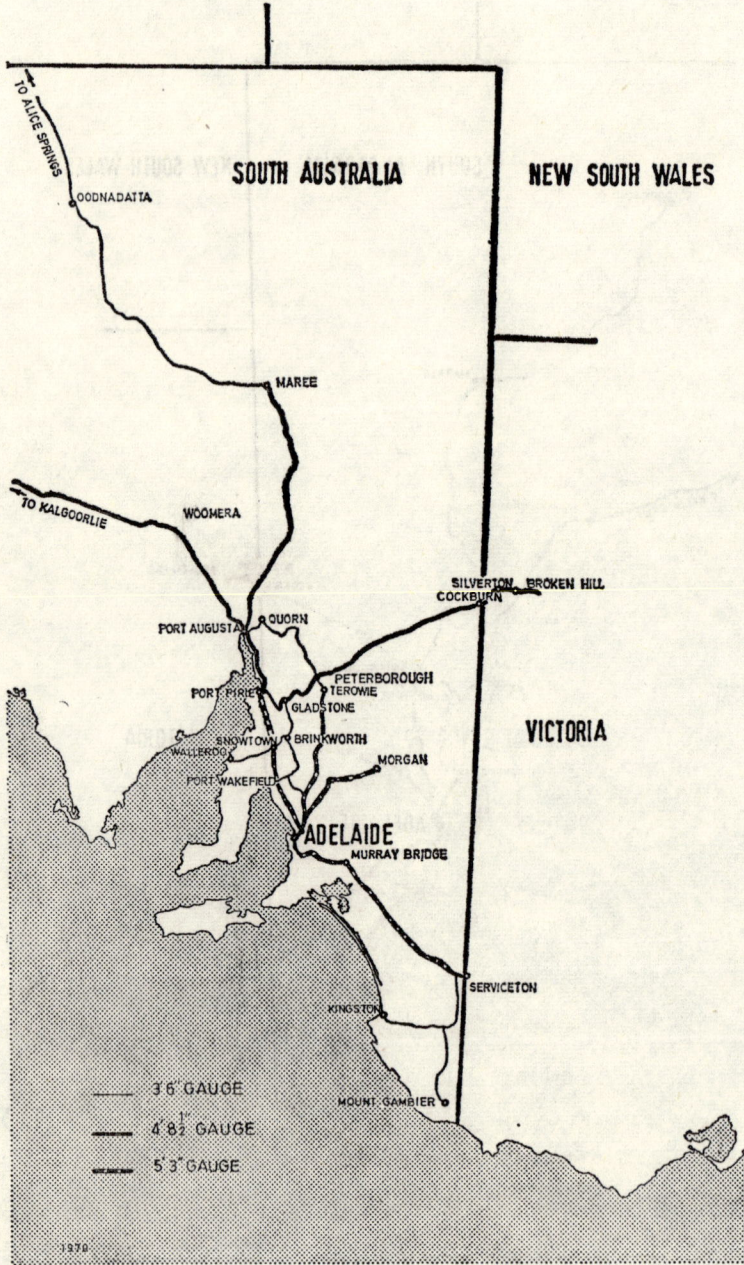

Map labels:
TO ALICE SPRINGS
OODNADATTA
SOUTH AUSTRALIA
NEW SOUTH WALES
MAREE
TO KALGOORLIE
WOOMERA
SILVERTON BROKEN HILL
COCKBURN
PORT AUGUSTA QUORN
PETERBOROUGH
TEROWIE
PORT PIRIE
GLADSTONE
SNOWTOWN BRINKWORTH
VICTORIA
WALLEROO
MORGAN
PORT WAKEFIELD
ADELAIDE
MURRAY BRIDGE
SERVICETON
KINGSTON
MOUNT GAMBIER

3' 6" GAUGE
4' 8½" GAUGE
5' 3" GAUGE

1970

Adelaide and lines north—1970

196

miles, and the branch from Roseworthy to Morgan. Both main line and branch traversed a rich agricultural countryside, but to a stranger it might seem strange that the broad gauge stopped short at what was then a mere hamlet, at Terowie, instead of pressing on over the remaining 14½ miles that would have brought it to the important cross-country junction of Peterborough, or Petersburg as it was known until World War I. Actually however the line from Terowie to Quorn was built before the Peterborough–Cockburn line; and it was not until the latter line was built that Peterborough became a junction. It is indeed astonishing to recall that until the year 1937 Terowie was a 'break-of-gauge' station on the Trans-Australian route, and that any through passenger between Adelaide and Perth had an additional spell on the 3 ft. 6in. gauge between the 5 ft. 3 in. of South Australia and the 4 ft. 8½ in. of the Commonwealth line!

Even in 1925 Terowie seemed no more than a 'back of beyond' station. Its photographs then showed the air of one of those remote junctions in the west of Ireland where some fascinating period piece of a narrow-gauge line connected with a sparsely-used branch of the Great Southern. But these South Australian lines were built to convey the produce of the land, rather than to provide through transcontinental connections. When no more than 25 miles out of Adelaide it turned away from the level coastal plains and climbed towards the Camel Hump Range. After changing from 5 ft. 3 in. to 3 ft. 6 in. gauge at Terowie the climbing eventually brought the line into Peterborough at an altitude of 1747 ft. above sea level. There the main north line intersected the historic cross-country line running from the New South Wales border at Cockburn to the then isolated rail-head of Port Pirie, on the Spencer Gulf. This 252-mile stretch of single line was originally constructed to form an integral part of the working of the great mines at Broken Hill. Coal and supplies of all kinds were needed for the working of the mines, and an outlet other than that by rail was needed for the products. Thus Port Pirie was established as a deep-water port nearest to Broken Hill, and a smelting works set up there; and over the intervening railway there flowed a highly-profitable reciprocal traffic —coal and supplies one way, the products of the various mines the other. Those who had constantly in mind the need for unification of rail gauges in Australia saw clearly enough that this line could well form an important stage in some transcontinental main line of the future. It is however only at the very time of writing this chapter that this long-anticipated project

197

has been achieved. This great event in Australian railway history is described in a later chapter.

At the time of the formation of the Commonwealth in 1901 two transcontinental lines were freely discussed; the east–west route from Port Augusta to Kalgoorlie, and a north–south route from Port Darwin to Port Augusta. A considerable stretch of the latter line was actually constructed under the administration of the South Australian Government, and was then known as the Great Northern line. At the turn of the century there was a weekly passenger service between Adelaide and Oodnadatta. A contemporary writer describes the journey thus:

Like few similar places, this part of the Australian continent possesses a charm which the most experienced and gifted writers have found hard indeed to describe. A passenger leaving Port Augusta by the morning train on a journey northwards for the first time, gains a unique experience of the Australian 'bush'. As the train gradually travels away from the more settled parts and passes over the lengthening gaps between each pair of stations, the quietude, in conjunction with the wide flat plains extending as far as the eye can see, mile after mile, and the most matter of fact traveller finds himself surrounded with an atmosphere which might almost be termed romance. The line consists of single track with sidings at the more important stations, and continues in this way right to the terminal station, Oodnadatta, a distance of 688 miles from the capital. . . .

The distances on the northern section of the railway between the stations frequently extend over twenty miles, and there are numerous parts of the journey, which, by being dead straight for many miles, would be a happy hunting ground for locomotive records, were they encountered on British lines. From near Ediowie, a station 310 miles from Adelaide to a point near Blackfellows Creek ($341\frac{1}{2}$ miles) there is the longest straight run in the State, a length of $34\frac{1}{2}$ miles.

The above was of course written many years before the construction of the standard-gauge Trans-Australian Railway, with its record-breaking straight length of 297 miles. One can however appreciate the writers' somewhat wistful longing for a little British speed on the journey to Oodnadatta, at a time when the journey from Adelaide took the whole of three days, with full overnight stops at Port Augusta and Herfott Springs. In distance the successive 'laps' were $259\frac{1}{4}$ miles, $181\frac{3}{4}$ miles, and 247 miles. Although an early start was made each day the staging points for the night's break were not reached until around 8 p.m. In referring to the map of 1905 it will be noticed that the first break was made not at the junction station of Quorn, but at Port Augusta, presumably on account of the lodgings available to travellers. The actual travelling time for the 737 miles from Adelaide to Oodnadatta via Port Augusta was 38 hr. 10 min., an average speed of 18 m.p.h. I would very much have liked to travel over this line, and its present continuation to Alice Springs, but unfortunately time did not permit of a trip, despite the incomparably faster journey times of today. Nowadays the run from Adelaide to Port Augusta takes only a matter of 5½ hours, instead of all day, and the 12.30 p.m. service from Adelaide, which runs twice a week, reaches Oodnadatta at 10.7 a.m. next morning. It takes another twelve hours to do the further 293 miles on to Alice Springs.

In mentioning train services on what is now called the Central Australian Railway, and is part of the Commonwealth system, I have drawn well ahead of my period, and I must now retrace steps from Quorn over the old 3 ft. 6 in. gauge line to Terowie, negotiate the break of gauge and continue southwards to Hamley Bridge, the starting point of the former 'Western' system of branch lines all originally on the 3 ft. 6 in. gauge. Their principal value in the 1905–15 period was to provide direct rail communication between Adelaide and the twin seaports of Wallaroo and Port Pirie. The latter was then reached by a junction with the Broken Hill line at Gladstone. These 3 ft. 6 in. gauge lines served some of the finest agricultural land in South Australia, and the significance of this is underlined when I recall that in the early days of this century South Australia was often referred to as 'the granary of the Southern Hemisphere'. Such of this traffic as was consigned to the capital or farther east, had to be worked via the 'break-of-gauge' station at Hamley Bridge, and at that period such aids to transportation as mechanised handling plants did not exist.

By the mid-1920s, while the 3 ft. 6 in. gauge system north of Terowie remained much the same, a notable extension of the broad gauge had been made by the construction of a direct line from Salisbury running almost due north, and cutting through the territory intersected by the 3 ft. 6 in. gauge lines spreading north-westwards from Hamley Bridge. By the year 1926 the new line extended to a junction with the cross-country 3 ft. 6 in. gauge line from Brinkworth to Wallaroo, at Snowtown; but even then

199

construction of the next stage onwards to Red Hill was in hand, and the final length into Port Pirie followed, reducing the distance from Adelaide to the former junction to 134 miles. The extension of this line into Port Pirie was only the prelude to the extension of the standard-gauge Commonwealth line southwards from Port Augusta into Port Pirie, 56 miles, and thus making possible, from 1937 onwards, a notable acceleration of the journey between Adelaide and the west. The old circuitous route via Terowie, Peterborough, and Quorn was then superseded by the direct run from Adelaide to Port Pirie, and making one change of gauge only from the 5 ft. 3 in. to the 4 ft. 8½ in.

The former Great Northern Line of the South Australian system is now part of the Commonwealth Railways, and as far as Maree, 213 miles from Port Augusta, it is laid to standard gauge. The method of working is considerably changed from that of former days. On two days a week the connecting service to the 12.30 p.m. from Adelaide leaves Port Pirie at 4.15 p.m., half an hour ahead of the Trans-Australian sleeper, but this train for the Great Northern line does not actually enter Port Augusta, but enters upon the Central Australian route at the junction of Stirling North four miles short of Port Augusta. The through carriages from Port Augusta are worked separately to Stirling North, and there marshalled into the train from Port Pirie. On the northern line Maree is reached at 10 p.m. and passengers there change into the 3 ft. 6 in. train, which is fully equipped with sleeping cars. Dining cars are now run throughout between Port Pirie and Alice Springs. Even with modern facilities however, and allowing no more than one day for sightseeing at the northern end of the line, it takes five days to travel from Port Augusta to Alice Springs and back.

Steam traction is virtually at an end in South Australia, but before passing on to modern running conditions on the lines north of Adelaide, I must refer to the locomotives that operated the 3 ft. 6 in. gauge lines prior to dieselisation. In later days the brunt of the work was borne by the class 'T' 2-8-0s which date back to 1903. They were neat and handsome engines, of typical British appearance, although they were wholly designed and all built in Australia. The cylinders, mounted outside, were 16½ in. diameter by 22 in. stroke; the coupled wheels were 3 ft. 7 in. diameter, and with a boiler pressure of 185 lb. per. sq. in. the tractive effort was 21,900 lb. At one time there were 84 of them at work, but six were sold

American influence: No. 500, dressed in the semi-streamlined style of the Southern Pacific's 'Daylight' trains, heads a freight near Eden Hills, South Australian Railways

to the Tasmanian Railways in 1920–1 and another five were converted for use on the 5 ft. 3 in. gauge. It is no small tribute to the excellence of the design and the standards of maintenance that they handled the whole of the mineral traffic in the Port Pirie–Broken Hill line for nearly fifty years.

In the last years of steam operation a number of Garratt articulated engines were used, but the first introduction was most unsatisfactory. This is perhaps an appropriate place to tell the story of the unfortunate Australian Standard Garratts, designed and built in frantic haste during World War II. The onset of war with Japan threw a heavy additional burden on to all the Australian railways, and new locomotives were most urgently required for the freight traffic. The Beyer–Garratt type was an obvious answer, because of its ability to provide high tractive effort for low individual axle-loading. At the time however Beyer, Peacock's were fully committed with large orders for the British Ministry of War Transport, and since the Western Australian Government works at Midland had built Garratts for their own use, the task of producing the new engines was allocated to them. Then, most unfortunately, personalities seem to have entered into it. From their world-wide experience Beyer, Peacock's must have had many designs that could have been used, practically without change. In normal times a locomotive engineer would naturally stipulate features of his own preference, and while taking full advantage of the experience of the manufacturers the engine would have something of a new look; but in wartime one would have thought that the nearest design existing could have been accepted, and built in the railway shops.

Instead of taking this seemingly obvious measure to obtain maximum additional engine power as quickly as possible, the then Chief Mechanical Engineer of the Western Australian Government Railways chose to design an entirely new Garratt in his own drawing office. Now the outstanding success of the Beyer–Garratt type in its later years was due to the gradually mounting wealth of experience in design, manufacture, and running of these big engines. Against this the drawing office at Midland was rushed, in shipwreck hurry, into a new design, vastly bigger than the smart little 2–6–0+0–6–2 'Msa' class, built in 1930. To stampede the entire design of these new engines through the drawing office in no more than three months, and then to sub-let much of the constructional work to numerous firms, was a gesture more heroic than expedient. The result was a near-disaster. An order for sixty-five was authorised, but by the beginning of

201

1945 only thirty-three had been completed and these were giving trouble. Some were allocated to Queensland, where they quickly earned a bad reputation; in Western Australia they were detested by the men, and when in 1951 the South Australian Railways purchased four of them as a stop-gap measure for use on the Port Pirie–Broken Hill mineral trains they ran them for less than a year.

The folly shown in trying to design something new was revealed by the subsequent action of the South Australian Railways. Still convinced that a Garratt was the right answer for this heavily-graded route they approached Beyer, Peacock's in 1952, and ultimately obtained ten splendid engines which were practically identical to the East African Railways '60' class. The only difference was that the Australians were to the 3 ft. 6 in. whereas the Africans were metre. It is interesting to recall however that both varieties were designed to be convertible in gauge. The E.A.R. class could be readily altered to 3 ft. 6 in. while the S.A.R. class could be converted either to 4 ft. 8½ in. or 5 ft. 3 in. Like their African counterparts these 4–8–2+2–8–4s were fine-looking engines, having a tractive effort of 38,400 lb. Even in 1953 however Beyer, Peacock's were not able to undertake the construction themselves, and these ten locomotives were built by sub-contract by the Société Franco-Belge at Raismes in France. They did excellent work, but due to the rapid onset of diesel traction their life was relatively short and by 1967 they had all been taken off main line work. I saw one of them on shunting duties at Port Pirie in 1969 in company with one of the old 4–8–0s.

I have written of the Port Pirie–Broken Hill traffic, but actually the South Australian Railways did not operate over the whole distance. Broken Hill lies 35 miles east of the State boundary, and in early days Adelaide wished to follow the precedent established on the Victoria–New South Wales borders to the east where several branch lines of the Victorian Railways crossed the Murray River and extended into New South Wales territory. But the New South Wales Government would have none of this at Broken Hill, and instead a private company, the Silverton Tramway, was authorised, to run between Broken Hill and the S.A.R. railhead at Cockburn. The line was opened on 2 January 1888, and this small private concern proved the most profitable railway in Australia. It was on this line that four large 4–8–2 locomotives of the Western Australia 'W' class were purchased, in 1951, from Beyer, Peacock's. One of these is now preserved at the narrow-gauge museum on the 'Puffing Billy' line at Menzies Creek. Although their life was short, they had a tremendous job to do on the Silverton line. The ore trains were marshalled into 1200-ton loads, and worked thus to Cockburn, where the S.A.R. Garratts took over. In 1961 these fine engines were superseded by the inevitable diesels; but now this line has been replaced by a new standard-gauge line on a new location from Broken Hill to the South Australian border, and this forms part of the Trans-Australia line from Sydney to Perth. Although lying 35 miles across the State boundary, the mining centre of Broken Hill is some 360 miles nearer to Adelaide than to its own State capital, Sydney, and a thrice-weekly passenger service is run via Peterborough, using South Australian stock.

Some interesting examples of the evolution of signalling practice are provided on some of these South Australian lines. When such highly sophisticated modern techniques are being introduced on railways of intense traffic and exacting operating conditions one is inclined to dismiss areas where perhaps the process of evolution is not so advanced, or where the traffic would not justify expenditure on electronic remote control, or similar modern methods. The skill of a railway engineer, whether dealing with locomotives, signalling, or rolling stock is not necessarily measured by the elaboration or magnitude of his works—sometimes, very much the reverse. One would regard with nothing but contempt a chief mechanical engineer who put large streamlined locomotives and sumptuous air-conditioned carriages on to a remote country branch line! So it is also in signalling. The working of the Cockburn–Port Pirie new standard-gauge line is a case in question. With single-line, heavy gradients, and long distances between passing loops this would at first sight seem to be a case for centralised traffic control in the style of the Victorian Railways standard-gauge line from Melbourne to Albury. There is however a vast difference in the density of traffic, and so the signalling arrangements have been designed as a kind of 'halfway house' between working with telegraphic train orders and a very minimum of fixed-signals, and full centralised traffic control, working the whole line, maybe, from a single panel, as in the case of the Melbourne–Albury line. The system actually installed goes by the general name of 'Absolute–Permissive Block'.

Historically it is a much older system of single-line working than C.T.C. and it was evolved in the U.S.A. when the need was felt to extend the advantages of automatic signalling to certain single-tracked routes. When using nothing except telegraphic train orders a certain degree of inflexibility can obtrude into the workings, where passing loops are far apart and one might have a succession of trains following each other in the same direction. While each of these might be given orders to proceed there was always the unsatisfactory alternatives, either of holding the second train until the preceding one had reached the next passing place, or allowing it to proceed after a certain time interval. With the first alternative, where passing places might be twenty miles apart the second train could be held for anything up to three-quarters of an hour, while with the second alternative there was always the risk of the second train making better time than the first, closing in upon it, and in conditions of bad visibility or restricted view of the line ahead in mountainous country proceeding to the extent of a rear end collision. The system known as 'Absolute-Permissive Block' was designed both to expedite train movements and provide greatly increased safety, while the timetable, amended as required by telegraphic advices, remained the basic method of train movement control.

The line is track-circuited throughout, and for opposing movements the block working is 'absolute'. That is, if an opposing train is in the single-line section the starting signal for a train travelling in the reverse way cannot in any circumstances be cleared. This, of course, is fundamental. In the long single-line sections a number of intermediate signals are installed. These operate like ordinary automatic signals on double-line, clearing sequentially as the previous train progresses through the section. With this facility, if there should be two or more trains following in fairly rapid succession in the same direction they can be permitted to follow as soon as the preceding train has cleared the intermediate signal next ahead. One could therefore have two or perhaps three trains following close after each other, all in the same twenty-mile single-line section, in complete safety, because each would be working to signal indications. Thus the name arose: 'absolute' for opposing traffic; 'permissive' for following traffic. Actually the system used for following trains is not what is normally understood by 'permissive' working on British lines. Permissive working is in force on certain slow-running freight lines where trains are instructed to proceed as far as the line is clear, and drivers crawl ahead until their engines are almost touching the rear of the train ahead. This method is used in automatic signal territory on double-line in South Australia. The great advantage of installing the 'absolute-permissive block' system on the Cockburn–Port Pirie line of the South Australian Railways is that the track-circuiting and signals can form the basis of a future C.T.C. installation when traffic increases to the extent that centralised control of all movements becomes necessary, in order to obtain maximum utilisation of the line.

In explaining the decision to put in 'absolute-permissive block' on the Cockburn–Port Pirie line I have referred to the economic factors involved, and the necessity to relate expenditure on signalling to the likely financial returns from such an investment. But there are certain aspects of railway working that cannot be measured in terms of hard cash, and one of these is the improved running and punctuality of trains. The coordination possible by grouping together in one signal box functions that previously were worked from a number of smaller boxes, eliminating the telephone conversations between signalmen, possible misunderstandings, and occasionally a little awkwardness that inevitably arises when individuals are working on their own and in isolated circumstances, is an advantage frequently stressed by operating men. Yet such concentrations cost money, and it is not always possible to justify the outlay in the possible savings of wages of operating staff. The experience of other railways may have been related in glowing terms in the technical press, but the published experience of others is no substitute for the hard experience of trying out the job oneself. While in Adelaide I was taken to see what I can only describe as a 'model' installation of a push-button electric interlocking at Balhannah, a delightful spot in the Mount Lofty Range on the main line to Melbourne. As a signalling installation it is no more than small; but it is beautifully designed and installed, and with the operating advantages already demonstrated it can well be the pattern for general signal modernisation on the busier lines of the State.

All too soon it was time to leave South Australia, and after a final burst of typical hospitality we boarded the 12.30 p.m. express for Port Pirie with no more than minutes to spare. Once again I had a privileged 'front seat' in the engine cab, this time on one of the English Electric '900' class diesels, put into service in 1951. Apart from their smartly-coloured livery these locomotives are similar in appearance to the familiar 'D200' class on British Railways, with the characteristic 'nose'-cab. The S.A.R. examples have the nose-cab only at one end, and are designed for working in multiple if need be, with two units back-to-back as we had experienced on the 'Overland' express. With a load of only 287 tons however only one diesel was needed. The locomotive was finished in a livery of red and creamy white, and the carriages have a colour that I can best describe as 'Furness' red. For those readers who are not familiar with the liveries of lesser English railways that 'red' was very appropriately the colour of iron ore, so much of which was carried by the Furness Railway in its heyday. Striking out northwards through the Adelaide suburbs, there are many level crossings, and our progress was at first slow. Signals obligingly checked us to 10 m.p.h. abreast of Islington Works, where I had a good sight of the lightweight streamlined Pacific No. 621 standing outside. This class, of which there were ten examples, was a 4-6-2 forerunner of the lightweight 4-8-4s of the '520' class.

After passing Islington we got going briefly at 50 m.p.h. but several checks for track relaying followed. On this stretch I noticed that the mechanical signal boxes have deep sunshades as one sees in Egypt and India; and so after twenty minutes' running we came to Salisbury, where our line diverged to the left from the old double-tracked main line to Terowie. Now we headed out into open, very flat country. The track was straight, and we worked easily up to 60 m.p.h. At some of the passing loops we slowed down to 30 m.p.h. because this fairly busy single line is worked on the electric staff system, and the exchange of staffs was done by hand. In this open country it was interesting to see the unusual width of the railway property. Enough land had been fenced off to provide a quadrupled track at some future time, if need be; and our single line in the centre seemed rather lost. Even while I was in Australia however consideration was being given to the building of a standard-gauge line from Port Pirie into Adelaide so that through working would be possible from Adelaide to Perth, both for passengers and freight. Whatever may eventuate in this respect, there is certainly plenty of space for a standard-gauge line alongside the 5 ft. 3 in. gauge line in this wide open countryside. Across the farmlands there was a fine backward view of the Adelaide Hills piling up towards the Mount Lofty Range. What I did notice also was a fine highway running parallel to the line between Virginia and Two Wells, and that it seemed quite deserted.

On a journey like this one naturally studies large-scale maps to see what lies to right and left of the line beyond that which can actually be seen from the train; and while we were standing at Kallora, awaiting line clear for a section ahead occupied by a freight train, I found we were lying almost exactly halfway between two townships named respectively Inkerman and Balaklava. One can only assume that some of the early settlers here were veterans of the Crimean War. We overtook the freight at Bowmans, where the route of the old 3 ft. 6 in. gauge line from Hamley Bridge to Wallaroo intersects the present line, and then continued to right of the Hummock Range into a very pleasant countryside of gentle rolling downland. There were sheep everywhere; at the stations were grain silos and as we headed north we left behind the springlike 'English' weather of Adelaide, and continued under cloudless skies. At some stations we saw double-decker sheep wagons, and alongside were double-decker loaders, so that both top and bottom decks could be filled simultaneously. At Snowtown we crossed the corresponding southbound train, which had connected with the Trans-Australian express leaving Perth on two evenings previously. It was hauled by another English-Electric diesel locomotive of the same class as our own. For the last stage of the run to Port Pirie, about 45 miles from Snowtown, I went back to the train and enjoyed the passing scene across the splendid wheatlands from the comfort of an open saloon carriage. The countryside is mostly quite flat on this stretch, though far away to the east was the line of hills in which Terowie lies. So, across the flats from Nurom we came into Port Pirie. We were a little behind the booked time of 3.48 p.m., on account of the delays experienced *en route*; but it had been a good journey and it was a pleasant farewell to the South Australian Railways.

CHAPTER SEVENTEEN

The amazing Trans-Australian line

To many readers of railway literature and particularly to those with a taste for the exceptional and the curious, Port Pirie will be known as the station where there was not only one break of gauge, but *two*; the place where trains on the 5 ft. 3 in., on the 4 ft. 8½ in., and on the 3 ft. 6 in. gauge could be seen simultaneously alongside. It was not always so, because the 4 ft. 8½ in. was a fairly late arrival; and it may seem a little strange at first to realise that this proliferation of gauges was in fact a very important step towards the elimination of one of the most serious and inconvenient breaks of gauge in all Australia. In the previous chapter I have told something of the build-up of the railway network to the north of Adelaide and how the rails were carried as far into the Northern Territory as Oodnadatta, with the aim eventually of getting through to Port Darwin. But today it is at Port Pirie that the journey westwards from Adelaide undergoes such a dramatic change. The station has been completely rebuilt since the days of the old three-gauge layout, and in a different location. but even so it still looks a rather unlikely place to be the starting point of a great transcontinental express.

In crossing the wide platform from the pleasant 5 ft. 3 in. gauge train that has brought us from Adelaide, one meets at once the portentous air of one of the truly great trains of the world. There is a long line of magnificently-appointed sleeping cars, at the doors of which stand smiling attendants, who in their very bearing embody that combination of travel experience, courtesy, and service that one meets on the 'Orient Express', on the 'Blue Train' in South Africa, or on 'Le Mistral'. But this is Port Pirie, out on the coastal flats of the Spencer's Gulf—not the Gare de Lyon, or Johannesburg Central! Near at hand are miles of sidings; an old 4-8-0 and a Beyer–Garratt locomotive are shunting, and there are works in the

PLATE 35. South Australian steam power

(a) The 'Overland' Express—Adelaide to Melbourne—at Eden Hills in 1951, hauled by '500B' class 4–8–4 No. 502

(b) Victor Harbour train near Lynton, hauled by lightweight 4–8–4 No. 526

PLATE 36. South Australian Railways: an A.R.H.S. special at Long Gully, hauled by 2–8–2 locomotive No. 700

distance. There seems to be no 'town' as such, and to the west are glimpses across the broad waters of the gulf. But to return to the 'Trans-Australian Express', some of the sleeping cars are of glittering stainless steel; others, equally impressive, have a terra-cotta coloured finish with the initials C.R. in huge raised stainless steel characters. 'C.R.' indeed, for we are now leaving the Government-owned systems of individual states and passing on to the Commonwealth Railways. And in stepping aboard this tremendous train of nineteen coaches, with its two diesel-electric locomotives coupled in multiple-unit, we are about to ride the rails of one of the greatest romances of modern transportation.

In the last decade of the nineteenth century, when in the British Parliament Joseph Chamberlain was Secretary for the Colonies, there was much talk of federating the individual Australian colonies into a single entity. I need not dwell here upon the many issues upon which opinion was divided among the colonies, except to say that for some time Western Australia stood resolutely apart. It was nevertheless felt strongly that without her federation could not be a success, and the inducement was offered that if she joined in the Federal Government would construct a railway to connect the easternmost railhead of Kalgoorlie to the South Australian system. One wonders now if the full implications of that offer were appreciated at the time; but with this and other assurances Western Australia came in, and the Commonwealth was inaugurated on New Year's Day 1901. Between Kalgoorlie and the nearest point on the South Australian system at Port Augusta there lay more than a thousand miles of virtually unexplored territory. The inhabitants were a relative handful of aborigines. In the whole history of Australian colonisation the few white explorers who had not met with disaster had returned with utterly negative results, convinced that the prospects for development were hopeless. Yet it was across this territory that the Federal Government was committed to build a trunk line of railway!

It is not surprising that it took a long time to get things going. Many years earlier the camel had been imported into Western Australia, and it was on camels that the first prospectors set out. More elaborate explorations were made with 'four-in-hands', the four being camels; and little by little the route was established. Much of the intervening country was so relatively flat, and so completely devoid of physical features and human habitation, that the line could be made completely straight for literally

o

hundreds of miles. It was however not until the year 1911 that the Federal Government approved the expenditure, and on 14 September 1912 the first sod was cut with great ceremony by the Governor-General of the Commonwealth, Lord Denman, at Port Augusta. No great engineering difficulties in construction had been anticipated. There were no great rivers to cross, no mountain ranges, with difficult cutting and embankment works—and of course, no tunnels. The problems were of a different kind altogether. In the entire 1051 miles between Port Augusta and Kalgoorlie there was not a single running stream, and the provision of water supplies for the construction gangs was perhaps the greatest undertaking of all. Wells had to be sunk, bores and reservoirs constructed, and as the line gradually advanced the task of maintaining supplies was enormous. Never in the history of world railways had a trunk line of such tremendous length been built through a country so completely lacking in natural aids. In crossing the American middle-west railway pioneers had to deal with wild animals and fiercely hostile Indians; but on the Trans-Australian line there was nothing—absolutely nothing!

The Commonwealth Railways Department had to organise the supply of all personal requisites and provisions for the workmen. It established stores, shops, lodging houses, along the route, with hospitals, post offices, savings banks, and all the requirements of a fully civilised community. After all this was not the era of Brunel and the Stephensons; this was happening within my own lifetime. The 'camps' were not the wild lawless communities of Blea Moor or Upper Clydesdale. The organisation provided for the constant supply of fresh meat and vegetables, there was a fully-equipped bakery, and as construction proceeded so the 'camp' was moved forward on rails to the next working site. Track laying began in 1913, and the work was continued with increased urgency through World War I. Mechanical track-laying machines were used, and at one stage the work was going forward at the rate of more than ten miles a week. In sucd conditions this was astonishing progress. It must be remembered that the hours of daylight are little more than twelve hours even in the height of the summer, while in that season the heat, and the almost complete absence of shade, could be trying in the extreme.

The territory traversed consisted of four quite distinct geographical divisions in that extraordinary 1051 miles of railway. Starting from Port Augusta, and covering a stretch that we unfortunately travelled over in darkness, the first division extends over nearly 400 miles of the so-called 'lake' country, through chains of vast flat pans of glistening salt. Hearing the description of this part of the line from various members of the train crew I determined that one day I must return and ride over this line in the daylight on a freight train. Then follows about 50 miles of almost pure desert—nothing but a long succession of sandhills. Following this is the incredible Nullarbor plain; a limestone plateau that extends for 450 miles, until the railway enters upon the granite plateau that covers the last 167 miles into Kalgoorlie. In this 1051 miles of railway there are only three stations that could be called in the least important, namely Tarcoola, 257 miles from Port Augusta; Cook, 513 miles; and Rawlinna, 816 miles. These were the original steam locomotive divisional points. The other 44 'stations' are mere crossing points, even today, though their names recall many personalities connected with Australian and Imperial history. Kitchener, Haig, Fisher, and Lyons have their immediate associations, while Cook, Reid, Hughes, and Denman have particular Australian significance, and above all there is Forrest—Lord Forrest—who in early days explored overland from Western Australia, and who, as Sir John Forrest, became the first Prime Minister of Western Australia.

Even before we have started on our way from Port Augusta, or from Port Pirie where the 'Trans-Australian Express' starts today, it may be asked why this line was ever built to the 4 ft. 8½ in. gauge. In 1917 when it was brought into service it involved a break of gauge at both ends to the 3 ft. 6 in. of Western Australia at Kalgoorlie and back to the 3 ft. 6 in. gauge of South Australia at Port Augusta. Even then however the urgent matter of gauge standardisation in Australia was a vital and controversial topic. To have built this new line on the 3 ft. 6 in. gauge with immediate and through connections at either end, would have been the easy way out. But without much doubt it would have slammed the door forever upon the ultimate prospect of gauge standardisation in Australia. As it was a wedge was driven between the non-standard systems at either end, and the solid fact of 1051 miles of 4 ft. 8½ in. gauge established between Port Augusta and Kalgoorlie. It had of necessity to be an absolutely self-contained system, as it was flanked at each end by lines over which its locomotives and rolling stock could not run; and along its vast length the 'stations' were spaced not because of the need to serve any local communities—of which there were virtually none—but to suit the operating requirements of the railways. Such intermediate points were sited to suit the coaling and watering requirements of steam locomotives, and the needs of changing and remanning them *en route*.

The fact that the 4 ft. 8½ in. gauge was chosen brought its problems in the selection of suitable motive power. It might have seemed natural enough to select well-proven New South Wales types, because these were the only 4 ft. 8½ in. gauge locomotives that were running or would be likely to run in Australia. It did happen however that the N.S.W. 'P6' class 4–6–0 and the 'K' class 2–8–0 were extremely good designs, both of which had by then the refinements of superheating and the experience of nearly twenty years of hard and successful service. In the midst of World War I however no locomotives could be spared from New South Wales, and so orders were placed with the North British Locomotive Company, of Glasgow, for 26 of the 4–6–0 type and 34 of the 2–8–0s. As experience developed in working this extraordinary line the locomotive workings were somewhat extended from the original turns, and by 1925 the locomotive rosters provided for three changes of engine *en route* from Port Augusta to Kalgoorlie, with lengths of run as follows:

Port Augusta–Tarcoola	257 miles
Tarcoola–Cook	256 ,,
Cook–Rawlinna	303 ,,
Rawlinna–Kalgoorlie	235 ,,

Because of the relatively slow rate of progress the engine crews did not work the same mileages as the engines, and intermediate changing points had to be set up. The method of crew working is much the same today, though the changing points are not necessarily the same.

When the line was first opened the electric staff system was in operation throughout, and every gang of workmen not located near a telegraph station, and every train was equipped with a portable telephone and apparatus for making connection with the electric staff wire at any point. In that way the station staff at either end of the section could be communicated with promptly in an emergency. Some of the staff sections were as much as 84 miles in length, the longest in the world. Experience in working has led to a considerable modification of these methods, as will be explained when I come to a more detailed description of our own journey. At that time the overall journey time between Port Augusta and Kalgoorlie was 37½ hours, an average speed of 28 m.p.h. It is now 26¾ hours. At the time the line was opened however, and for many years afterwards, the service consisted of three passenger trains a week in each direction, and in those days, long before the introduction of regular passenger and air mail services, an excellent connection was provided in conjunction with the Western Australian railways with the fortnightly mail steamer from the United Kingdom, which arrived at Fremantle on alternate Tuesdays. By using the railway passengers could save at least 48 hours on the journey from London to Melbourne, and three days from London to Sydney. At that time, of course, the journey throughout from Fremantle involved changes of gauge at Kalgoorlie, Port Augusta, Terowie in South Australia from 3 ft. 6 in. to 5 ft. 3 in. gauge, and finally the change back to the 4 ft. 8½ in. gauge at Albury.

From the very outset however the Trans-Australian trains were equipped with sleeping cars of the finest contemporary types. There was of course no such thing as air-conditioning then; but electric fans were installed, and showers for first-class passengers. The dining cars provided excellent fare, and a very popular feature was the lounge car, fitted with very comfortable armchairs, a piano, and a news service providing telegraphic advice of the world's press news, posted daily in the lounge car. These facilities serve to emphasise the complete isolation that took place when a Trans-Australian train set out from Port Augusta, or Kalgoorlie. The passengers and crew alike were out in the wilds for a day and a half on end, completely cut off from world affairs. While preferential treatment was naturally given to first-class passengers, very good second-class accommodation was also provided, including four-berth sleeping cars. A normal train of the early 1920s consisted of seven coaches, including dining and lounge car, and accommodation for both first- and second-class passengers. It is certainly significant of the difficulties of working and the need for many engine changes that a stud of 26 passenger engines of the 4–6–0 type was needed to operate a service of three trains a week in each direction. Goods traffic over the line was slow in developing, though with all vehicles fitted with the Westinghouse brake the odd wagon, or sheep van, could be attached to a passenger train.

By now it is time to be leaving Port Pirie on our modern journey, in splendid air-conditioned stock. At the time of our journey however, in the early Australian spring, weather conditions were delightful, and one rather missed the opportunity of being able to open windows. We left Port Pirie at 4.45 p.m., but how conditions might have been that night over the sandy portions of the route, without air-conditioning, I do not know. Nor, unfortunately, was there any chance of seeing this part of the line. By the time we left Port Augusta, at 6.14 p.m., it was practically dark. The standard-gauge line between Port Pirie and Port Augusta was opened in 1937, and this opening run of 57 miles takes the line on very level country up the eastern shores of Spencer's Gulf. The scene westwards across the water was very attractive, with the sun setting in a cloudless sky over the low hills on the far side of the gulf. In the foreground the ground was covered with a very dwarfed scrub, and this was the prelude to seeing hundreds of miles of it, and nothing else, in full daylight on the following day. The speed was around 50 m.p.h. and so we came towards the head of the gulf, passed through the junction at Stirling North, and joined the track of the one-time 3 ft. 6 in. gauge line that was once the only eastward connection from the standard-gauge Trans-Australian line. So we came into Port Augusta, at dusk; it had the appearance of a wooden 'shack' town, and the sight of an occasional aborigine on the platform fully confirmed the impression that we were now really heading into the 'outback'. The 57 miles from Port Pirie had been run non-stop in 86 minutes.

We left again at 6.20 p.m., and travelling now through a land without a glimmer of light, it is a good opportunity to say something of the train itself. The two-berth 'twinette' sleepers are generally the same as those we enjoyed on other Australian night trains. They convert into a delightful private saloon for day travel. The single-berth sleepers are of a novel design. They are known as 'roomettes' and are ingeniously designed to serve as a private sitting room by day, and a single-berth sleeping cabin by night. The layout is longitudinal, instead of the transverse berths of the twinettes, and to afford the maximum amount of space inside the roomettes the vestibule between them, running from end to end of the car, is 'wavy' in its direction. The vestibule is kept of an even width throughout, but by thus weaving its way, or snaking its way as it might be described, it provides additional and very acceptable space inside the rooms. Making one's way through a 'roomette' car *en route* for the dining car is an unusual and sometimes amusing experience. A fellow traveller suggested that the zig-zag path through these cars had been designed to facilitate the uncertain trajectory of any who had enjoyed an extra-convivial spell in the buffet car!

214

The whole atmosphere of what may be termed the 'social' part of the train is very pleasant. The lounge car, with its piano and deep armchairs, is more like the saloon of a ship than part of a railway train. Almost without exception the passengers are making a lengthy journey, and with the air-conditioned carriages there is little chance for getting out, even if the intermediate stops gave any inducement to do so. It is much the same as being on board ship. The dining car menus are attractively pictorial, and in keeping with the way passengers 'get-together' on the long journey, meeting time and again at successive meals, these souvenir menu cards have a space on the back for autographs, appropriately headed by a fine colour picture of one of the diesel-electric locomotives now working the train. As mentioned previously the lounge car with its piano, and 'club' comforts, is not a recent innovation. A non-air-conditioned prototype was operated on this railway from the early 1920s. Today the hotel or ship atmosphere is strengthened by the serving of coffee after lunch and dinner, in the lounge, rather than in the dining car. There are, I must add, good 'operating' reasons for this, in addition to providing a pleasant touch of gracious living. With a train of nineteen coaches, conveying a total of 230 passengers, each main meal had to be served in at least three sittings, and 'coffee in the lounge' meant that sitting time in the dining car could be reduced.

While we were at dinner the stewards told us to look out for a large cluster of lights on the northern horizon. This was the celebrated Woomera rocket range. After this brief intermission the windows lapsed once again into an impenetrable darkness. In steam days it was daylight by the time Tarcoola was reached, 257 miles from Port Augusta. A traveller who made the journey in the year 1925 wrote of Tarcoola:

Here we were entertained with the antics of a few of the aborigines who were soon on the track by the train begging for food and coppers. One bright boy gave an exhibition of boomerang throwing, and reaped a good reward. He could bring the 'wood' right back to his hand. For the rest, the standard charge for posing to be photographed was 6d.

At Ooldea many aborigines could often be seen, for this became a kind of rendezvous for nomadic bands. At that period the lengthy stops for locomotive purposes gave ample opportunity for most of the passengers to climb down, and walk around. On our trip Tarcoola was reached at

12.47 a.m. and Ooldea passed without stopping shortly after 5 a.m. Up to then we had been working on Central Australian time, but on reaching Cook at 7.10 a.m. we changed over to Western time, and put our watches back a further hour and a half.

At this stage, to whet the appetite of other travellers as well as our own for some future occasion, I may quote from a description of this part of the line that appeared in the monthly bulletin *Railways of Australia Network:*

A few miles from Port Augusta the train skirts the head of the Gulf and turns westward, seeming to fix its course by the strange, flat-topped hills that stand out like islands in a sea of myall and mulga scrub.

As the hills fade into the rich purple and red distance the express enters the moon-like 'lake' country through chains of vast flat pans of glistening salt. Some of these 'lakes' have an area of several square miles, but are merely shallow salt beds. When covered by rain water they have a bluish look, like inland seas, surrounded by bluffs and wooded slopes.

The train then crosses Lake Windabout and skirts the Island Lagoon, a large salt lake with a remarkable hilly peak rising from its midst like a miniature volcano.

Tarcoola, the largest settlement between Port Augusta and Kalgoorlie, was named after a horse that won the Melbourne Cup. From the low rugged hills at the back of the town, gold deposits were found early in this century. After leaving Tarcoola, the train passes the boundary fence of Wilgena, a typical sheep station covering 1,920,000 acres of saltbush country.

The train is now sweeping past the crest of hills formed from age-old accumulation of fine dust, a tangled mass of ridges covered with mallee gums, myall, black oak, silky oak, native cork, and many other shrubs and bushes. East or west there is not a fence in over 800 miles.

Such is the part of this remarkable railway that we passed in darkness. I must now revert to our own personal experience.

For some little time before reaching Cook I had been astir, because from this divisional point I was to have a spell on the footplate. As dawn broke I looked out upon the most amazing scene I have ever seen from a train window. We were running at about 55 m.p.h. through a countryside that was completely flat as far as I could see from a single large window, and covered with the same low scrub that we had seen between Port Pirie and Port Augusta on the previous evening. Over this queer landscape, dun-coloured in the last minutes before sunrise, was spread the most superb cloudless sky. The travelling inspector who was looking after our needs brought an early cup of tea, and on arrival at Cook I climbed down, and walked forward the considerable way to our leading locomotive. We had a pair of GM diesels, with 3000 engine horsepower between them, but on reaching the front end, and climbing into the cab, I saw that the seemingly limitless expanse of flat, dwarf scrubland not only extended to one side of the railway but in every direction, ahead of us, in rear, and on both sides. The sun was now up and almost directly behind us, and the scrub partook of a soft bluish-grey colour.

Before starting away, something must be said of the present arrangements for locomotive manning over this route. With an absolute minimum of habitation in the entire 1108 miles between Port Pirie and Kalgoorlie it is only at the two ends that there are such things as locomotive depots. The diesels work throughout, and they are remanned at various points *en route*. The crew that I joined at Cook, and which had just taken over, were Kalgoorlie men, and were working home in two stages. They were on the third stage of a four-day cycle, in which they had done Kalgoorlie-Rawlinna on the first day, and Rawlinna–Cook on the second. At Rawlinna and Cook there are well equipped, though necessarily small hostels in which enginemen rest between turns. In steam days, with slower running the remanning of locomotives had necessarily to be more frequent, to avoid inordinately long hours. The locomotives themselves worked through between Port Augusta and Kalgoorlie, though not continuously; they, like the enginemen of today, worked forward stage by stage on a cyclic basis, the difference being that the engines eventually worked right through, whereas the crews from Port Pirie and Kalgoorlie now work out and home at each end.

From the cab of the diesel, while we awaited the right-away from Cook, I looked ahead along that extraordinary 'straight' that extends for 297 miles. The actual commencing and finishing points are the mileposts 496 and 793 from Port Pirie. At Cook we had already traversed 73 miles of this straight, and now we set out on its amazing continuation. The bluish-grey scrub, never more than twelve inches or so from the ground, is known as saltbush. It is said to provide good fodder for sheep, but there were no sheep to enjoy it, nor was there any other sign of wild life. It is the absolute 'nothingness' of the Nullarbor Plain that creates such a unique and compelling atmosphere. The ground on each side of the formation, and where

217

the scrub does not grow, is a yellowish brown; but beneath a cloudless blue sky the colour is rich despite the inevitable sense of emptiness. Nowadays the track is heavily ballasted with the indigenous limestone of the plain, but when the railway was first built the sleepers were laid on the surface with no ballasting worth the name. For the first stages of the run I had in the cab we could not develop the normal passenger train speed of 60 m.p.h., on account of re-ballasting; but we had plenty of mile-a-minute running afterwards. In the aggregate the line is level on this stretch; there are numerous slight undulations following the lie of the land. This can be observed most readily by noting the rise and fall in the line of telegraph posts beside the line.

It was an eerie sensation to be travelling such a land. Checking times and mileposts I reckoned that fairly soon we should be coming to the next station, and I began to peer ahead along that sunbaked single line of railway. Then I described a few specks on the far horizon, and as they were gradually revealed as low buildings I realised that here was an exact counterpart of the first appearance of islands, or ships at sea. We were sighting the buildings of Denman over the curve of the earth! It was only that curve that prevented us seeing further. Generally stations and other buildings first became visible about eight to ten minutes before we actually passed through. Denman was cleared in due course, and we continued across the plain. After another forty minutes of what could well be described as completely featureless running we sighted Hughes in the same way; but here, after two minutes of approach, in which the full extent of the few small buildings was becoming apparent over the curve of the earth we saw a piercing light. This was the headlight of the freight train we were due to cross at Hughes. An English reader might well question why it is necessary to keep headlights on in such brilliant weather, in such conditions of incredibly clear visibility. This is done for the benefit of men working on the line, for without the headlight it would be hard to tell from the speck in the distance whether a train was going or coming.

We first sighted that headlight just over five minutes before we came to a stop at Hughes, alongside an immensely long freight train drawn by three diesels. Here I left the engine of our train and went back to breakfast after a truly unique one and a half hours in the cab. It was then eight o'clock, but such was the extent of this vast plain we were crossing that it was not until after 12 noon that day that I first noted in my travelling diary the sight of a tree! Many of the incidentals of travel in that incredible wasteland were nevertheless fascinating to recall. We crossed the State border from South Australia into Western Australia at 8.53 a.m.; at Forrest, where there is an aircraft landing strip, we crossed a ballast train, and as the sun mounted ever higher into the cloudless sky we saw many mirages. Near Mundrabilla the countryside was almost plain desert. We took the straight track at the crossing place there at a full 60 m.p.h., and then entered upon a further stretch of the blue-grey saltbush. The altitude along this part of the line was between 550 and 600 ft. above sea level.

After a time the novelty of the wilderness began to wear off and one fell to wondering how, if ever, such a vast open space could be utilised. Our driver had remarked earlier: 'No one knows what is below this surface. There could be gold, iron-ore, nickel—but there's no one to dig and find out!' At Loongana however there are deep ballast pits and a limestone crushing plant, for providing ballast for the permanent way. The track certainly seems in splendid shape, and the riding of locomotives and coaches was impeccable. After passing Loongana the country grew flatter and more featureless than ever for a while, as we continued on this seemingly endless straight track at 60 m.p.h. Nearing Nurina there is actually a slight curve, and at Haig there was a small belt of trees. But the landscape was still very much that of the Nullarbor Plain, and with this same landscape passing unceasingly outside the windows it was the hour of the aperitif, and we made our way to the lounge. In daylight, with the fierce relentless sun outside, one noticed new features of that pleasant air-conditioned car. The bar is furnished with red padded armchairs; in the piano-lounge the upholstery is in green moquette, with thick pile carpets, tasteful curtains, and soft background music by radio. At 60 m.p.h. the riding was so quiet that one tended to lose all sensation of railway travel.

At Wilban, reached at 12.45 p.m., we stopped, and waited to cross the corresponding eastbound 'Trans-Australian Express', and while at lunch the conductor told us where shortly we might see kangaroo. We were now definitely passing out of the Nullarbor region, and near Naretha, having spotted many kangaroo, we were coming into low bush country. There was saltbush on the ground, but now it was among gum trees. At Kitchener, at 3.16 p.m., I went down to the rear end to spend some time with the guard. Earlier in this chapter I mentioned that when the line was first opened in 1917, and for some years after, it was worked on the electric staff system. Now that system is no longer used, and the operation is regulated by telegraphic train orders. The guard showed me the order under which they were then running, which instructed us to proceed to Zanthus, and cross eastbound goods No. 440, which was being hauled by engines GM 32 and GM 22. Both of these were the same type as our own engines—the standard for both passenger and freight on the line. We reached Zanthus first, and had to wait nearly half an hour for the freight. We then received an order to make another 'cross' at Curtin, nearly a hundred miles further on.

Zanthus is a pretty settlement, set deep among the gum trees. It was pleasant to climb down for a while, and enjoy the fresh air, for at 4 p.m. the heat of the sun was rapidly diminishing and there were already signs of evening coming on. After all it was no more than early spring. We went on into thick bush country where the soil is real Devon red. It was most beautiful in the evening light, and when eventually we came to Curtin and stopped to cross the freight it was growing dark. We had been climbing steadily from Kitchener, and we were now more than 1100 ft. above sea level. The timetable provides ample margin for lengthy waits to cross opposing trains, and despite the 'meeting' at Zanthus we were slightly ahead of time. We dined with the last rays of daylight of this most memorable day slanting across the dining car, and so after 1108 miles of the Commonwealth Railways we drew into Kalgoorlie, shortly before 7.45 p.m.

CHAPTER EIGHTEEN

Western Australia—earlier days

At the 129th meridian we had entered the vast, sensationally-developing land of Western Australia, and had already travelled for 450 miles across it by the time we came to Kalgoorlie; but until quite recently the great standard-gauge transcontinental line had been an establishment somewhat apart from the indigenous 3 ft. 6 in. gauge systems in Western Australia itself. These had originated from the logging trade, and from the maritime rivalry between Albany and Fremantle. But before coming to consider what might be termed the 'old' railways of Western Australia, it is just as well to fix in mind something of the vast extent of the country, even in comparison with the rest of Australia. In Perth I was given two maps that vividly illustrated this matter of size. Both show the outline of Western Australia with the outlines of other countries superimposed upon it. The first shows that Western Australia could comfortably accommodate New South Wales, Victoria, the whole of New Zealand's two main islands and Tasmania, while the second shows, still more easily fitted in, the whole of the British Isles and the American state of Texas, with a great deal of space still to spare.

From the 129th meridian to Perth is a modest 820 miles, and the distance from the south of the north coast of the State is considerably more than that; and when it is appreciated that in 1868 the total population was only 15,000, the very humble start to railway transportation, which began three years later, will equally be appreciated. The first railway was indeed a privately-owned timber line from Busselton, on the coast some 120 miles south of Fremantle, into the nearby forests. In the following year another logging railway was opened from Rockingham, about 18 miles south of Fremantle, into the appropriately named Jarrahdale. In view of more recent developments it is interesting to recall that the first Government-owned railway in Western Australia was built to assist the lead and copper

221

mining industry, that was even then developing favourably far to the north of Perth, the capital city. This first Government line ran from the port of Geraldton, about 300 miles north of Perth, to Northampton, a distance of 33¼ miles. For some reason, probably due to the remoteness of the locality from the capital of the colony, great difficulties were experienced in getting this project under way. Work was started in October 1874, but it was not until nearly five years later that the first public service was operated. This line started its existence, or rather its pre-existence, as a 3 ft. gauge line; but this was changed to 3 ft. 6 in. before the line was brought into service.

So far, it will be seen, no railways had been constructed at or near Perth. But then the beginnings of the line that was eventually to provide a continuous chain of railway communication right across Australia were seen in the opening of a Government line from Fremantle, through Perth to Guildford, a distance of 20 miles. Extensions came rapidly, in very hilly and difficult country, amid the heights of the Darling Range, and very soon a rail link was established between the agriculturally rich Avon valley, lying on the eastern side of the Range, and the twin centres of Perth and Fremantle. The line reached Northam in 1886, while another fork from Spencer's Brook had taken the railway southwards to York. By that time there was a continuous line of railway for 90 miles between Fremantle and York; but having been built to serve the intermediate logging and agricultural interests it was very curving and had many gradients as steep as 1 in 40. The 'branch', as it was then considered, from Spencer's Brook to Northam was only five miles long. By August 1886 the principal line had been extended a further 21 miles south to Beverley. It was then that interests other than those of the Government began to enter the arena of Western Australian railway development.

I have previously told how the newly-established mail steamer service from England favoured Albany rather than Fremantle as a port of call. In the early days of the colony a system of land grants was in operation, and a private company known as the Western Australian Land Company was offered a grant of 10,000,000 acres in return for the construction of a railway from Albany to join the existing line at Beverley. The line would have been about 243 miles long, so that the grant was roughly equivalent to 40,000 acres per mile of railway. This was considered excessive, and the proposal hung fire, until a London syndicate negotiated a revised offer with the Government on the basis of 12,000 acres per mile of railway. This agreement was concluded in 1884, and the line built in good time. The Government line to Beverley was completed by August 1886 and there was a through line of communication between Perth and Albany when the Land Company's line was opened for traffic in 1889. This line was known as the Great Southern Railway, and although taken over by the Government in 1896 it is still, to this day, known as the Great Southern Railway. The departure of the last mail by road was made something of an occasion in Albany. It was a covered wagon drawn by four horses, but it was not so very long previously that motive power for the mails had been provided by camels. On the new line it was only at Beverley that anything of a town existed. The intervening places were mere 'bush' stations, where originally there was an air of domesticity about the arrangements. There were no such persons as porters; the stationmasters handled the goods and their wives issued the tickets.

The successful promotion of this line led to a further agreement under the Land Grant System for construction of a line running due north from Midland on the main Government eastern line, to Walkaway, on the Geraldton line, 277 miles to the north. The agreement was concluded on the same basis as that for the Albany–Beverley line, namely 12,000 acres per mile of railway; but the enterprise came very near to complete failure through lack of funds. The situation was saved however by the floating of a new company in London, known as the Midland Railway Company of Western Australia Ltd. This company took over the concession, and the line was opened for traffic in 1894. Although Midland is the name of the junction where it originates, the description Midland is only appropriate as representing a link between the Government-owned lines in the Perth and Geraldton districts. If English railway names were to be adopted 'Great Northern' would seem to have been more appropriate than Midland. Perhaps however there were home ties that settled in favour of the latter name. Names or not, the Midland of Western Australia remained a privately-owned railway until as recently as 1964, and like the Great Southern, the name is still in official use within the Western Australian Government Railway organisation.

Shortly before the opening of the Midland Railway however there had come the momentous discovery of gold in Western Australia, and the names of Southern Cross, Coolgardie, Boulder, and Kalgoorlie became household names on the Stock Exchanges of the world. The prospect of

223

fabulous riches drew men towards 'The Golden Mile', as it had done earlier in Australia at Ballarat and Bendigo, and equally to the diamond diggings at Kimberley in South Africa. People of every estate flocked to Western Australia, and the need for improved means of transport became very urgent. An extension of the Eastern line for 170 miles from Northam to Southern Cross was projected by the Government. This passed through easier country than the line through the Darling Range, and the steepest gradient was 1 in 60. The entire line was opened in a single stage on 1 July 1894. It was followed by another $60\frac{1}{4}$ miles on to Boorabbin just two years later, while the final 78 miles to Kalgoorlie was completed and opened for traffic on New Year's Day 1897. The arrival of the first train at Kalgoorlie, carrying the Ministerial party, was the occasion for a great popular demonstration. Lord John Forrest and the special guests were photographed in front of the double-headed train, while crowds of workmen and other sightseers climbed on to every vantage point including the tops of the carriages, so as to be in the picture.

The opening of the line was not however the end of difficulties in transport to and from the goldfields. When my wife and I were in Western Australia in September 1969, we became very much aware of what prolonged droughts can mean to the inland regions. The situation in the Kalgoorlie district was extremely serious, and though at that time the concern primarily was for farming and livestock, I began to appreciate something of the conditions that could have prevailed on the railway in such circumstances in the days of steam haulage. The line to the goldfields had indeed not been opened very long before they were in dire trouble. While the stretch of line between Northam and Kalgoorlie is not so completely devoid of natural water supply as that over the Nullarbor Plain, it was necessary at the outset to provide reservoirs at nineteen places, and of these only five were replenished by gravitation; the remaining fourteen were dependant upon a pumped supply, using steam pumps.

During the very dry summer of 1898, when extreme drought conditions prevailed for many weeks, the intermediate water supplies between Northam and Kalgoorlie failed completely. Fortunately a reasonably ample supply remained at Burlong Pool reservoir, near Spencer's Brook in the Darling Range, and the engineers had to resort to the dire expedient of pumping from this reservoir all the water needed for operation of some 270 miles of line to the east of this location. Special water trains were run,

PLATE 37. Diesel-hauled expresses

(a) Victorian Railways: the 'Overland', with a pair of 'S.300' class locomotives

(b) South Australian Railways: the 12.30 p.m. Adelaide to Port Pirie service, connecting with the Trans-Australian express of the Commonwealth system

(c) The 3 ft. 6 in. gauge 'Ghan', on the Central Australian line of the Commonwealth system near Alice Springs

PLATE 38. South Australian vintage steam

(a) 'RX' class 4–6–0 (5 ft. 3 in. gauge) on down Sedan freight at Pallamanna

(b) 3 ft. 6 in. Beyer–Garratt (4–8–2 + 2–8–4) on down ore train at Warnertown

(c) 3 ft. 6 in. gauge 'T' class 4–8–0 on Peterborough freight train at Port Pirie

and the extra train movements involved, and additional utilisation of locomotives, led to a high degree of disorganisation. The railway staff rose to the emergency magnificently. Senior officers and local supervisors alike worked for days on end with practically no rest; how the locomotives were kept going was nothing short of a miracle. Through these efforts however, whatever disorganisation there might have been among the internal working arrangements of the railway, very little delay resulted in the operation of the advertised services. Nevertheless it was a very close-run thing, and in his report for the year 1898, the General Manager, referring to the critical period from 10 December to 2 January, wrote:

The scarcity of water had reached a very acute stage indeed, and nearly caused a cessation in the train services on some portions of the goldfields lines. The year proved to be the driest since the opening of the railway from Northam.

To keep the service going, 55,440,000 gallons of water in 42,000 water travelling tanks each capable of holding 1320 gallons and upwards had to be conveyed on ordinary and special water trains. . . .

The task will be better appreciated when I add that this water-carrying involved a total of 228,606 additional train miles during that critical month. In respect of the period from 10 December to 2 January, this would represent a train mileage of something like 8000 a day! No wonder the resources of the line in locomotive power were strained, ironically enough with every additional train requiring in itself more water. The locomotive superintendent aptly summed up the situation when he reported: 'The experience gained on this occasion has made it clear that a local supply of suitable water must be obtained at Kalgoorlie and Coolgardie, and I propose to recommend that condensers be erected at these points capable of condensing, together, 70,000 gallons of water per day.'

It is interesting to review the overall situation of the Government railways of Western Australia at this period, and the following statistics will make clear the extent of the system itself, and the rolling stock available for working it. First of all, as to mileage, the lines open on 30 June 1898 were:

Eastern Railway: Fremantle to Kalgoorlie and branches	474	miles
South Western: to Bunbury etc.	166.2	,,
Midland: Geraldton to Mullewa etc.	109	,,
Great Southern: Beverley to Albany	243	,,

P

This made up a total of 992.2 miles, and to work it the administration had 186 locomotives, 289 carriages, and 4478 wagons. These statistics make an interesting comparison to those of a British railway of what might be termed 'medium' busyness of that period, midway between the high intensity of the London and North Western, and the sparseness of the Highland. Taking the Glasgow and South Western as this example, its locomotives worked over about 550 miles of line, and to operate the services then run the stock required was 400 locomotives, 1300 carriages, and 18,000 wagons. On an average this was one locomotive to every $1\frac{1}{4}$ miles of line, compared to one for every $9\frac{1}{4}$ miles on the Western Australian Government Railways.

It will be appreciated that the expansion of these railways into a main line system took place largely in the last decade of the nineteenth century, and this is to some extent reflected in the high quality of the coaching stock in use at this relatively early date in their history. Of the 289 carriages mentioned previously upwards of 200 were bogie vehicles, including no fewer that eighteen sleeping cars. The journeys between Perth and Kalgoorlie, or Perth and Albany, could most conveniently be done at night, and in addition to the 'sleepers' the administration operated a number of American-type saloons with high clerestory roofs, resembling the Pullman type of car in outward appearance. For day travel consideration had naturally to be given to the extreme heat experienced on the inland sections during the summer, and the bogie passenger stock in service at the turn of the century was equipped with sunshades as then in general use on the Indian railways. These were formed of horizontal boards outrigged from the side of the coach, and extending downwards to a level roughly that of the top of the windows. The interiors of the carriages were thus shaded from the direct rays when the sun was at its highest and hottest. On many Indian carriages one had to duck under the sunshade when entering a compartment, but on some Western Australian carriages the sunshade was cut away over the doors.

As originally built, Perth station had only one long platform for through traffic, with terminal bays at each end, with an all-over roof in the central portion covering the platform line and the two through lines adjoining. The station buildings, and headquarters offices of the Government Railways, were handsomely styled in a neo-classical form of architecture. At first there was no more than a single storey; but a second was added in 1893, with a fine central portico. At that time a very elaborate enlargement was proposed, with a third storey, and a magnificent clock-tower. A contemporary description commented: 'When the imposing pile of buildings is completed Perth will probably possess the finest railway station to be found in any of our colonies (excepting, of course, India).' The actual extensions were added on each side, but the third storey, and the great clock-tower, never materialised. Since then the traffic-handling facilities of the station have been considerably increased, and reference to these and other developments are included in a later chapter. Of course the construction of the standard-gauge line from Kalgoorlie, and the building of the new terminal, has removed the transcontinental passenger traffic from the original station, leaving it now free to deal with increased efficiency with the purely Western Australian services.

The discovery of gold at so many places in the State, leading to the unprecedented rush of traffic on the newly-opened line to Kalgoorlie, was, naturally, followed by the inevitable slump; but when the gold fever had subsided the State began to develop to a remarkable extent its lesser natural resources, in timber, in coal, and in its capacity for growing grain. In years long before the development of long-distance road haulage the burden of transportation fell almost entirely upon the railways, and extensive traffics were built up serving the principal ports of Fremantle, Bunbury, Albany, and Geraldton. In the years before World War I Western Australia had virtually no outlet to the east, and so her exports even to other parts of Australia all had to go by sea. Main traffic depots grew up at Fremantle, Midland, Northam, Collie in the coal areas in the southwest, Narrogin—a general 'cross-roads' on the Great Southern lines—and Kalgoorlie. The latter did not assume major importance however until the opening of the Trans-Australian line in 1917. Northam and Narrogin were the principal concentration centres for the wheat traffic, and in the early 1920s the average length of haul for the wheat trains was as much as 140 miles.

Operation of the long and difficult line from Perth to Kalgoorlie was maintained originally with nothing more powerful than a series of small 4–4–0s, twenty-four in number, with coupled wheels only 3 ft. 6 in. in diameter, and a tractive force of 10,374 lb. The mainstay of the main line service was however a class of sixty-eight 2–6–0s, of slightly greater tractive power. These were afterwards supplemented by some 4–6–0s of still

227

slender proportions but considerably greater power. All three classes, 4-4-0, 2-6-0, and 4-6-0, had outside cylinders, and were of typically British appearance, with straight running plates and a very neat outline. The 4-4-0s have now all been taken out of traffic, and one of them is preserved; but examples of both 2-6-0s and 4-6-0s are still in service in jetty and general shunting duties at Bunbury. I was fortunate enough to find two of these old veterans on the shed during my tour in good positions for photography.

While on the subject of really old Western Australian locomotives I must mention the curious 'Double-engines' built in 1879 by the Avonside Engine Company of Bristol, for the Geraldton–Northampton line. There were two of these engines, designed on the celebrated 'Fairlie' principle of articulation so familiar from the almost phenomenal success of the engines of that type on the Festiniog Railway. The Western Australian 'Fairlies' had a comparatively short life. They were much larger and more powerful than the Festiniog engines, weighing $33\frac{1}{2}$ tons, against 20 to 22 tons, and having a tractive effort of 8307 lb. against 5410 lb. They ran, of course, on the 3 ft. 6 in. gauge, as against the 1 ft. $11\frac{1}{2}$ in. of the Festiniog, and were built after the Avonside Engine Company had built the second Festiniog Fairlie, the *James Spooner*, in 1872. The two Western Australian Fairlies spent only nine years at Geraldton, for in 1888 they were transferred by sea to Fremantle, and used for a further five years on the main Eastern line. In 1893 both of them were taken out of traffic. One was sold, and the other dismantled. Of the latter one half was rebuilt as a 2-4-2 tank engine, and the other half installed as a stationary engine to drive machinery in Fremantle workshops.

In 1902 and 1903 some considerably larger main line engines were obtained from the United Kingdom; these were 4-6-2s for passenger and 4-8-0s for goods. Neither class were large engines, and both had a distinctly 'South African' look about them. The 4-6-2s came from Dübs, and the first of the 4-8-0s from Nasmyth Wilson. All the 4-6-2s have now been scrapped, but when I was in Australia in 1969 no fewer than 34 of the original 57 of the 4-8-0s were still on the register, though only eight of them were actually in traffic. These 4-8-0s are class 'F', using saturated steam, and 'FS' superheated. At Bunbury I found two 'FS' and one 'F' class on the shed. The last mentioned, still looking smart and business-like, is not far off her seventieth birthday. The Bunbury 4-8-0s, together with others stationed at Narrogin and Collie, are engaged in the heavier kind of shunting work.

Mention of the junctions of Narrogin and Collie leads me on to a discussion of the general traffic situation as it built up in the early years of the present century. I have mentioned earlier the Great Southern line from Beverley to Albany. There was also the coastal route from Perth southwards to Bunbury, and its continuations to Busselton and Northcliffe. Between these two lines which ran roughly parallel to each other on either side of the Darling Range, a network of cross-connections grew up of a surprisingly comprehensive nature, seeing that they served a widely-scattered rural community, with little in the way of major industry to produce an all-the-year-round traffic. At harvest time the railway was loaded almost to bursting point. Collie was a concentration point for the coal traffic, but this was not heavy, by any ordinary standards. As a result of these circumstances, and the fact that Western Australia was completely isolated from the rest of the continent until 1917, the practice grew up of working many 'mixed' trains.

Having seen something of modern traffic working on this railway, it is astonishing to reflect upon the profound change that has come over Western Australia. In the years of which I am now writing, when the only serious alternative to railways was haulage by camel over rough, scarcely-made tracks, the settlements and occupations of a small and scattered population virtually dictated railway policy. With such a wide range of territory and so few people to serve, an immense amount of light 'roadside' business was put on to the railway. It was very much in the English country station pattern of pre-1914 days, except that much of the business did not extend to a full wagon load. It was extremely difficult to secure efficient utilisation of the wagon stock, and at that period the annual averages showed a movement of less than 20 miles a day, all the year round. Seeing that this average included the peak period of the grain harvest, when every locomotive and wagon that could turn a wheel was pressed into service, the conditions over the rest of the year can well be imagined. Another feature of the working that pleased no one was the relatively low revenue derived from the peak traffics. At the end of the 1914–18 war period conveyance of hay, straw, chaff, and wheat, together with fertilisers, accounted for nearly 40 per cent of the ton-miles hauled, and yet it produced no more than 20 per cent of the total revenue. On the other hand

229

general goods haulage, included all the small consignments picked up at local wayside stations, only accounted for 6 per cent of the traffic, yet produced 20 per cent of the earnings.

Here indeed was a paradox for the management, but it amply explains why such attention was given to the light roadside business, and why arrangements for it to be conveyed on passenger trains were continued for so long. In this connection however Western Australia had other operating difficulties. Unlike the eastern states, a considerable proportion of its goods stock was not fitted with continuous automatic brakes. The fact that Western Australia had chosen the vacuum, rather than the Westinghouse, was of no consequence, in that the railway system was isolated and no question of interchange with other railways was involved; but even in the early 1920s only about 70 per cent of the total wagon stock was vacuum fitted. Most of the remainder was piped through, but careful attention had to be given to the consist of both all-freight and mixed trains, especially where descent of the very steep gradients on parts of the line was involved. This general pattern of traffic working persisted until after the end of World War I, until the development of road haulage upon the rural communities began to make itself felt. In the early 1920s against the total of about $4\frac{3}{4}$ million train miles run on the Government system no less than 1.1 million miles were run with mixed trains. Of course it was the passenger who objected to the mixed-train principle. With the attaching and detaching of wagons at intermediate stations, and the loading and unloading of small consignments, progress could be unbelievably slow. The management did not mind; it was good paying traffic! It is only fair to add that the working of mixed trains was carefully watched, and if passenger or goods business on any particular route showed signs of preponderating one way or the other, distinct passenger or freight services were substituted.

The type of freight wagons in use reflected the nature of the traffic, and the continuing strong influence of traditional British methods. Most of the stock was four wheeled. The 'coal-boxes', as they were termed, were small and open, though a number of special double-decker wagons were introduced for the sheep traffic. There was no such thing as bulk-handling of grain in those days. It was bagged up at the farms, and stacked high on to open wagons for despatch to Fremantle, or other ports. I have dwelt rather on early conditions in Western Australia to emphasise the nature of the railway system that was built up, and to contrast it with the magnificent developments that are now taking place over the same—or nearly the same—tracks. This is not to deprecate in any way the system as it existed until comparatively recent times, which was adequate for its original purpose, and which rendered excellent service to the community. It is rather to stress how organisation and methods that would have been totally inadequate in this present age have been completely replaced, by one of the most progressive administrations I have ever had the pleasure to study.

Before leaving the W.A.G.R. of the past I must say something of the suburban service around Perth, from which densely-used residential lines radiate in three directions: to Fremantle, to Midland, and to Wungong. The services were developing rapidly by the year 1909–10, and to provide for heavier loads and more rapid acceleration between stations some very handsome 4–6–4 tank engines were obtained from the North British Locomotive Company. These engines, which were generally of the traditional British appearance, had 4 ft. 6 in. diameter coupled wheels, and the Walschaerts valve gear. The one distracting feature was the sandbox on the boiler top, roughly midway between chimney and dome, and shaped to look like a glorified dustbin! This latter was for a short time a speciality of the Western Australian railways. These tank engines were fitted with cow-catchers at both ends, to enable them to work without the necessity of turning at the suburban terminal points. A development of this class, superheated and including a number of modern detailed improvements, was produced at Midland Works in 1946. A total of eighteen was built. All these engines are still on the register, and ten were in active service in 1969, based on Midland and East Perth depots. They are now mainly engaged on local goods and shunting work in the Perth metropolitan area.

CHAPTER NINETEEN

Western Australia:
the great standard-gauge project

Kalgoorlie: a warm starlit evening in early September 1969. We had just arrived on the Trans-Australian express from Port Pirie, and we were about to do something that would have been impossible to travellers a mere three months earlier. For the great train in which we had journeyed across the Nullarbor was going forward to Perth. There was no longer a break of gauge at Kalgoorlie. The connection had actually been made just over twelve months earlier; the first through freight ran from Port Pirie to the west coast in November 1968, and the passenger service followed in June 1969. And so, instead of changing trains, I climbed down to watch the pair of Commonwealth diesels couple off, and a single Western Australian diesel of 3300 horsepower back down to our lengthy train. Behind that simple operation lay ten years of some of the most remarkable railway development seen anywhere in the world this century. Ever since the completion of the Commonwealth line from Port Augusta to Kalgoorlie in 1917, the continuation of a standard-gauge line through to Fremantle had been a greatly desired development; but the recession in trade following the end of World War I and the world depression that followed, virtually eliminated any economic justification for such a development, and it was not until the 1950s that circumstances suddenly became very favourable. Then it was the discovery of a vast iron-ore deposit at Koolyanobbing, some 36 miles to the north-east of Southern Cross, and some distance away from the existing 3 ft. 6 in. gauge main line of the Western Australian Government Railways.

The Broken Hill Proprietary Company decided to install plant to the value of $10,000,000 (roughly 4¾ million pounds sterling) for the mining

The Lonely Road: A trans-Australian Express crosses the great Nullarbor Plain in 1969

of the ore, and to build a comprehensive iron and steel 'industry' at Kwinana, on the west coast about ten miles to the south of Fremantle, for the tremendous sum of $100,000,000. In 1960 the necessary agreement was signed with the State Government, and this was contingent upon the construction of a standard-gauge railway from Kalgoorlie that should pass through Koolyanobbing and then proceed via Southern Cross and Northam to Kwinana. The railway was envisaged as an integral part of the great new iron and steel industry projected—a 310-mile 'belt conveyor' between one establishment and the other. Such was the magnitude of the deposits existing at Koolyanobbing, and the relatively assured prospects of the export trade from Kwinana, that the construction of the railway was readily agreed to. It was first and foremost for the conveyance of heavy minerals and other freight; but it would also have the immense publicity and tourist value of eliminating yet another 'break of gauge' in the system of inter-state passenger traffic. Quite apart from the considerable diversion from the existing route that would be necessary at the eastern end in order to pass through Koolyanobbing, there were equally to be no half-measures elsewhere. There was to be no mere laying in of mixed-gauge tracks over existing routes; the whole project was to be looked at afresh, to obtain the finest possible route for the very heavy traffic that was just waiting to be conveyed.

In Chapter Seventeen of this book I have referred to the modest way in which the railways of Western Australia originated, and how the line leading eastwards from Perth into the Darling Range was routed to suit the logging trade, wriggling its way on severe gradients and still more severe curves to reach Spencer's Brook. A survey of the Avon valley, somewhat to the north of the existing alignment, showed that the average gradient between Northern and Midland would be 1 in 200. To obtain such a gradient uniformly through this 72 miles of country would however involve very heavy intermediate constructional works. In view of the importance of the traffic offered the decision was to build this new route not only to a gradient *not exceeding* 1 in 200, but on such alignments as to permit of continuous running at 70 m.p.h. by passenger trains, and 50 m.p.h. by the heaviest freights. An Englishman inevitably recalls the constructional policy on the Settle and Carlisle line of the Midland Railway, by the great Tasmanian engineer Sharland. There was no skirting of obstructions, with awkward curves; if a rocky eminence lay in the direct path there was only one way to deal with it, to blast clean through! And that is just what has been done on the new standard-gauge line between Northam and Midland.

The sleeping car attendant on the 'Trans-Australian Express' called me with a cup of tea at 4.30 a.m., for I was to ride the big diesel from Northam down the Avon valley. At that hour it was still quite dark, but when we left at 5 o'clock the powerful headlight of the locomotive so lit up the line ahead that I could see much of the magnificent engineering that has been put into the new line. This section is laid with mixed gauge, and had been in use for just over three years; but the earthworks still have a very new look, and the engine headlight showed up vividly the stretches where great cuttings had been hewn from the solid rock. We literally glided along. Although the speed was not high by Western European and British standards, I rarely remember travelling on a smoother-riding locomotive, while my friends in the cab pointed out some of the major engineering features. Leaving out of consideration for the moment the great new marshalling yards at Avon and Toodyay, and the new station at Northam, it was remarkable to find that such uniformity of gradient, and smoothness of alignment, had been achieved without recourse to a single tunnel. Some of the cuttings, particularly that through Windmill Hill near Toodyay, are certainly very deep and their construction in difficult geological conditions brought severe problems to the engineers. But the result has been a magnificent piece of railway. My first acquaintance with it, from the locomotive cab, in darkness, was impressive enough. I was later to visit some of its most strategic points in daylight, and to see something of its colossal freight traffic.

First however I must finish the account of my journey into Perth. Descending the Avon valley the skill of our driver and the capacity of the locomotive were displayed in the maintenance of a steady comfortable speed on the continuously descending gradients. The 'L' class, with an engine horsepower of 3300, are the most powerful diesel-electrics yet to be brought into service on any Government railway in Australia. They have the Co+Co wheel-arrangement, and a maximum axle-load of $22\frac{1}{2}$ tons. The new standard-gauge line has certainly been built as a maximum-capacity route, and the limit of axle-loading laid down by the civil engineer is no less than $23\frac{1}{2}$ tons. The superb grading and alignment is supported by a massively ballasted road bed. These great diesels of Class

234

'L' are finished in a livery quite distinctive from the green and red of the 3 ft. 6 in. Western Australian diesels; the 'L' class are pale blue with a broad central band of sky-blue edged with yellow. All the standard-gauge diesels are finished in this style. The 'L' class are fitted with regenerative braking, and while this is a great asset in providing very smooth running with a heavy passenger train when descending a moderate gradient, it is invaluable with mineral trains of the immense tonnages now worked over this line.

Daylight was coming before we emerged from the hill country; but the change in the landscape came quite suddenly, and then we were running through vineyards and fine agricultural land. We swung alongside the 3 ft. 6 in. gauge line of the old Midland Railway at Millendon, about five miles short of Midland, where the original 3 ft. 6 in. gauge line to Spencer's Brook and Northam struck off into the hills. We had then covered 67 miles from Northam down the new line in just over 70 minutes, and had comfortable time to make an easy run through the outer suburbs of Perth to make a punctual arrival after our long run across more than half the length of Australia. The original Central station, fine though it was, and now modernised to handle the busy present traffic on the 3 ft. 6 in. gauge line, would have been totally inadequate to accommodate the lengthy standard-gauge express trains. In Chapter Seventeen I have described the various amenities provided for the long journey from Port Pirie. Such facilities are even more necessary now that through running between Sydney and Perth has been inaugurated by 'The Indian Pacific' service. So an entirely new standard-gauge terminal station has been built in Perth, at a locality a little removed from the city centre, but easy enough of access. The new station has a main platform that is more than long enough to accommodate the longest trains likely to be run on 'The Indian Pacific' service, but it is provided with an awning for almost its entire length. There is no more dismal end to a long and otherwise comfortable journey than to arrive and have to detrain on an open platform in pouring rain! This aspect of travel has been well provided against at Perth new terminal. As at Brisbane South there is only one long platform. The station is designed for the transcontinental traffic, and the trains are not expected to come in at commuter frequency—not yet anyway!

Having seen the new line for the first time as a passenger, it is only natural that I have written of the passenger facilities first; but as previously explained it was the prospect of heavy and sustained mineral traffic that provided the justification for building this splendid new railway. Actually however iron ore was not the first traffic to be conveyed over the new line. Following the opening of the new Avon valley line between Midland and Northam in February 1966, such good progress had been made during that year east of Northam that by November a further hundred miles of standard-gauge line was ready, to Merredin. This new line followed the old route fairly closely, with improvements in grading and alignment to secure better running. At the Perth end the new standard-gauge freight line encircling the city on the south side and approaching Fremantle from the south was also ready, and on 11 November 1966 the first commercial use was made of the new railway. Merredin is a junction point of five routes, and a concentration centre for the very extensive grain traffic of the eastern wheatbelt. Except for the new railway all lines converging on Merredin are 3 ft. 6 in. gauge, but the advantages of the new railway are such that although laid with mixed gauge throughout mechanical transfer facilities are installed for transferring the grain into standard-gauge wagons.

These transfer plants are to be seen also at Avon Yard, near Northam, and as near to Perth as Midland. At each place end-tipplers and a special form of shovel facilitate rapid discharge of the grain into under-rail hoppers, which have an intake rate of 400 tons per hour. From these hoppers the grain is fed to garner bins to await loading into standard gauge wagons. And what wagons they are too! Specially designed to afford rapid loading and discharging, they are huge bogie vehicles carrying a pay-load of up to 75 tons each. The cylindrical bodies of some are constructed entirely in aluminium, and have a tare weight of only 19 tons. The steel wagons are painted a soft yellow colour, happily indicating the colour of ripe grain. They make a striking sight sweeping through the countryside behind an 'L' class diesel-electric locomotive in its smart blue and white livery. The grain trains are made up into block loads of 35 wagons, representing a gross trailing load of 3300 tons. If one of the 'L' class locomotives is not available a pair of the 'K' class, of 1950 horsepower each, are used. The first commercial use of the standard-gauge railway was in the running of these block grain trains from Merredin to Leighton Yard on the seashore, near Fremantle. The run of 198 miles is made in six hours.

Extending eastwards from Merredin the new line followed the track of the old one, with appropriate improvements in grading and alignment, as far as Southern Cross, a further 74 miles, and this represented the most easterly extent of the grain traffic on the standard-gauge line. Beyond Southern Cross the 3 ft. 6 in. gauge continues on its old course to Kalgoorlie, but the standard-gauge line now strikes out on its own, making a wide sweep to the north to reach Koolyanobbing, and in April 1967 the first iron-ore trains commenced running over the 310 miles from the mines to Kwinana. The location of this latter plant will be seen by reference to the map of the railways in the Perth district. It is estimated that the main deposit at Koolyanobbing contains about 40 million tons, and that in the area a total of nearly 100 million tons exists. The scheduled train service is now delivering 1·3 million tons a year to Kwinana, and if the present demand continues it will be appreciated that there is a staple traffic for the new line for many years—quite apart from anything else. For economical transport it was appreciated that the ore should be conveyed in maximum load trains, and the standard formation is 96 of the special bogie wagons, representing a trailing gross load of 9000 tons. To haul these immense trains, each more than half a mile long, three of the 'L' class locomotives are used, coupled in multiple, representing an engine horsepower of 9900.

The designing of locomotives, wagons, and track has all been carefully co-ordinated. I mentioned earlier that the track has been designed to permit of a maximum axle-load of $23\frac{1}{2}$ tons. On most railways this maximum would only be approached on the driving axles of the locomotives, but on the Western Australian standard-gauge line the entire moving loads of these block freight trains have been designed near to the limit of axle-loading. The special grain wagons weigh 94 tons fully loaded, and so do the special 'WO' class open iron-ore wagons. So, with a standard 96-car loaded ore train the permanent way has got to withstand the passage of 402 axles, each carrying a load of $23\frac{1}{2}$ tons, when a triple-headed train comes thundering along at 50 m.p.h. At present there are five of these trains a week. When I was visiting some signalling installations in the Avon valley I saw one of them come past. It was a railway sight never to be forgotten. But while iron-ore and grain provide very important traffic on the new line, they are far from being the only ones, although others do not fall so conveniently, perhaps, into the

237

conveyorbelt technique in running block loads. For ordinary freight traffic a number of special new vehicles have been designed for the standard gauge, and this brings me to consideration of the extensive new marshalling yards that have been already commissioned, and of the vast Forrestfield–Kewdale project now in an advanced stage of construction.

Despite the successful inception of the standard-gauge line, and the advantages derived from the elimination of break-of-gauge activities at Kalgoorlie, the Western Australian Government Railways remain primarily a 3 ft. 6 in. gauge system, on which a very high proportion of the internal freight traffic of the State will continue to be carried. In many respects the construction of the standard-gauge line to Kalgoorlie, with feeder lines to the great works and yards on the coast near Fremantle, has increased the complexity of railway operation in the Perth metropolitan area by introducing a second gauge where only one previously existed. But as in everything else today the responsible authorities in Western Australia have 'thought big' over their railway problems, with the result that a magnificent concept of freight handling has been developed, and is in process of realisation in the Forrestfield–Kewdale scheme. As its name might suggest this project consists of two separate, but closely related, installations. Kewdale is the large new freight terminal for general traffic serving the whole of the Perth area, and will provide for all incoming and outgoing goods on both the standard and the narrow gauge, while Forrestfield is the huge new marshalling yard lying just over a mile away, and which will provide for the sorting of incoming traffic, and the marshalling of outgoing traffic into economical train loads for the many different destinations involved. Beside the yard runs the new standard-gauge line on which the huge block-load trains of grain and iron-ore pass from Midland, to Leighton on the one hand and Kwinana on the other.

This great complex was one of the first installations my railway friends in Perth took me to see, and my first reaction was of their good fortune in having almost limitless space! I thought immediately of the complications that had surrounded the design and construction of the new marshalling yard at Melbourne, and of the constraint placed upon the engineers in many British yards, where complicated stage work was involved in transforming an old, out-dated layout into a modern one. Forrestfield is virtually in open level country, while Kewdale goods terminal, itself in open ground, is nevertheless near enough to the city centre to facilitate efficient despatch and receipt of goods. The fact that it is a little way out is an advantage in that road vehicles coming and going are not likely to suffer from the street traffic congestion that seems inevitable in all modern cities. In the marshalling yard area and in the goods terminal the standard- and narrow-gauge lines have, for the most part, been kept entirely separate, though some interlacing is needed, with provision of mixed gauge tracks. When I was there the plans for mechanised marshalling in the Forrestfield yard were in no more than a preliminary stage, and the laying in of the nests of arrival and classification sidings was in progress. While we were inspecting the entrance to the yard at the north end one of the block grain trains, double-headed with two 'K' class locomotives, came down the through line at full speed—a great sight. While I would be the first to admit that diesel locomotives have not the glamour or the emotional appeal of steam, there is something deeply impressive about the mass-transportation of huge loads of this kind and of the integral part they are playing in the phenomenal industrial development of Western Australia.

There is one very important new traffic, that is not conveyed on the standard gauge, and which runs neither over the new line in the Avon valley nor passes through Forrestfield yard. The name Jarrahdale would immediately suggest the historic logging trade of Western Australia, but in this new age it has assumed an entirely new significance. In the old forest areas large deposits of bauxite were discovered, and the production of alumina was enterprised by the firm of Alcoa of Australia Pty. Ltd. at Kwinana. Jarrahdale is only 28 miles from Kwinana, and a new 3 ft. 6 in. gauge line has been built to connect the two. The bauxite is mined by open cut, and road hauled to the railhead. There the ore, crushed to particles of less than one inch, is conveyed by belt to automatic loaders, where the special new bauxite wagons are loaded at the rate of 60 tons every five seconds! Like all new wagons for iron-ore and grain traffic on the W.A.G.R., the 'XB' hopper wagons were specially designed for the job, and they each carry up to 63 tons of ore. Because of the short distance involved a single train of 21 wagons was all that was needed, at the time I was in Australia. The turn round at each end is rapid, and with a regular schedule of three runs a day a million tons of ore is being carried from Jarrahdale to Kwinana each year.

On the standard-gauge line between Perth and Kalgoorlie, as finalised, the three major intermediate points of traffic concentration are at Koolyanobbing, Merredin, and Northam. The first named is concerned almost entirely with iron ore, while the other two collect agricultural produce and general merchandise. The new line is single-tracked eastwards from Northam, and the two sections East Northam–Merredin, and Merredin–Koolyanobbing, are each signalled by independent centralised traffic control installations. The section from East Northam to Merredin is 110 miles long, and the section east of Merredin approximately 100 miles long. On each stretch the crossing loops are roughly eleven miles apart. All traffic on both sections is controlled entirely by signal indication, with electric operation of all the main line points. Centralised traffic control was until fairly recently one of the wonders of modern railway operation, particularly when the introduction of electronic methods made possible extreme rapidity in the transmission of control and indication codes. Nowadays however C.T.C. is the recognised method of operation, and on the new line while there are local power interlockings at the larger intermediate places, such as Avon Yard, near Northam, and at Merredin, the rest of the line is controlled from no more than three signal control panels.

Taking first the section between Merredin and Koolyanobbing, in this length of 100 miles there are eight passing loops. Two of these are nothing but passing loops, remotely controlled from the push-button panel at Merredin, while another four have sidings in addition. Of the remaining two, which have three running lines, Southern Cross is a typical example and the track diagram is shown on the accompanying plan. At Koolyanobbing, the place of origin of the enormous ore traffic, the layout of the crossing loop and sidings is almost exactly the same as that of Southern Cross except that there is a 'siding' nearly three miles long leading to the loading point for the iron-ore trains. In preparing the signalling arrangements for this stretch of line, throughout the 100 miles between Merredin and Koolyanobbing, account had to be taken of the non-existence of any reliable public electricity supply. The railway engineers had therefore to install a power line of their own alongside the track. Another peculiarity faced the signal engineers in the approach to Koolyanobbing. For many years it had been found necessary to protect the rich wheatlands that extend westwards from this point from the ingress of rabbits, emu, and

240

PLATE 39. Trans-Australia line

(a) Making a reconnaissance

(b) Ploughing by camel during construction of railway

(c) Track-laying near the South Australian border in 1916

PLATE 40.

(a) The 297-mile 'straight', as finely ballasted today, and seen from the cab of a diesel

(b) Flash-back to 1917: the first train leaving Kalgoorlie for Port Augusta on October 25, and hauled by two N.S.W. type 4–6–0 locomotives

SOUTHERN CROSS

DIAGRAM OF SIGNALLING
STANDARD GAUGE

ALL DIMENSIONS IN YARDS

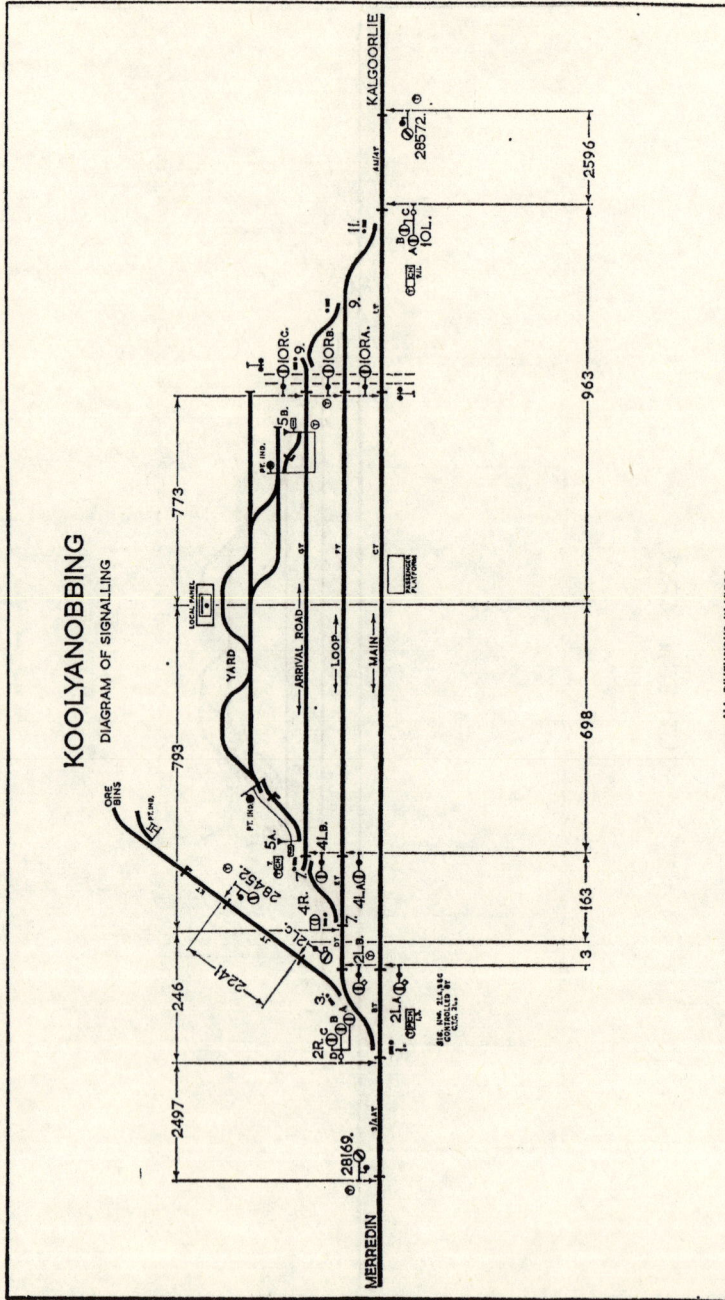

KOOLYANOBBING
DIAGRAM OF SIGNALLING

MERREDIN

KALGOORLIE

ORE BINS

YARD

ARRIVAL ROAD

LOOP

MAIN

LOCAL PANEL

PASSENGER PLATFORM

2497

246

793

773

698

963

2596

163

3

2B|69.

28452.

28572.

ALL DIMENSIONS IN YARDS

other predatory livestock, from the undeveloped inland areas; and a fence had been erected, extending for hundreds of miles. The railway crosses the fence near Koolyanobbing, and here a reinforced concrete pit was constructed 15 ft. by 12 ft. and 5 ft. deep and the railway carried over on steel girders. This had been found successful in preventing the movements of pests where the track passes through the fence. But it was not possible to use normal track-circuiting across the pit, and a special device for proving the clearance of trains through the section had to be devised.

In studying the layout of the crossing station at Southern Cross it will be noted that the signals at the entrance to the loop include one unit for each alternative route—either along the main line or into the loop. The signals themselves are of the colour light 'searchlight' type, displaying red, yellow, or green as the case may be; but on the Western Australian Government Railways no use is made of route indicators. With the relatively simple layouts concerned separate signals are used, in the old British tradition of the splitting signal at a junction. Electric operation of all points on the running lines is controlled from the C.T.C. panel at Merredin, where all track circuits throughout the 100-mile section are indicated on the illuminated diagram. On this section there are a number of level crossings, two of which can be seen on the right-hand end of the layout at Southern Cross. Flashing lights are installed to protect these crossings, warning road traffic of the approach of a train, while an outer home signal is also provided, as an additional facility for the regulation of railway traffic.

I travelled over this section in the middle of the night, but on a subsequent occasion I was able to visit Northam, and to inspect the similar plant that regulates traffic working between that place and Merredin. An entirely new station has been built at Northam, very much in the modern style, and in a pleasant room in this building is the control panel for the East Northam–Merredin section. It is a fine example of modern railway operating practice, combining extreme compactness with maximum operating convenience. The layouts of the crossing loops on this section are all identical save that in some cases the additional running lines and siding accommodation is not provided. On the traffic-master panel there is only one set of operating buttons. These are common to all stations, and to operate a particular function the controller must first press the station selection button. This connects the appropriate electronic equipment, and lights a lamp near to the station name on the track diagram to confirm that the particular station has been correctly selected. Then all the function buttons on the traffic-master panel are in direct contact with the equipment at the selected station. Thus, to take an example, while there is only one button on the master panel, for the entering points at the western end of loops, the selection of a particular station enables the points at that place to be operated. On the East Northam–Merredin section, with nine intermediate stations or loops, the traffic-master panel has only one-ninth of the number of buttons that would be needed if individual operation was used.

Northam today is a key point in the operation of the standard-gauge line, and although grain traffic is here transferred from narrow- to standard-gauge wagons it is also the concentration centre for much traffic from the 3 ft. 6 in. gauge lines which is not transferred to the standard gauge, and which continues either to east or west on the narrow gauge. Foremost among these feeder routes is the Great Southern main line from Albany, which joins up with the east–west routes in a system of triangle junctions. I was taken to see the magnificently sited Avon Yard just to the west of Northam, where marshalling of both standard- and narrow-gauge traffic takes place. Never, surely, can a great marshalling yard have been set in such majestic scenery, though the steep flanks of the valley and the sweeping curves of the river provided many problems both in design and construction for the civil engineers. The yard master's office is a fine modern building, in which the operating floor has a signalling control panel for regulating all the train workings in and around the yard, and its entry and departure from the main running lines. The track layout is spacious, arranged in a picturesque series of sweeping curves within the confines of the Avon valley. Elaborate arrangements are made for floodlighting at night, and it was of course in these conditions that I first saw the yard as we passed in the Port Pirie–Perth express.

The new line down the Avon valley is laid with mixed gauges, but at the west end of the yard the gauges separate for eastbound trains, with the standard-gauge lines going in a wide sweep to the south of the yard, and the narrow-gauge to the north. In between are the separate sorting sidings for standard and narrow gauge, and the facilities for transfer where necessary. Avon Yard is yet another of the features of equipment that

PLATE 41. Consummation of the 'Trans' in February 1970

(a) The inaugural 'Indian Pacific' in two sections, prior to departure from Sydney

The two sections combined in one huge train and hauled by three diesel-electric locomotives crossing the Nullabor Plain on its through run from Sydney to Perth

PLATE 42. The Ministerial Special to Kalgoorlie, Western Australia on January 1st 1897, on the occasion of the completion of the line from Perth

make the 'Standard-Gauge Project' so impressive an example of a completely *new* railway, with every facet designed to the very finest modern standards yet completely integrated one with another in their overall functioning. I have already emphasised how locomotives, wagons, and track were designed to secure maximum utilisation of each in respect of loading. The signalling, traffic control, and yard facilities are likewise coordinated, and there is one final feature that I must specially mention. In view of the vast distances involved and the sparsely-populated nature of much of the country traversed, radio communication has been established at the iron-ore loading site at Koolyanobbing, and at the grain loading bins at Merredin. There is also radio communication from end to end of the lengthy ore trains running between Koolyanobbing and Kwinana, and on the grain trains between Merredin and Leighton. Yet a third installation of radio communication is on the 3 ft. 6 in. gauge bauxite ore trains between Jarrahdale and Kwinana.

CHAPTER TWENTY

The railways of Perth today

In no more than three rooms in the headquarters offices at Perth Central station one can watch the fascinating spectacle of the remote control and running of traffic many miles away on three quite distinct routes; on the standard-gauge main line between Midland and East Northam laid for most of its length with mixed-gauge tracks; on the new standard-gauge freight line between Midland and Leighton Yard, and also on the 3 ft. 6 in. gauge line running southwards to Bunbury, over the 43 miles between Armadale and Coolup. These are, to some extent, the 'neon-lights' display of the Western Australian Government Railways in the Perth area, though of course completely unheeded and unknown to the ordinary traveller. The 'neon-lights' aspect is revealed quickly enough to the privileged visitor. In these days one can however get a little *blasé* towards the applications of C.T.C., and be inclined to pass them off as 'Oh yes; another C.T.C. job.' I hope I never get to that stage myself, because I believe C.T.C. in its more sophisticated forms is still only on the threshold of its application to modern railway operating. Here in Perth however, before coming to discuss the long stretches of line that are remotely controlled from the station offices, the interesting developments in the metropolitan area itself must be described.

All over the world today the problem of commuter traffic into and out of large cities is one of the greatest 'headaches' in transportation. Railways become congested and the peak-hour trains shockingly over-crowded. One can see this situation in every continent in the world. Frustrated business people take their own cars, to increase congestion in the city streets and introduce the most acute problems of parking, while the railways with diminishing traffics find it difficult to raise the capital needed for major improvements. By world standards Perth is not a large

246

From Kalgoorlie & Eastern States

Millendon

Dual gauge to Northam only

GUILDFORD

BASSENDEAN

MIDLAND

INDIAN

OCEAN

SUBIACO

PERTH

KEWDALE

CLAREMONT

WELSHPOOL

SWAN RIVER

LEIGHTON YARD

NORTH FREMANTLE

FREMANTLE

ROBB JETTY YARD

ARMADALE

COCKBURN

SOUND

GARDEN ISLAND

BYFORD

KWINANA industrial area

MUNDIJONG

From Bunbury

———— 3'6" Gauge

▬▬▬▬ 4'8½" Gauge

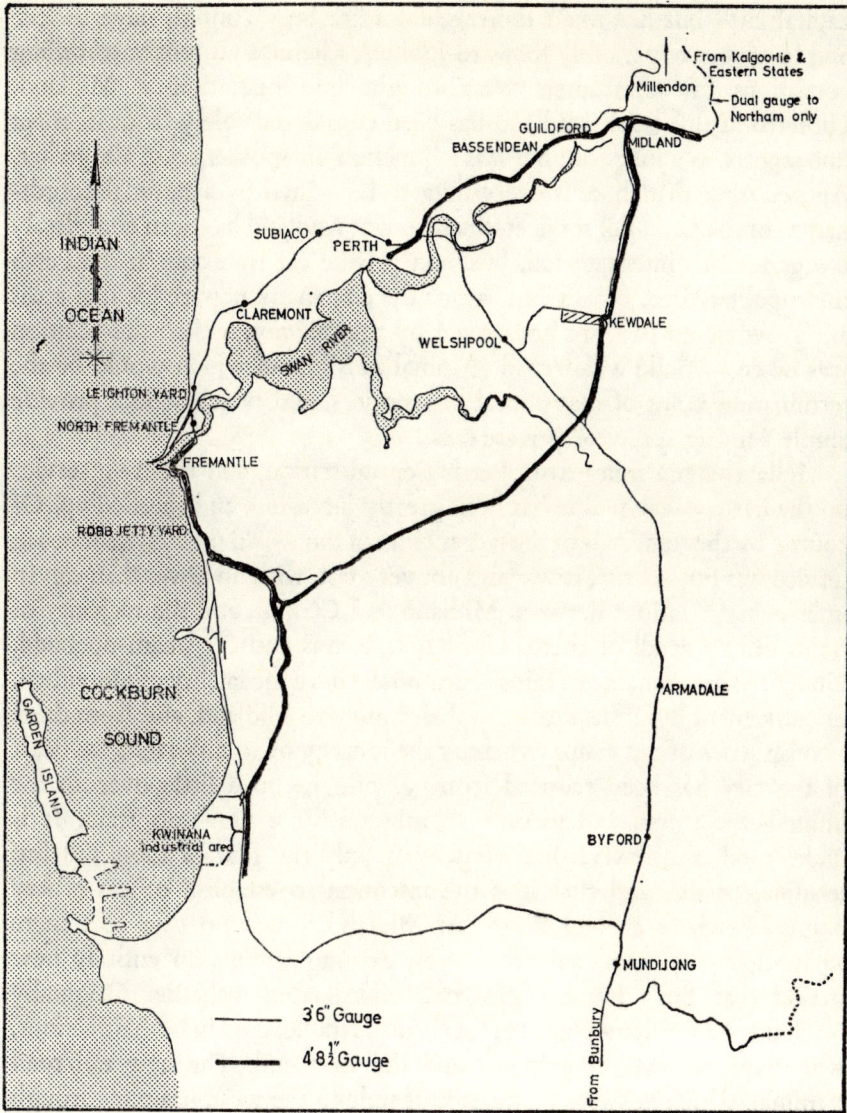

Lines in the Perth district

247

capital city, but her main thoroughfares are busy enough nevertheless, and in 1968 a remarkably forward-looking scheme to improve travelling conditions for commuters was brought into operation at Midland. Hitherto in this book Midland has been considered solely from its main line aspects, as a junction; but it is a 'junction' in another sense altogether. Appreciating that there is everything to be gained by a rational coordination of road and rail services, the layout at Midland has been completely reorganised to integrate rail, bus, and private car transport in the Perth metropolitan area. North and east of the city many new residential areas are growing up that are not served by the railway, and so the decision was taken to build a rail/road terminal at Midland which would be the terminating point of many local bus services, and which would provide ample parking space for private cars.

Midland is ten miles from Perth Central station, and the train service on the narrow-gauge line has been greatly increased, and speeded up. Of course, by the standards of the larger cities of the world the Perth suburban service was not intense. It was also not very fast, with no fewer than eleven intermediate stations between Midland and Central, and the majority of trains calling at all of them. Until 1954 it was entirely steam-operated. Under the new scheme of things commuters have the facility of individual, or convenient bus transport from their homes to Midland, and from there a lavish series of fast trains, whereby the journey of 10 miles into the heart of the city has been reduced from 30 minutes to a little over 20 for limited-stop trains, and to only 16 minutes for a non-stop train. It is understood, moreover, that Midland is only the first of these rail/bus terminal points, and that it is the intention to establish others at key points elsewhere around Perth. At Midland it was no case of a mere enlargement, or modernisation of an existing layout; an entirely new station was built for the rail/road coordination scheme. Originally Midland had one long platform for through traffic, used in both directions, with bay roads at the east end and the west end. The new rail/road terminal, which lies about a quarter of mile to the west, has one through platform for running in either direction, and three bay platforms for city-bound trains terminating at Midland. Taking the Midland complex as a whole therefore, old and new stations combined, the platform capacity has been more than doubled. From this one can readily appreciate how smoothly the greatly increased passenger service could be handled.

248

Alongside this extensively modernised narrow-gauge layout runs the new standard-gauge main line from Northam and the east. The mixed-gauge lines that exist down the Avon valley separate into standard and narrow gauge where the new line comes alongside the former Midland Railway main line at Millendon; but there is intersection between standard and narrow gauge at Midland West, for locomotives to cross into the Workshop Area, and the steam locomotive running sheds, that are adjacent. The rail/road terminal station is controlled by power signalling of the latest type, with a relay interlocking push-button panel, and this interlocking also controls the junction, about half a mile to the west of the terminal, which takes both standard- and narrow-gauge lines to Forrestfield yard and the great new goods station at Kewdale. This is the route taken by the 96-wagon, 9000-ton iron-ore trains from Koolyanobbing to Kwinana. From this junction into Perth the standard-gauge line is no more than single-tracked as it thenceforward becomes largely a passenger line. The narrow-gauge line is of course double-tracked, and the suburban stations consist mostly of a single island platform.

Another important scheme of improvement has recently been completed on the eastern side of Perth. As mentioned in Chapter Eighteen of this book the Central station is a through one. From the west the suburban line from Fremantle comes in, and then at the important junction of Claisebrook the line to Bunbury and the southwest diverges from the double-tracked main narrow-gauge line to Midland. It was on the Bunbury line that a major traffic difficulty had already built up, and was likely to get considerably worse in future years. Immediately beyond Claisebrook, the Bunbury line curving round to the south crosses the Swan River on a long viaduct. This latter was built in the early days of railway development in Western Australia, before traffic grew to anything like its present extent, and it is only single-tracked. The cost of doubling would now be inordinately high. But with modern operating methods it was not the single-tracked section over the Swan River that was causing the major difficulty. Two and a half miles from Claisebrook, just beyond the suburban station of Rivervale the line made a level crossing with the Great Eastern Highway; this would not have been critical in itself, but at Rivervale there is also a large yard giving access to a cement works. Furthermore, the single-tracked section over the Swan River

249

viaduct was continued to the Rivervale interlocking. Inevitably traffic peaks on both road and railway tended to coincide, and many yard shunting movements had to be made over this very busy level crossing. There were frequent road blocks, endless complaints, and not a few accidents.

The problem was tackled as in so many places elsewhere in Western Australia, in the most thoroughgoing manner, and at Rivervale the sources of trouble were completely removed, albeit by the construction of quite extensive new works. The necessity for shunting across the main lines and over the level crossing at Rivervale itself was eliminated by doubling the line as far back as Goodwood in the direction of Perth, and controlling access to the yard and cement works from there instead of from Rivervale, while the level crossing was eliminated by the construction of an underpass by which the Great Eastern Highway would be carried under the railway. These kinds of operation are of course easier said than done, and a considerable amount of stage work was necessary in the diversion of lines and temporary signalling while the Main Roads Department of the State was carrying out the necessary excavations to carry the highway down to the level where it could pass under the railway. There was also considerable stage work in signalling during the alterations in the track layout and provision of the additional running line between Rivervale and Goodwood. But such clear thinking in the first place, backed by resolute action, cannot fail to succeed in such a case, and the ultimate result has been a positive transformation in working.

I had the privilege of seeing the signal box at Claisebrook, then however known as East Perth, from which the single-line section over the Swan River is controlled. Claisebrook is primarily a mechanical interlocking, with rod-worked points, and the few colour light signals operated by electric circuit-breakers attached to the tails of the full-sized levers. It is a picturesque elevated box carried on stilts as it were; but within the limits imposed by the many rods extending downwards to operate points in the immediate vicinity a new relay room has been constructed, or rather, suspended, to contain the numerous items of electrical equipment for the remote control of the section over the Swan River, and of the interlocking at Goodwood, where the single-line section now ends, and the double-line automatic signalling commences. This remote-control interlocking is operated from a small panel mounted on the instrument shelf at the right-hand end of the existing mechanical interlocking frame in Claisebrook signal box. In Western Australia, although such rapid progress has been made with the installation of colour light signalling, not only on the new standard-gauge line but also elsewhere, as at Midland, the old standard semaphore signals are still much in evidence, and these are of the picturesque somersault type, for main running movements. For shunting and subsidiary movements revolving disc signals are used, as in Victoria.

There is still a considerable amount of steam locomotive working in Western Australia and the large running sheds at Midland and temporary small sheds at Claisebrook continue to be active. Ten of the later 4-6-4 tanks, built in 1945-6, were in use on metropolitan goods and shunting work when I was in Australia in 1969, while a number of the big 'V' class 2-8-2s were still in service between Midland and York, working over the new mixed-gauge line up the Avon valley as far as Avon Yard. But in the Perth area steam has ceased altogether on the passenger workings, and freight is diesel-hauled on the narrow-gauge lines except the 'V' class runs just mentioned. The changeover to diesel haulage on the principal express passenger services of the State began in 1954. Prior to this one of the most popular locomotive classes for passenger working was one acquired in unusual circumstances. During World War II the British Ministry of War Transport ordered a number of Light 'Pacific' type engines from the North British Locomotive Company for service on the 3 ft. 6 in. gauge lines in the Sudan. Before they could be delivered however the collapse of the enemy in Northern Africa had occurred, and these engines were no longer required. The Western Australian Government Railways purchased fourteen of them in 1946 and they put in some excellent work on express passenger services from Perth. When I was in Australia all fourteen were still in existence, though thirteen of them were stored out of service. The remaining one was on occasional duties from Midland shed.

A large amount of the local passenger working is now performed by diesel-mechanical railcars. The first of these came from England in 1954 at the time when the first general move towards dieselisation took place in Western Australia. They came from the A.E.C., which company supplied the diesel railcars extensively used on the Great Western Railway, in England, before World War I. The design has since been developed in Australia to meet increasing needs and a large number of similar cars have been built at Midland Works. The power units are combined power and passenger cars, and are arranged for coupling with any variety, either English or Australian build, with a number of trailers to form a train of the required length, and to be operated by one man. Each car provides accommodation for about a hundred passengers. More recently some very handsome twin-railcar sets have been supplied by the Commonwealth Engineering Company of Sydney. These are also diesel-mechanical, with one power car and one matching trailer manufactured by the W.A.G.R. permanently coupled as a two-car unit. The superstructure and panelling of these cars is in stainless steel, with the panelling on the sides in the form of fluting for the full length of the car, while the roof is similarly featured in corrugated form. These cars were only just coming into service when I was in Perth, but I can well appreciate that both on the score of their fine appearance and attractive accommodation they will prove very popular.

I have several times referred to Midland Works. It is an establishment geared to a remarkable versatility of output, and one which has played a most vital part in the great resurgence of activity that had taken place on the Western Australian railways in recent years. It is a works that can undertake anything—literally anything! In the anxious years before the outbreak of World War II Government officials concerned with potential war production visited a number of the larger railway works in Great Britain to ascertain what these shops might possibly undertake in an emergency. They quickly realised that there was little in the way of mechanical engineering production that they could *not* do. So it is equally at Midland. The W.A.G.R. still has some 150 steam locomotives in regular service, and in the advancing age of the diesels this does not mean that the older breed is being neglected, or run down. I was to see for myself later that the modern freight engines were being well maintained. Midland has to do this, while embracing all the newer techniques and shop facilities for maintaining the new diesels. I have referred earlier to the special wagon stock designed for the new traffics. Much of this new stock has not only been designed but built at Midland. Railcar trailers, aluminium-clad bauxite wagons, refrigerators, high-capacity covered bogie vans, the capacious open bogie wagons for iron ore have followed each other in rapid succession from the Midland assembly lines.

In no respect however has Midland moved to some extent even ahead of the times further than in the modernisation of the main line passenger

252

PLATE 43. Western Australian Government Railways: a grain train, hauled by two 'K' class diesel-electric locomotives in the eastern wheat belt

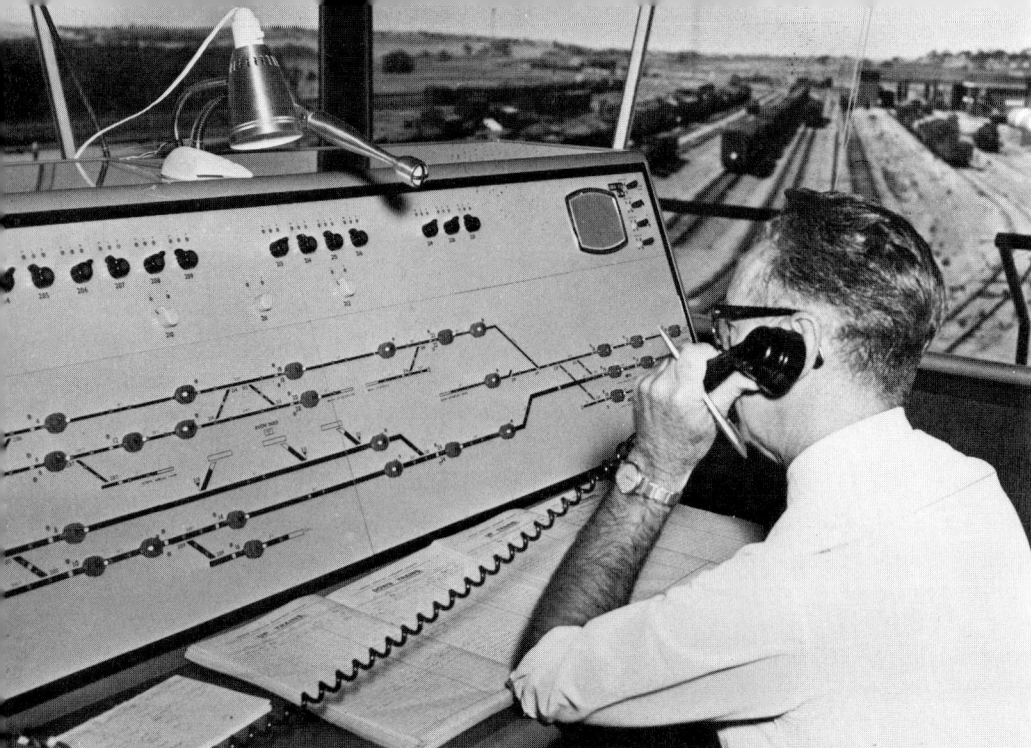

PLATE 44. Avon Yard—new standard gauge line

(a) The signalling control panel: thick lines on the diagram are standard gauge tracks, the thinner lines along the upper portion are the 3 ft. 6 in. gauge

(b) An aerial view of the yard looking towards Northam. The 3 ft. 6 in. gauge through line runs along the upper left-hand side of the yard, while the standard gauge through line sweeps round to the right beneath the photographer

rolling stock. Since the summer of 1969 so much attention has been focused on the through standard-gauge express trains between Perth and the eastern states that the positive metamorphosis of the stock for the purely domestic express train services has been partly obscured. From 1961 onwards a most vigorous programme of modernisation was applied to all the express trains on trunk routes. As in other parts of Australia communication between the capital city and the more distant country areas of Western Australia is maintained by night trains. All these services now have named trains, with travel facilities fully equal to those on the well-known intercapital expresses in the eastern states. Over the Great Southern line there are 'The Albany Progress' and 'The Albany Weekender'; between Perth and Geraldton, over the former Midland Railway line, there is 'The Midlander'; on the long run north to Mullewa, over the line branching from the Avon valley line at Toodyay, there is 'The Mullewa', and on the eastern main line, in addition to the transcontinental expressed there is 'The Kalgoorlie'.

These night trains, all on the 3 ft. 6 in. gauge, include first- and second-class sleepers, a buffet lounge for service of refreshments on the journey, and ordinary coaches for passengers joining or leaving intermediately and not requiring sleeping berths. The sleeping berths are finely equipped, though perhaps not quite so lavishly as on the transcontinental trains; but the interior decoration is delightful. Automatic ceiling ventilation, electric fans, and refrigerated drinking water is provided throughout. As on the 'narrow'-gauge trains elsewhere in Australia there is little suggestion inside the coaches that one is travelling on a sub-standard-gauge line. The overall width of the modern coaches used on these overnight country passenger trains is 8 ft. 9¾ in. Externally they are very smartly finished in a livery of larch green and cream.

Best known of all, among the fine modern trains constructed at Midland, was of course the 'Westland'. It is a little sad to have to speak of this train in the past tense, but with the inauguration of through services between Port Pirie and Perth in July 1969 the 'Westland' ceased to run. As a named train it commenced running in March 1938, providing connection at Kalgoorlie with the standard-gauge 'Trans-Australian Express' of the Commonwealth system. The journey between Perth and Kalgoorlie was made by night in each direction, and bookings were restricted to inter-state sleeping berth passengers. Like the 'Trans-Australian Express' of the

Commonwealth Railways the 'Westland' had its lounge car, and a well-equipped dining car. The lounge facilities on this train did not extend to a piano, but it was very cosily equipped otherwise. The basic passenger formation was supposed to be only three first-class and three second-class sleepers, together with the dining car and the lounge car. This may have been the case during the first six years of its running, when the train was steam-hauled; but a well-known photograph taken when the train was running on the 3 ft. 6 in. gauge tracks of the new line down the Avon valley shows a diesel locomotive hauling no less than eighteen vehicles on the downhill run from Northam.

The first main line diesels to operate in Western Australia were the Metropolitan Vickers 'X' class, imported from England in 1954. They were of no more than moderate power, having a Crossley engine of 1105 horsepower. This class is used extensively on the overnight country services of today, but on the 'Westland' it was superseded by the more powerful 'A' and 'AA' classes. These Australian-built locomotives have engine horsepowers of 1425 and 1650 respectively. They are essentially a main line job, whereas the 'X' class was introduced as a general-purpose machine with a high route availability. They are in fact the most powerful single-engine units in the world operating within the limit of a 10-ton axle-load. I will defer further comment on these excellent little locomotives until my final chapter, which includes some notes I made on a journey with one of them on the delightful daylight 'Australind Express'.

Perth can certainly be proud of its railways today. A peroration to this chapter may seem superfluous; but in scanning the overall scene and taking in the rail/road terminal at Midland, the remodelling at Goodwood, the C.T.C. installations controlled from the Central station, and the activities of Midland Works—all covered in this chapter—one must also add the new standard-gauge terminal, the Midland–Kwinana standard freight line, not to mention such huge projects as Forrestfield Yard and Kewdale goods terminal, noticed in Chapter Nineteen. With the intrusion of a little steam, and some signalling period-pieces to set beside the modern C.T.C. installations, one could scarcely find, in a relatively small area, so much major development, nor so much all-round railway interest.

254

CHAPTER TWENTY-ONE

Modern W.A.G.R. motive power

In using the adjective 'modern' in the title of this present chapter I am intending to cover locomotive practice on the Western Australian Government Railways since the end of World War II, this including the majority of the steam locomotives that are still in service, together with references to the various types of diesels introduced since 1954. From what I have written in the immediately foregoing chapters it will have been appreciated that in the 4100 miles of railway operated by the W.A.G.R. in those years just after the war there was a great diversity of physical conditions. Although the system served much agricultural land, where water was good, a greater proportion of the total mileage ran through arid waterless regions where the necessary provisioning for steam locomotives had always been a major problem. Again, the existence of rich coal deposits in the area of Collie not only provided a valuable staple traffic, but a ready-made source of locomotive fuel. Thus the W.A.G.R. was at one and the same time an ideal field for the introduction and development of diesel traction and equally for the continued development of steam power. In both these respects the system provides an interesting study in a logical and entirely parallel development.

The first step in what could be termed the modern development of W.A.G.R. motive power took place while the war was at its height, and arose from the need to provide additional power for the coal traffic from Collie. In 1943 a new design of heavy freight locomotive was designed at Midland, and the first example built in the railway shops. This was the 'S' class 4–8–2, and having a tractive effort of 30,685 lb. was by far the most powerful class so far introduced on the system. In outward appearance they gave an impression of being much larger and more powerful than they really are. They have the full-length casing over all the boiler mountings used on the Australian Standard Garratts referred to in Chapter Sixteen, and this is carried up to the full height of the cab. The coupled wheels are 4 ft. in diameter, but the two cylinders are no more than 19 in. diameter by 24 in. stroke. Nevertheless they are capable of hauling 1200-ton loads over certain routes. All ten engines of this class are still in service in the Collie area. There are two varieties of tender used with these engines. The large one has a capacity of 5000 gallons of water, and 7 tons of coal, while the smaller one carries more coal (9 tons) but considerably less water (3500 gallons). Although ranking high in the W.A.G.R. power stud the overall weights in working order are no more than $126\frac{1}{4}$ tons, with large tender, and $119\frac{1}{4}$ tons with the smaller one.

Apart from the purchase of the fourteen 'light' 'Pacifics' of Class 'U', originally designed for the Sudan, and referred to in the previous chapter, the first appreciable development in the realm of main line power after the war was the purchase of 35 new 'Pacifics' of the 'P' series. This series had originated with the importing in 1924 of twenty-five engines of this wheel-arrangement from the North British Locomotive Company. In the light of experience gained with these engines an improved version was built at Midland in 1938, and the new series of 1950 incorporated many improvements in detail design, though not any increase in nominal tractive effort. The cylinder dimensions, coupled wheel diameter, and boiler pressure remained the same. The new engines, which like the original 'P' class were built by the North British Locomotive Company, included many refinements that were then being adopted on modern locomotives in most parts of the world, such as roller bearings on all carrying axles, and mechanical lubrication was provided for the coupled axle guides. Seventeen of the class, designated 'PMR', had roller bearings throughout. Numerous modern fittings were incorporated to reduce the time spent in servicing. When first introduced they handled main line passenger traffic between Perth and Kalgoorlie, in addition to mixed traffic duties, but on the introduction of diesel traction in 1954 they were transferred to goods workings. All except one were still in service when I was in Australia in 1969, working on the lines in the south and south-western areas of the State. Their leading dimensions were, cylinders 19 in. diameter by 26 in. stroke; coupled wheel diameter 4 ft. 6 in. and boiler pressure 175 lb. per sq. in. The tractive effort is 25,855 lb. In these engines the old dustbin type of sandbox was abandoned; and while the provision

PLATE 45. W.A.G.R. modernisation

(a) The new station and control offices at Northam

(b) Dual gauge lines and signalling at Toodyay yard

Dual gauge track and points at entrance to Kewdale freight terminal, Perth

PLATE 46. Bulk transport of iron ore

(a) The mechanical loading plant at Koolyanobbing

(b) Ore train *en route* to Kwinana, hauled by four 'K' class diesel-electric locomotives

of a sandbox on the top of the boiler hardly improves the appearance of any locomotive, the saddle form used on the 'PM' class is a great improvement upon most.

In the following year a remarkable new design of the 4–8–2 type was introduced. More powerful modern locomotives were needed for the high proportion of the total system mileage laid with 45-lb. rails, and permitting no greater axle-load than 10 tons. Further requirements were for longe-range successful operation on the low-grade Collie coal, and in the areas where water is scarce and of high salinity. An initial order for twenty 4–8–2 locomotives was placed with Beyer, Peacock and Company, but this was subsequently increased to sixty. The world-wide experience of this famous firm was never utilised to greater advantage than in assisting the W.A.G.R. in the design of these engines. Every inch a utility job, it was nevertheless the most handsome locomotive design yet seen in Western Australia, in which all modern aids to efficient working were incorporated in a notably clean outline. The fact that a smart new livery of medium green, with black and white lining, was inaugurated on these engines added to the very favourable impression they made on arrival in Australia. But neat outlines and smart liveries do not, in themselves, get the work done, and it is necessary to take a slightly more technical look at these fine engines to appreciate their sterling worth.

There is first of all the special design of the boiler. Collie coal burns slowly, with a rather long flame, and a firebox with a volume that is high in relation to the grate area is ideal for burning this fuel to the best advantage. The grate area is considerably smaller than on the majority of recent W.A.G.R. locomotives, being 27 sq. ft. against 35 sq. ft. on the 'P.M.' Pacifics; but the shape of the firebox, and the provision of a large combustion chamber, makes for almost ideal conditions of working. Again, although the boiler barrel looks very long it is actually not so, because the combustion chamber extends for some 4 ft. ahead of the rearmost coupled axle. The inner firebox and combustion chamber is of Colville's special firebox steel, and is entirely of welded construction, not only providing for reduction of weight but a greatly improved design. The construction includes the fitting of a thermic siphon and has two arch tubes, which promotes rapid circulation of the water in the boiler and improved steaming capabilities. Externally the boiler-top is astonishingly free of 'gadgets'. The sandbox is incorporated in the same

R

casing as the steam dome, and the finely-shaped chimney would do credit to the most elegant age of steam locomotive design on the British home railways.

The maximum axle-load is actually that on the trailing truck under the cab, carrying 10.3 tons. The load on each of the coupled wheels is only $9\frac{3}{4}$ tons, through very clever designing. The cylinders are 16 in. diameter by 24 in. stroke, the coupled wheels 4 ft. in diameter, and the boiler pressure 200 lb. per sq. in. This provides a tractive effort of 21,670 lb. —no more than a moderate-powered engine, but a highly versatile one. For example, tests have shown that loads of no less than 900 tons could be hauled with ease at 35 m.p.h. on level track, while on a 1 in 80 gradient the rostered maximum load is no less than 435 tons. Accessories include the Hadfield power-reversing gear, developed by the builders primarily for the large Beyer–Garratt locomotives, and electric lighting. The importance of locomotive headlights has been emphasised in previous chapters of this book, but on the 'W' class 4–8–2s additional points are provided for inspection purposes, as an aid to servicing. At many places in remote country districts where these engines work yard lighting would be non-existent, and an electric lighting system on the engine itself is certainly preferable to the traditional flaming oil-can of old. Taken all round the 'W' class is a splendid example of steam locomotive practice of the 1950s, and it was a pleasure to see so many of them in active service. The whole class is still at work, and as designed they are used in all steam areas on the system. With their notably light axle-loading there are no routes where they cannot be routed.

The first diesel locomotives were introduced on the W.A.G.R. in 1953, and were of shunting and short-haul types; but in March 1954 delivery was taken, from England, of the first of the 'X' class 2–Do–2 diesel-electric main line locomotives, and the superseding of steam in certain areas began. An order for no fewer than 48 of these locomotives had been placed with the Metropolitan Vickers Electrical Company, but at that time the general superseding of steam was not envisaged. The new diesels were intended primarily for the Eastern and Northern lines where the water shortage is a constant source of difficulty, quite apart from occasional crises in the recurring conditions of absolute drought. At the same time however the conveyance of coal from the Collie area to Perth and Fremantle was presenting an increasing problem in haulage, and in

1954, again in consultation with Beyer, Peacock and Company designs were prepared for a new heavy main line freight engine. This time the physical limitations were considerably less severe than with the 'W' class 4–8–2s, and a maximum axle-load of 15 tons was permitted. The new engines were designed to work trains of 1250 tons throughout from Collie to Perth, and on level track to take no less than 1600 tons. The detail designing was done by Beyer, Peacock and Company, but the actual construction was sub-let to Messrs Robert Stephenson and Hawthorn Ltd.

The result was another very handsome but thoroughly modern locomotive, designated Class 'V', and first put into traffic in April 1955. These engines, of which twenty-four were built, could well be described as a much enlarged version of the 'W' class, including the same special design of firebox and boiler. With less restriction in the matter of maximum axle-loading it was not necessary to use a leading bogie and 2–8–2 wheel-arrangement made for a very compact locomotive, capable of rounding curves of 330 ft. radius. Like the 'W' class 4–8–2s the second and third pairs of coupled wheels had thin flanges. Like the 'W' class the smokeboxes are equipped with spark-arresting apparatus, which is very necessary when using the soft Collie coal, and particularly so when working in the 'dry' areas. Bush fires are one of the greatest hazards in many parts of Australia, and locomotive working needs to be carefully safeguarded to reduce the emission of sparks to an absolute minimum. These fine engines are used on the Great Southern Line between York and Albany, and also on the Eastern main line between Midland and York. Their use on the latter section is diminishing with the further introduction of diesels. The dimensional details of these engines are: cylinders 19 in. diameter by 26 in. stroke; coupled wheels 4 ft. 3 in. diameter; boiler pressure 215 lb. per sq. in., and tractive effort 33,630 lb. They are the most powerful non-articulated engines ever to run on the 3 ft. 6 in. gauge in Australia.

The introduction of the diesels followed the usual pattern on many railways, and of course in its early stages it was confined to the only gauge then existing in Western Australia, the 3 ft. 6 in. As previously mentioned the first type, as in the United Kingdom, was for shunting and light branch duties, but the main line locomotives of the 'X' class which followed early in 1954 were at once put on to lengthy hauls, working in diagrams in which the utilisation could be high. Engine changing at intermediate points could be eliminated, and full advantage taken of the greatly reduced time necessary for servicing such units. But before going further into the workings some reference to the technical details of the locomotives themselves is needed. They were specified, like the 'W' class steam 4–8–2s, for use practically everywhere on the system, and as such were restricted to a $10\frac{1}{2}$-ton axle-load. The engine horsepower is 1105, and they are believed to be the most powerful locomotives in the world for such a light axle-loading. Their tractive effort on starting is 28,000 lb. compared to the 21,760 lb. of the steam 4–8–2s. At a speed of 35 m.p.h. the diesels have a tractive effort of 5600 lb., or roughly $2\frac{1}{4}$ tons. The total weight in working order is 78 tons.

Some of the problems in design connected with diesel electric locomotives are well illustrated in this class. A vast amount of mechanical and electrical machinery is neatly accommodated behind the plain, rather featureless exteriors, and anything that can be done to reduce the size and weight of individual components is always welcome. The Western Australian Government Railways use the vacuum brake on the narrow-gauge lines, and the brake cylinders are large, because the pressure difference available for braking is only about 10 lb. per sq. in. compared to about 50 lb. per sq. in. with the air brake. In the United Kingdom it had become the practice to use air brakes on both diesels and electric locomotives, because of the greatly reduced size and weight of the cylinders that could thus be employed. The locomotive brakes are vacuum-controlled, in conjunction with the vacuum brake valve used for control of the train brakes. This feature is also used on the 'X' class diesel-electrics of the W.A.G.R. Despite their relatively high power, the heavy seasoned traffics in Western Australia, in addition to the frequent incidence of severe gradients, often required greater power than can be provided by one locomotive, and of the 48 units of the class 20 are fitted for multiple operation of two locomotives operated by one crew. In the steam areas also, double-heading is common at times of the heaviest freight traffic. The 'X' class locomotives are smartly turned out in the standard green livery with broad red bands, and they are named after native Western Australian tribes.

The introduction of these locomotives was a great success, and by the years 1956-7 the 48 units were responsible for 30 per cent of the total freight train miles of the W.A.G.R., which then amounted to 6,800,000 per annum. In passenger service they worked throughout over the 380 miles between Perth and Kalgoorlie, over the 340 miles between Perth and Albany, and over the 600 miles between Perth and Meekatharra, at the extremity of the line running north-eastwards from Geraldton. Until the year 1960 these 48 locomotives were the only main line diesels operating in Western Australia, and their early achievement of hauling 30 per cent of the entire mileage run on the State railway, passenger and freight was sustained. They have now been relegated to lighter duties, but are continuing to do very good and reliable work. One cannot expect any spectacular performance from them, as their maximum speed is restricted to 50 m.p.h. I rode No. 1019 of this class between Perth and Bunbury on the 'Australind Express', and found her an excellent and smooth-riding locomotive.

In quoting the high proportion of the total train miles run by these locomotives when they had the field to themselves, as it were, it must be borne in mind that they were allocated to the jobs most favourable to diesel traction. They had the 'plums', and showed a very high percentage utilisation in consequence. This was greatly to their credit; but it has been a well-known phenomenon in countries all over the world that as the diesel fleet grows, and more and more duties are taken over from steam, so the chances of very high utilisation lessen. With many 'odd' jobs to be done the opportunity for working out diagrams for maximum utilisation grows less, and inevitably the less important units of the fleet spend a higher proportion of their time standing, waiting turns, and so on. In Western Australia, that situation does not yet seem to have been reached, though with the opening of the standard-gauge line many 3 ft. 6 in. gauge diesels have been released from duties formerly carried on the narrow gauge east of Northam, and the availability of these locomotives will undoubtedly lead to the taking of further steam locomotives out of regular traffic. But the problems of the peak agricultural traffics remain, and it is likely that the steam locomotives made redundant will be stored rather than scrapped.

The year 1960 saw the introduction of considerably larger and more powerful diesel-electric locomotives for the heavy main line work on routes where the axle-load of 15 tons could be permitted. This was the 'A' class, built in Australia by the Clyde Engineering Company

261

of Granville, New South Wales. Later locomotives of this same class were built at Bassendean, Western Australia, by the Commonwealth Engineering Company, and were the first diesel-electric locomotives to be built in the State. These are of the Co–Co type and have an engine horse power of 1425, but apart from the technical details of their equipment the physical design of these locomotives is indicative of an interesting trend in diesel-electric locomotive development. In early days, arising from the fashions in styling set in the U.S.A., and followed in the first British classes, the external casing was built out to the limit of the loading gauge, presenting a smooth and to some extent streamlined exterior. This can be seen on the British-built 'X' class already discussed in this chapter, while the casings were frequently distinguished by the so-called 'nose'-cabs, in which there was a forward extension below the front windows. Certain British engineers brought up on steam insisted on this shape, as a modest form of protection for enginemen hitherto accustomed to having a long boiler between them and the front buffer beam. Manifestation of the American 'General Motors' and the British 'English Electric' style can be seen in the main line diesel-electric locomotives of New South Wales, Victoria, and South Australia, the working of which has been described in various earlier chapters of this book, and of course on the Commonwealth locomotives operating between Port Pirie and Kalgoorlie.

While such styling makes for a neat exterior and facilitates the application of various distinctive styles of painting, it can make things damnably inaccessible for maintenance! Of course on locomotives regularly running at very high speed, such as the 3300-horsepower 'Deltics' on the East Coast Route of the United Kingdom, a smoothed exterior is desirable for the reduction of air resistance. This becomes of increased importance when regular running at 90 to 100 m.p.h. is involved; but in the very week that I was writing this chapter I had occasion to go through the engine room of one of the 'Peak' class, 2500 horsepower diesel-electrics of British Railways, and it was as much as I could comfortably do to make my way along the narrow passage beside the engine. Maintenance work cannot be ideally done in such conditions. In this respect the Western Australian 'A' class, and the still more powerful 'C' class introduced late in 1962, represent a considerable change. On these locomotives a simple casing, of which the sides consist of almost entirely a series of removable covers, is erected just over the machinery, and the walkway, which is so constrained on a totally enclosed design, is on an open platform *outside*. The driver's cab extends to the full width of the frames, and access to the walkway is by a door in the front.

This design does not lend itself to such a stylish appearance as the older form, but for locomotives habitually running at no more than moderate speeds it is a much more practical arrangement. The cab is at one end, and when working passenger trains, or long-haul freight, it is customary to have the cab at the leading end. But after all, when working the reverse way, it is no different to driving a steam locomotive and scanning the road ahead past a long boiler. In any case, with the diesel there is no exhaust steam to beat down and obscure the view. These latest Western Australian locomotives are similar in their physical design to the standard main line locomotives in Queensland on which I rode between Gladstone and Rockhampton. The 'C' class of Western Australia are also of the Co–Co type, and have an engine horsepower of 1535. At the time of their introduction they were the most powerful 3 ft. 6 in. gauge locomotives operating anywhere in Australia. The first examples were built by the English Electric Company of Australia, at Rocklea, Brisbane. Like the 'A' class they have a maximum axle-load of 15 tons.

Both the 'A' and the 'C' class diesels are designed for general service, and have been used in passenger and freight service alike. Their introduction enabled multiple-working with 'X' class to be dispensed with on the heavy Westland sleeping car express between Perth and Kalgoorlie, while in heavy freight working the 'C' class has been found capable of hauling loads of 500 tons of mixed traffic at about 11 m.p.h. on a 1 in 40 gradient. The 'C' class have duplicate driving controls in the cab. On some locomotives, notably the large steam Beyer–Garratts in South Africa, when they are run 'backwards' for any length of time the driver has a somewhat awkward stance, or 'sit' twisting round on his seat to scan the road, while keeping the major controls readily to hand. On the 'C' class the provision of a complete duplicate set of controls, arranged in the appropriate positions for forward or backward running, makes things easy for the driver.

In early chapters I have written at some length about the striking development on the standard gauge in Western Australia; but it is now most important for me to emphasise that the modernisation of really heavy railway freight workings in the State are certainly not confined to the standard gauge. The W.A.G.R. is still essentially a 3 ft. 6 in. gauge line and a remarkable example of heavy mineral transport is to be seen in the north, in the iron-ore line from Koolanooka Hills. The Western Mining Corporation has an annual export commitment, to Japan, of 750,000 tons of iron ore. This is shipped from Geraldton, 136 miles from Koolanooka, and eight block-load trains are operating, 'round the clock', in what is another example of 'conveyor-belt' railway service. On this duty the 'A' class diesels are operated in pairs. They are marshalled so that the cabs are outwards and the driver thus obtains the clearest possible lookout whichever way the pair of locomotives is running. In the chapter dealing with the standard-gauge project, in which the Forrestfield–Kewdale complex outside Perth was described, I mentioned a further new railway, built on the narrow gauge, namely the special line for the conveyance of bauxite ore from Jarrahdale to Kwinana. This latter is another 'conveyor-belt' job.

It was in 1963 that another new railway of 28 miles was built specially for this latter traffic. The target output set was put at a million tons per annum, and it was calculated that a single modern train would suffice for this duty. An important consideration however was that the new line leading from the Darling Range would have very heavy gradients. There would be no difficulty from the viewpoint of providing motive power since the loaded trains would be running in the downhill direction. It was a matter of brake power. For even though the trains would be fitted with continuous brakes throughout, the factors involved in descending long gradients of great severity introduce a number of serious technical difficulties. An 'A' class locomotive was therefore set specially aside for this duty, and equipped with dynamic braking, in addition to the standard brake equipment. Although it has no more than an indirect bearing upon locomotive power, it is interesting to add that through efficient mechanised handling, in both loading and unloading of the ore, the output has been pushed considerably beyond the original target of a million tons per annum, but since I was in Australia a double-consist as well as the single train is now necessary to deal with the transport of this increased output.

During the last few years two further classes of diesel-electric locomotive have been introduced in Western Australia for the narrow-gauge lines. These are the 'AA' class of 1650 engine horsepower, and the 'R' class for heavy freight working, of no less than 1950 engine horsepower. Both are of the Co–Co type, but while the 'AA' is a mixed traffic job, suitable for main line passenger of goods, with a maximum speed of 62 m.p.h., the 'R' class is designed for maximum load haulage at slow speeds, and at 11 m.p.h. can exert a tractive force of no less than 50,200 lb. Both classes are nevertheless built within the general limitation of the W.A.G.R. narrow-gauge main lines, where the axle-load is limited to $15\frac{1}{2}$ tons. The 'AA' class were built at the Granville works of the Clyde Engineering Company, and the 'R' class by the English Electric Company at Rocklea, Brisbane. Both are particularly fine examples of modern Australian locomotive construction.

CHAPTER TWENTY-TWO

The 'Indian Pacific'

At various points on our journey through Australia in August and September of 1969 we saw magnificent new sleeping cars, in stainless steel, carrying the proud and significant legend 'Railways of Australia'. Until comparatively recent times the only stock operated jointly in Australia was on the Overland service between Melbourne and Adelaide. The completion of the standard-gauge line west of Kalgoorlie enabled the splendid red cars of the Commonwealth system to be worked through to Perth, but the approaching completion of the standard-gauge link right across Australia meant that the new passenger train service between Sydney and Perth would pass over the tracks of four systems: New South Wales, South Australia, Commonwealth, and Western Australia. It was as much a national project as the construction of the Trans-Australian Railway itself in 1917, and so what better title for the new jointly operated stock than 'Railways of Australia'?

When two sections of the 'Indian Pacific' set out from Sydney, in the late evening of 23 February 1970, it was not merely the inauguration of an epoch-marking train service, but the consummation of many years of hard, unobtrusive engineering effort. East of Kalgoorlie there were no spectacular constructional works to be completed; no Hawkesbury River to be bridged; no Blue Mountains to be negotiated. The right-of-way was there already. It is true that in Western Australia the splendid new standard-gauge line between Kalgoorlie and Perth was a major link in the line of continuous railway communication on the 4 ft. 8½ in. gauge from the Pacific to the Indian Ocean, and that this new line included some vast earthworks in the Avon valley. But, as told in an earlier chapter of this book, the standard-gauge line in Western Australia was built primarily for the bulk conveyance of iron ore from Koolyanobbing to Kwinana.

266

That it already existed to form a vital link in the Indian–Pacific route was fortuitous.

The situation in New South Wales was quite different. There was the similarity that great natural resources lay at Broken Hill, and that an immense industrial development had flourished there for upwards of ninety years; but the railway outlet had been into South Australia, rather than to New South Wales, and this had led to the establishment and rise in importance of Port Pirie as the place of shipment. The construction of the long line of communication to the State boundary at Cockburn had been made on the 3 ft. 6 in. gauge; likewise the 30 miles of the privately-owned Silverton Tramway, from the State boundary into New South Wales to the centre of the mining activity, at Broken Hill. All this development, railway and mining alike, was well into its stride before the end of the nineteenth century. While it could be regarded as a triumph for South Australian enterprise to secure the major share of the transport and shipment of mineral riches lying wholly within New South Wales, there was good reason for this preferment, in that Port Pirie was 247 miles from Broken Hill, against the 699 miles from Broken Hill to Sydney. Furthermore, for very many years after the South Australian development Broken Hill had no railway communication at all with the eastern districts of New South Wales.

Eastwards the nearest railway was at Parkes, 422 miles away, across a country that was virtually desert: an arid, unpopulated land, practically devoid of water. In the mid-1920s, when the spirit of the age in Australia was one of great optimism, the New South Wales Government Railways enterprised an extension westwards from Parkes. It was pointed out that a connection to Broken Hill would shorten the distance from Sydney to Port Pirie and the west by 267 miles over that via Melbourne and Adelaide, though as things were then there would still be two breaks of gauge, because of the incidence of the 3 ft. 6 in. gauge of the Silverton line and of the South Australian Railways. The extension of the New South Wales Government Railways from Parkes to Broken Hill was completed in 1927, to much the same standards as those accepted for the Trans-Australian line of the Commonwealth on its opening in 1917. Where there was any ballasting at all it was plain earth; but in many places the sleepers were laid on the surface of the ground. No more than light locomotives were permitted to run, and speeds had necessarily to be kept low.

Furthermore the completion of this link did not have the effect of diverting through east to west traffic from the older route through the capital cities.

At the time this was understandable enough. Main line passenger business was almost entirely from city to city, such as Sydney to Melbourne, and Melbourne to Adelaide. Despite the construction of the Trans-Australian line there was little interchange of passenger business between Perth and the eastern states of the Commonwealth. Traffic was largely confined to that between Western Australia and South Australia. All this, be it remembered, was long before the establishment of any regular civil air services. The construction of the standard-gauge line of the Victorian Railways between Melbourne and Albury had the effect of still further consolidating the route through the capital cities for through east–west traffic, because introduction of the rapid and efficient bogie-changing facilities for freight vehicles at Port Pirie and Dynon yard, Melbourne, coupled with the faster running on the well-laid inter-state main lines, was ample compensation for the shorter distance via Broken Hill. In consequence, by reason of its light utilisation and the character of its construction at the outset, the standard-gauge line of the New South Wales Government Railways between Broken Hill and Parkes was accorded the minimum of maintenance necessary to carry the light traffic prevailing, and until some six or seven years ago it was totally unfit to bear heavy locomotives and rolling stock such as would be essential for the operation of a through express service between Sydney and Perth.

A tremendous problem faced the management and engineers of the New South Wales Government Railways. Except in regard to the terrain, and the volume of traffic, the project was closely analogous to the electrification of the London Midland main line between London, Liverpool, and Manchester, in that a new railway had to be built over the tracks of the old one while the traffic continued to flow. During my own visit to Australia in 1969 time unfortunately did not permit of a visit to the works on this remote part of the 2461-mile transcontinental route. They were then in full swing; but from many railwaymen I met I gained a vivid impression of the extraordinary conditions under which the task of upgrading this 422 miles of line had to be planned and executed. But before referring to the engineering work involved, the physical and climatic conditions need more than a passing mention. As in all parts of the Australian 'outback', whether desert or otherwise, the route of the railway

268

between Parkes and Broken Hill is subject to severe and prolonged conditions of intense heat. The thermometer may be registering temperatures of more than 100 deg. F. for weeks at a time; everything is completely dried up, and the hot prevailing winds carry continuous clouds of red dust. There is scarcely a town worth the name in the entire 422 miles between Parkes and Broken Hill, and provision of living accommodation for the gangs engaged on the job was a major consideration in the forward planning, so efficiently carried out by the Chief Civil Engineer's department of the N.S.W.G.R.

Coming now to the actual work, it goes almost without saying that the whole line had to be relaid from end to end; but what was more important was that it had to be completely ballasted, up to first-class main line standards. It was estimated that roughly one and a half million tons of crushed stone ballast would be needed. To have conveyed such a tonnage from existing supply points would have been out of the question, but fortunately there was good rock existing at many points along the route. To rationalise the work, and to integrate the provisioning of ballast along the line with the stage-by-stage improvement of the road bed, and other necessary works in the general upgrading of the railway, two quarries were opened, one near Broken Hill from which ballast for the western half of the line was obtained, and the second at Shepherds Hill, nearer to Parkes. It will be appreciated that the running of 'work trains', with the associated dumping of the ballast *in situ* had to be programmed so as to cause the minimum of interference with ordinary traffic, on a single-line railway then provided with crossing loops of no more than moderate length. It was not merely a matter of providing new ballasting. Over lengthy stretches of line the old, primitive earth-ballast had to be dug out and removed, and ultimately there was some $1\frac{3}{4}$ million cubic yards of this stuff to be disposed of! The new quarries quickly attained a high degree of productivity, and at the peak of their achievement one was producing 45,000 tons of crushed rock a month, and the other more than 30,000 tons.

The human side of the task needed as much careful planning as the engineering and the special train movements. Such settlements as existed in the 422 miles between Parkes and Broken Hill had grown up largely to serve the needs of the men engaged in maintaining the line. They were widely dispersed, and the facilities they offered were those of remote outposts, in the Australian 'outback'. They would have been quite inadequate

s

to supply the needs of a big labour force moving steadily from one point to another as the job progressed. It was realised that the work would not only be arduous on the desert conditions, and sustained heat, but also to quote the vivid expression used by a senior officer of the N.S.W.G.R., *lonely*. Mobile camps were organised, providing good sleeping accommodation and amenities, while the men worked a ten- to eleven-hour day, for eleven days in each fortnight, the shifts being arranged to provide three rest days in this period. By these measures the work was pushed rapidly ahead, with the physical labour of ballasting and track laying kept to a minimum by the use of modern mechanised track-laying equipment. The gangs worked outwards from Broken Hill and Parkes respectively, completing the work as they went. The complete rebuilding of the existing railway was not the only task to be done. To bear the heavy loads of modern traffic the embankments had to be widened, and the passing loops lengthened to 6000 ft. to accommodate maximum-length freight trains. Extensive modernisation of the signalling had also to be carried out.

It is interesting to study the make-up of the Indian Pacific route, as finally constituted. The following table sets out the mileages, and the character of the sections concerned.

Mileage	Section	Description
277	Sydney–Parkes	N.S.W.G.R. main line
422	Parkes–Broken Hill	N.S.W.G.R. line upgraded
30	Broken Hill–Cockburn	Silverton Tramway replaced
217	Cockburn–Port Pirie	S.A.R. gauge converted
1108	Port Pirie–Kalgoorlie	Trans-Australian Railway
407	Kalgoorlie–Perth	W.A.G.R. new standard-gauge line

From its commencement of regular service from 1 March 1970 the 'Indian Pacific' has been worked by the locomotives and crews of the various systems over which it runs. It is electrically hauled over the first 97 miles from Sydney, through the Blue Mountains to Lithgow, and then N.S.W.G.R. diesels continue the journey to Cockburn. The South Australian Railways then take a turn, while from Port Pirie onwards the Commonwealth Railways are responsible, with a succession of crews manning the one pair of diesels on the long 1108-mile run to Kalgoorlie.

Then finally, the Western Australian 3300-horsepower diesels take over, as on my own run over the Trans-Australian Railway described earlier in this book. It has been suggested that at some future time engine-changing may be obviated and that a single locomotive or pair of locomotives might work through from Lithgow to Perth; but such a practice would envisage a degree of unification of locomotive policy between four different railway systems that certainly does not exist at present, quite apart from some reconciliation between the widely varying requirements of power output on the various stages of the journey. To quote a single example: to haul a heavy sleeping car express up the long ascent from Perth to Southern Cross requires a locomotive of considerably greater tractive power than of working the same train at a maximum speed of 60 m.p.h. over the comparatively level gradients of the Trans-Australian line.

The 'Indian Pacific' expresses are made up to a minimum load of twelve coaches, though these are likely to need strengthening on frequent occasions. Each set train makes a round trip from Sydney to Perth and back once a week. The departures from Sydney are on Mondays and Thursdays each day at 3.15 p.m., and the corresponding departures from Perth are on Sundays and Thursdays. The total journey time is $65\frac{3}{4}$ hours westbound, and 64 hr. 20 min. eastbound, and between Perth and Port Pirie the new trains run in the timetable path of the former Trans-Australian expresses. At the time I made my own journey right across the continent the 4.45 p.m. departure from Port Pirie ran on five days a week; now, with the addition of the 'Indian Pacific' service there is a daily departure from Port Pirie for Perth at 4.45 p.m. The average speed throughout from Sydney is approximately 38 m.p.h., with the journey involving two whole days, and three nights in the train. The timing is arranged so that with the departure from Sydney at 3.15 p.m. passengers can enjoy the magnificent scenery of the Blue Mountains in daylight. It is perhaps a little unfortunate that in neither direction is the Avon valley in Western Australia traversed in daylight. Not only is the westbound train due in Perth at the early hour of 7 a.m., but the eastbound departure is at 9.30 p.m. Still one cannot have the best of both worlds, and of the two splendidly scenic stretches the Blue Mountains are by far the most spectacular.

CHAPTER TWENTY-THREE

'Australind to Bunbury'

On reaching Perth our 5000-mile pilgrimage on Australian railways was nearly ended. The many items of railway interest that I then visited in and around that fair city, and indeed far out into the Darling Range, were reached by road; but there was one last trip to be made by train—into the south-west. So, on our last full day in Australia we made the delightful day excursion to Bunbury. This is one of the many lines in far places of the world that are familiar to me, on paper at any rate, through my signalling work; and it was not long after the end of World War II that I was associated with plans for a C.T.C. installation between Armadale and Brunswick Junction, covering the major part of this line from Perth to Bunbury. But before describing our journey, or any part of the present equipment and working, the interesting and characteristic story of the early days of this line must be recalled. As at Albany, the coastal terminus of the Great Southern line, construction began at Bunbury itself, in this with no more than a local line to Boyanup in 1891. Its object was to convey agricultural produce from a particularly rich farming district into Bunbury. But such a line could not remain isolated for long, and by the end of August 1893 the 110 miles of the South-Western line had been constructed between East Perth and Picton, where the local line from Boyanup was joined on the outskirts of Bunbury.

The line became a busy one after the opening up of the coalfield at Collie and the construction of the connecting line to Brunswick Junction, some 12 miles to the north of Picton. Collie itself lies only 20 miles to the east of Brunswick, and it is a straightforward haul from the colliery districts to Perth and Fremantle over the South Western main line. It was the single-tracked section between Brunswick and Armadale, roughly 80 miles, that was studied for C.T.C. operation. The control panel was

PLATE 47. Signalling in Perth

(a) The modernised cabin at Claisebrook (formerly East Perth)

(b) C.T.C. Control Panel: Armadale–Coolup section

PLATE 48. Western Australian steam

(a) Massed power around the Bunbury turntable

(b) Class 'FS' 2–8–0, at Bunbury

(c) One of the Class 'W' 4–8–2s, No. 921 on the Bunbury turntable

designed and built to cover the entire section; but at present only the stretch between Armadale and Coolup is actually under C.T.C. operation. The panel is one of those housed in the W.A.G.R. headquarters offices at Perth City station, and there, for the second time in Australia, I was able to watch the running of a train by which I travelled. In Melbourne, at Spencer Street offices I watched the progress of the 'Intercapital Daylight' over the standard-gauge line between Melbourne and Albury, while here in Perth I had watched the running of the 'Australind' on which we were to travel on the following day. The C.T.C. system installed between Armadale and Coolup is of the earlier type, as developed in the U.S.A., and using a multiplicity of small electro-mechanical relays for switching instead of the modern electronic methods. It is ideal for the traffic conditions on a line such as this, but the transmission times of the control and indication codes are not rapid enough for lines carrying a heavy traffic and requiring more intense utilisation of the line wires on which the codes are sent.

The 'Australind' daylight express, taking its name from the coastal district near Bunbury, where there are extensive and valuable deposits of mineral beach sands, is a most attractive little train. We were travelling at a relatively quiet period, and it was made up to no more than four saloon coaches and a van. I could however well imagine that in the holiday season it loads to almost embarrassing tonnages. The coaches are beautifully equipped, and the engineering features included to ensure comfortable travel in all seasons are most comprehensive. We made our journey in the early Australian spring, in the temperate weather of this western seaboard, and the arrangements between cars to exclude dust and draughts were not so apparently necessary. In the heat of the summer such amenities as cooling fans would be well appreciated. The train is equipped throughout with a public address system, for announcements and the broadcasting of soft background music. A hostess travels with the train, though as I spent most of the time in the engine cab it was only my wife who was able to appreciate this lady's services. Our locomotive was one of the 'X' class diesel-electrics No. 1019, and from this unrivalled 'front seat' I was able to see the line to the best advantage in the company of a friendly crew and very informative locomotive inspector.

Leaving Perth City station at 9.30 a.m. we ran cautiously over the junctions at Claisebrook, and over the single-tracked section over the Swan

River Bridge, and then made our way at moderate speed through the south-eastern suburbs. The names presented the usual delightful Australian mixture of adopted British titles, with Carlisle, Welshpool, Queens Park, and Higham following in rapid succession. In Chapter Twenty of this book I described how the very inconvenient level crossing at Rivervale had been eliminated by the construction of a road underpass; but as we drove into the outer suburbs there were many more level crossings, including one with an important main road at Welshpool. On this outer suburban section the signalling is of the typically British semaphore type, using the somersault design of arm. Near Welshpool is the junction with the line leading into the new Kewdale freight terminal and at Kenwick, the next station beyond Higham, we crossed the new standard-gauge line leading from Midland to Kwinana, and so heavily used by the iron-ore and the grain trains from the new line. By this time we were heading out into open country, of a soft, pastoral kind, with the beautiful hills of the Darling Range near at hand on our left. This 3 ft. 6 in. gauge line is finely maintained, and I was able to see later some of the heavy traffic it conveys, even though the day was a Saturday, and freight business was easing off for the weekend. The underline bridges are of a picturesque timber trestle construction. A run of just half an hour from Perth brought us to Armadale.

Up to this point speed had not been permitted to exceed 45 m.p.h.; but leaving again at 10.6 a.m. we got away in good style for a run of 32 miles to Pinjarra, entirely over single line, and controlled by the C.T.C. panel in Perth City station. Needless to say we made no speed records. The line maximum is limited to 50 m.p.h. and we had to slow down for the various loops, usually to about 40 m.p.h. The most important intermediate station is Mundijong, where this line is intersected by the new freight line from Jarrahdale to Kwinana, built specially for the transport of bauxite ore. The 21-wagon train that shuttles backwards and forwards three times a day over this 31-mile long railway is another of the great sights of Western Australia. Since the time of our visit a second train of 58 wagons has been added. The Class 'XB' and 'XC' hopper wagons were specially designed and built at Midland Works, and their pneumatically-operated 'Bomb-bay' type of doors permit of the almost instantaneous discharge of up to 63 tons of bauxite on to the conveyors at the Kwinana refinery. Now, double-consist trips bring a total of 3654 tons of ore to Kwinana, and this process is repeated three times a day, week in, week out. The wagons themselves are very distinctive in appearance, with bright yellow underframes, and 'natural' aluminium-coloured bodies. We passed Mundijong at speed, and continued through a lush park-land countryside reminiscent of some Midland shires of England. Covering the 32 miles from Armadale to Pinjarra in 46½ minutes was indicative of our pleasant leisurely rate of travel through this delightful countryside. For the most part the land west of the Darling Range was level, and extended thus as one looked towards the sea.

Continuing from Pinjarra, still under C.T.C. control, we seemed to be travelling along a flower-strewn path! As in South Australia between Adelaide and Port Pirie, and over the Nullarbor Plain, the railway property is much wider than the single-track line presently needs, and the profusion of wild flowers growing on either side gave this floral impression. In just over ten minutes from Pinjarra we approached Coolup, and the end of C.T.C. working. Here we slowed down to 15 m.p.h. to pick up the electric staff, and under this method of working we continued for the rest of the journey to Bunbury. At Waroona, reached at 11.18 a.m., the impression of an English countryside grew even stronger, with cows grazing, and the most dazzling profusion of dark purple, yellow, and blue flowers growing wild in the meadows, and within the railway boundary on either side of the line. We were now running continuously at 50 m.p.h. between loops, and some that are now normally unattended were passed at full speed. The eight miles from Waroona to Yarloop took just twelve minutes, and at this latter place there was a long freight train in the loop waiting to follow us southwards. It was headed by one of the 'P.M.R.' Pacifics, No. 726, purchased from 1949 onwards from the North British Locomotives. In these regions, in fact, we were the only diesel-hauled train, and the preponderance of steam was to become more and more apparent as we drew nearer to Bunbury.

From Yarloop we continued at a steady 50 m.p.h. through fine cattle country, on a very straight track, where the railway boundary was lined with tall trees, for miles, or so it seemed. It put me irresistibly in mind of the priceless malapropism committed by a rustic of our acquaintance in Wiltshire, who once described the approach to a certain stately home as flanked by 'a retinue of trees all paralytic to each other'! At Harvey, a station beside orange groves, we crossed a northbound freight train hauled by another of the 'P.M.R.' class Pacifics. Station stops were more numerous

275

now, but each was very smartly discharged. Despite the exceedingly rural atmosphere, the arrival of 'the train' was never the occasion of those social little platform parties that so characterised many a country station in the west and south-west of England. Now alas the country stations of England have nearly all gone, and a traditional, if not very efficient, feature of British railway working gone with them. We slowed to 15 m.p.h. to exchange 'staffs' at Benger, and so at 12.30 p.m. came to Brunswick Junction, where the line to Collie connects. Here, appropriately enough, was one of the fine 'V' class 2–8–2s waiting to proceed northwards on a heavy freight. From Brunswick the line is rather more undulating than hitherto; but we were now on the last lap and the short gradients did not unduly trouble our locomotive. After a final burst of 50 m.p.h. running we approached Picton Junction, and after passing through, at 15 m.p.h., ran cautiously over the last few miles into Bunbury terminus. The 115-mile journey from Perth had taken just over three hours.

Approaching the terminus, on the right-hand side of the line was a sight to set the blood coursing through the veins of every steam locomotive enthusiast, not merely an old-time roundhouse, but one absolutely packed with locomotives. It was a Saturday afternoon and they were stabled for the weekend. As soon as we had taken leave of the enginemen of the Diesel No. X1019, Inspector Pimmell, who had been such an informative guide on the run from Perth, took me over to the shed, and in the quietude that then reigned I was able to walk among the locomotives parked cheek by jowl on the shed roads and round the turntable. The light was splendid for photography, and my exposures were many. The two modern classes, the lightweight class 'W' 4–8–2s and the big 'V' class 2–8–2s, were there in force. A little 'Z' class diesel-mechanical shunter was put to good use in pulling one steam locomotive after another out on to the turntable for photographing. In addition to the more modern engines there were several of the 'F' class 4–8–0s on shed. The photograph reproduced facing page 273 gives some impression of the spectacle these engines presented, radiating star-fashion from the turntable. I could not help thinking how fortunate for me it was that the shed practice at Bunbury did not follow that of Inverness, on our own Highland line in steam days, when all the engines round that famous central turntable had their 'noses' tucked into the confines of the shed, and only the backs of their tenders protruding!

But photography was not all 'jam', even at Bunbury. In the dark recesses of the shed were two of the 'S' class 4–8–2s, as well as two 'Pacifics' of the 'P.M.R.' class. There are however limits to which one can extend the readiness of friendly shed staff to oblige, and to get one of the 'S' class or a 'P.M.R.' on to that turntable would have involved a major operation in shunting. Fascinating in their very antiquity however were the 'G' class 2–6–0 and the little 4–6–0 No. 123, and fortunately both of these were well positioned for 'capture'. These old engines, retained at Bunbury for shunting, are modestly attired in plain black, and they show their humdrum present-day role, in their workaday, ungroomed condition, beside the attractive green livery of the 'V' and 'W' class main line engines. They also operate 'The Leschenault Lady', a vintage train stationed at Bunbury and used for various excursions. I could have lingered for hours in this old steam shed, with its rich variety of locomotives; but time was not on my side. The turn-round time of the 'Australind' allowed for little more than this brief look round the shed and for lunch; and so, regretfully, we returned to the station for our last journey on the railways of Australia—for the time being at any rate. Together, my wife and I enjoyed the beautiful country traversed by the 'Australind' from the train; the beautiful wild flowers, the distant views of the Darling Range, and the modern facilities afforded by the train itself. We were back into Perth dead on time, at 6.10 p.m.

That evening a friend newly arrived from England called at our hotel, and brought in all the latest news from home. We in turn told him of the wonderful experiences that had befallen us since we left Heathrow nearly five weeks earlier. It had been, first and foremost, a railway pilgrimage, and though many other things had been interspersed, our hosts nearly everywhere were railway folk, and there was a railway background to nearly all. It was therefore of the Railways of Australia, and of their men and women, that we talked mainly on that last night. Since then, telling the story of our journey to audiences in Africa and at home, and to groups of engineers on the continent of Europe, I have many times had occasion to reflect upon the trend of railway affairs in Australia, and to look at it in perhaps longer perspective than the immediate atmosphere of bustle and enthusiasm that seems to permeate all activities from Brisbane, in the north-east, to Perth. Taking a completely world-wide look, there is no doubt that railways are passing through the most critical phase that

277

their long history has so far experienced. The recession and contraction in progress at home is nothing to what the railways of the U.S.A are experiencing. One meets, as I did only a week before writing this chapter, intelligent and straight-thinking men who still believe that the only logical step from present difficulties is to scrap the lot and turn the tracks into motorways. I argued as logically and objectively as I could against such a creed, and inevitably found myself quoting examples of modern development from Australia, only to receive the *riposte* 'Well, of course, you're a railway enthusiast.'

I am; and I hope I always shall be, but in quoting this incident it is merely to show how one who has been there, and seen for himself, is indelibly impressed with the spirit of enterprise and the sheer business acumen that permeates the whole field of Australian railway activities today. It is not spirit of prestige, no mere waving of the flag, that has led to the building of great new lines like those from Moura to Gladstone, from Koolyanobbing to Kwinana, or even the 31-mile Jarrahdale line. These are tough commercial enterprises, while another feature of Australian railway working that left a most lasting impression, and which has created much surprise and interest among those to whom I have spoken of it at home, is the present popularity of the train for long-distance inter-city travel. Because of the great distances to be covered there is an easily formed idea—outside Australia—that railways would be completely outmoded for journeys between Sydney and Melbourne, for example. Quite the contrary; the night sleeping car trains, not only between these two cities but also to Adelaide and Brisbane, are booked to capacity every night. And the reason is not difficult to find. An air journey, no matter how fast the speed of transit, consumes part of the working day particularly if one's home is some distance from the airport; whereas a night express train leaves some time after the end of the business day, and lands one in the heart of the city soon after breakfast.

This is not all. The Trans-Australian service between Port Pirie and Perth was to me a phenomenon. Although arrangements for our own journey were initiated nearly two months in advance, such were the passenger bookings that it was not until we actually reached Port Pirie that it could be confirmed we had a twinette berth on the train. While not altogether a 'between time', our journey was not made at a peak period, and yet that immense train was booked to capacity. So far as through

278

passengers to Perth were concerned this is an instance where air travel saves a complete business day. In view of the popularity of the service between Port Pirie and Perth I could quite understand the confidence with which the Railways of Australia combined to introduce 'The Indian Pacific'. At a time when great and old-established long-distance trains in other lands, like 'The Twentieth Century Limited', are being withdrawn, this Australian enterprise, based on the prospects of expanding and excellent business, is most heartening to all who still have faith in railways as a major, if not entirely dominating, factor in transportation.

On the following morning there was a little gathering at Perth Airport; four Australian railway folk had come to bid us farewell. Two were Queenslanders whose hospitality we had greatly enjoyed in Brisbane, and who were then on holiday; the others, high officers of the W.A.G.R., hailed respectively from New Zealand and England. As we talked of many other railwaymen, and their wives and families who we could now call mutual friends, the great distances of Australia seemed to slip away, and the world itself became a smaller place. After all it was approaching noon, and that evening we were due to dine in Johannesburg! Inevitably we were drawn to those delightfully picturesque pools in the airport gardens where the fierce and symbolical black swans of Western Australia swim. It was a natural foreground to some final group photographs, and then the loud-speakers began to tell us it was time to board the big jet—first stop, Mauritius.

The Railways of New South Wales, 1855–1955. Dept. of Railways N.S.W.

Victorian Railways to '62. Leo J. Harrigan. Victorian Railways

A Hundred-Year History of the P. & O. Boyd Cable. Ivor Nicholson & Watson Ltd., London, 1937

A Century-Plus of Locomotives, New South Wales Railways 1855–1965. Australian Railway Historical Society

Railways of Australia. C. C. Singleton and David Burke. Angus & Robertson Ltd., Sydney, 1963

Power Parade 1854–1954. Victorian Railways Public Relations and Betterment Board

Brief History of the Western Australian Government Railways. W.A.G.R., Perth

A Short History of Australia. Manning Clark. Tudor Distributors Pty. Ltd., Sydney

The Railway Magazine. 1897 to date

Australia. Frank Fox. A. & C. Black Ltd., London, 1910